The Parklands

Trails and Secrets from the
National Parks of the
United States

gestalten

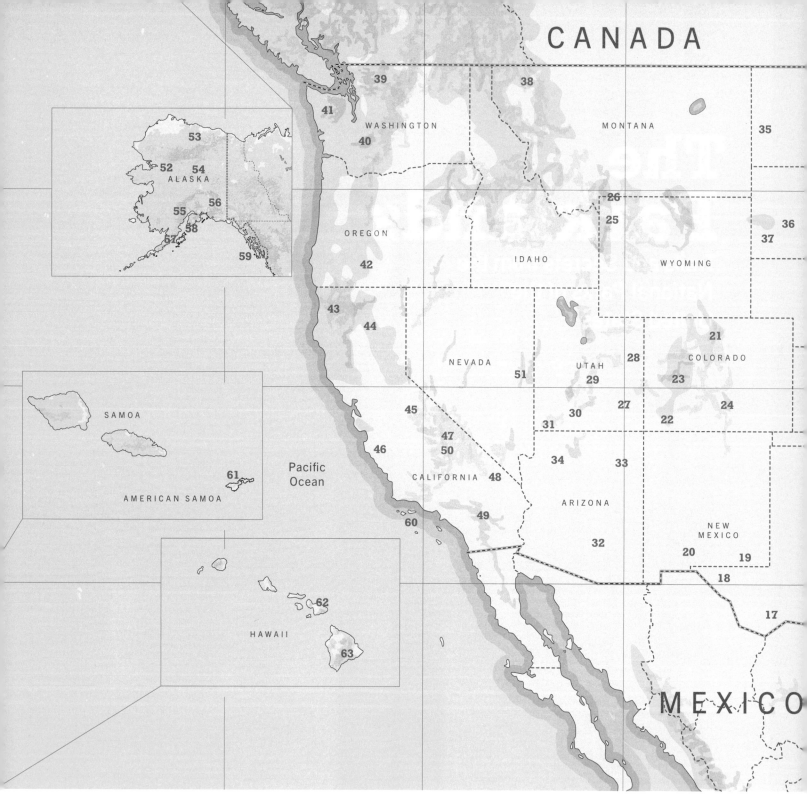

Leave It Better Than You Found It

Introduction letter from Keith Eshelman, co-founder of Parks Project.

March 1, 2022, marked 150 years since the designation of Yellowstone National Park, the world's first protected parkland. At the north entrance of the park, just outside of Gardiner, Montana, a stone arch stands above a two-lane road crossing from private into public land. With its cornerstone laid down by President Theodore Roosevelt in 1903, the arch frames the rolling hills behind it, beckoning the adventurous and curious alike. Emblazoned into its stone reads "For the Benefit and Enjoyment of the People."

With the designation of this parkland came the beginning of change. The foundation of the world's first park marked a shift in mentality, in attitude, of how some people conceived of land and a new conversation began—what is public land and why should it exist? While the conversation was—and is—not without controversy and devastation toward Indigenous communities, it was a new way of thinking and marked the beginning of a revolution of thought about our natural wonders and most majestic places.

With each new establishment of a national park, we make a promise to ourselves and the generations that will walk their boundaries long after we are gone. It's a promise to protect these places. It's a promise to remember what they stand for. It's a promise that in spite of all of our flaws—as people, as a society, as a nation—we are protecting something bigger than ourselves.

In the face of threats to parks by development and climate change, the fate of our most delicate, wondrous parklands is in our hands. We should see this as a privilege, not a burden. Through volunteering and advocacy, we have the power and honor of protecting our national parks. "We the people" have the privilege of looking after these places together—our public lands are spaces for everyone, regardless of where we come from or what language we speak.

We have the privilege to hand down the gift that has been given to us, the opportunity to protect a world full of wonder and beauty for generations of people we will never meet. Our commitment to leaving these places better than we found them is our most powerful instrument and the single thing that will ensure that all parklands—existing and yet to come—will remain protected and preserved forever.

Founded by Keith Eshelman and Sevag Kazanci, Parks Project believes that parks are places to exercise and unwind, but they are also important places for wildlife and preserving cultural history. Since 2014, Parks Project has created apparel and home goods, and aims to transform park enthusiasts into park champions. A portion of every sale goes to supporting conservation education and advocacy.

Steps Through Time: The History of National Parks Conservation

From the pioneering endeavors of a few nature lovers to the implementation of national programs, conservation efforts over the years have been as diverse as the wild lands they strive to protect.

By the mid-1800s, the eastern United States was mostly developed, and wild lands were privately owned. But the West was a different story. The new frontier boasted vast acres of federally-owned land gained by seizure from Native Americans and war with Mexico. Ambitious businessmen and hopeful settlers were eager to expand and exploit these newly-available resources.

It was glacier-carved Yosemite in California that inspired early conservation actions. As settlers claimed land and loggers threatened the sequoias, public outcry over the destruction encouraged Abraham Lincoln to enact an 1864 law giving Yosemite to California to protect as a state park.

Four years later, John Muir arrived—widely considered the country's first enviromentalist. He was traveling through Yosemite and the Sierra Nevada, chronicling his adventures for *The Century Illustrated Monthly Magazine.* Around the same time, geologist Ferdinand Vandiveer Hayden led an expedition to Yellowstone in Wyoming to document the bubbling pools and erupting geysers, both natural wonders thought to be urban legends.

Moved by what they experienced—Muir in Yosemite and Hayden in Yellowstone—both men began to advocate for the conservation of these lands. The conservation movement was born.

Exploration Leads to Designation

The most obvious marker of success for early conservationists was the creation of the first national park. In 1872, President Ulysses S. Grant designated Yellowstone a national park, the first in the world. Yosemite earned its designation, along with Sequoia and Kings Canyon, in 1890.

Outdoorsman and future president Theodore Roosevelt formed the Boone and Crockett Club in 1887—the first organization to address conservation issues. In 1892, Muir founded the Sierra Club, and in 1894, Roosevelt lobbied Congress to pass the Yellowstone Game Protection Act to enforce laws against the illegal hunting of buffalo.

Later, under Roosevelt's presidency from 1901–1909, he extended the protection of lands to include wildlife and places of historic importance. By the time he left office, his efforts had led to the creation of five national parks, 18 national monuments, and 150 national forests.

The Parks, United

Though the list of national parks was growing in the 1910s, there was no single agency to manage them. Much of the work fell to the Buffalo Soldiers: all-Black military regiments who fought during the Civil War, and who continued to serve afterwards in various capacities.

From 1891–1913, these U.S. Army soldiers battled wildfires, curbed animal poaching, and constructed roads and trails in the national parks. Captain Charles Young—the first ever Black superintendent of a national park—achieved some of the most impressive improvements, including building a road to the world's largest trees in Sequoia National Park.

Finally, in 1916, Congress created the National Parks Service (NPS): one entity to oversee the parks under the mission of maintaining lands "by such means as will leave them unimpaired for future generations."

Stephen Mather was assigned director, followed by Horace Albright. Under Albright from 1929–1933, the NPS expanded east of the Mississippi River and brought national monuments and military parks under the NPS umbrella. Mather went on to found the National Parks Association, which eventually became the National Parks Conservation Association.

A 19th-century wood engraving of Lower Falls at Yellowstone, the country's first national park. Of the three most impressive waterfalls carved out of the rocks by the Yellowstone River, Lower Falls is the tallest.

The creation of the Civilian Conservation Corps (CCC) under Franklin D. Roosevelt took a major step toward preserving the parks, giving men employment (left) and halting the destruction of habitats that had been seen through lumbering, among other activities (opposite). In the South parks were subject to the same segregation laws as in other institutions and facilities, and it was not until the 1950s that they were lifted (below).

From Grassroots to Government

When America entered the Great Depression, conservation of distant wildlands became a low priority for many struggling Americans. President Franklin Roosevelt, however, saw an opportunity.

FDR used his time in office (1933–1945) to create the Civilian Conservation Corps (CCC), resolving two critical issues: unemployment from the Great Depression and environmental harm.

The CCC employed millions during its near-decade run and raised awareness of the outdoors and protecting natural resources. In the national parks, the CCC planted trees, built campgrounds and trails, improved wildlife habitats, preserved historic sites, protected shorelines, and re-vegetated rangelands.

The conservation movement of the latter 20th century gained more momentum under Secretary of the Interior Stewart Udall. From 1961–1969, he was responsible for legislation like the Wilderness Act, the Endangered Species Preservation Act, the National Trails System Act, the Wild and Scenic Rivers Act, and the Land and Water Conservation Fund.

Reflecting on the Past, Focused on the Future

There is much to praise about the early conservationists. From John Muir's impassioned arguments for preservation to FDR's sweeping legislation to improve the national parks, there is no doubt these efforts paved the way for what we enjoy today: 63 Congressionally designated parks that protect the country's scenic beauty, wildlife, and ecosystems.

But it has come with a cost. Vast, federally-owned national parks were only made possible by the violent displacement of Indigenous people during the colonization and westward expansion of the continent. They lost homes, access to sacred sites, and a connection to their heritage. And while the NPS has worked diligently to right these wrongs, it is a dark underbelly to an otherwise bright spot in our conservation history.

Today's conservationists continue to strive for a balance between progress of society and preservation of the natural environment that sustains us. The national parks are integral to these efforts. Through ecotourism, research initiatives, volunteer opportunities, and more, the NPS offers myriad ways to uphold its original ethos: maintaining wild lands for exploration while keeping them pristine for future generations.

A Park Ranger's Guide to Proper Etiquette

Following proper etiquette helps preserve the national parks' beauty, both for your fellow visitors and for future generations. We have put together a list of the six cardinal rules for visiting a national park, as well as eight lesser-known or unexpected rules. The National Park Service is a vast system that spans a huge variety of climates and ecosystems, so make sure to check the specific etiquette and guidelines for each park before your visit.

Be Respectful of Others

The national parks are there for everyone's enjoyment, so a golden rule of park etiquette is that your actions should not prevent someone else from enjoying the park. If you're camping, make sure to respect the quiet hours posted in the campground. While on trails, refrain from playing music through a speaker. Most visitors are there to enjoy the tranquility of nature, so if you must listen to music, please wear headphones. Our advice is to turn your devices off, take a deep breath, and enjoy nature's soundtrack.

Don't Feed the Animals

Most of the food we give to animals (bread, potato chips, fries) does not contain the nutrients animals need to survive in the wild, which can make them sick. Feeding animals also causes crowding, a surefire way to spread disease between wildlife. And, most importantly, feeding wildlife often trains them to approach and cross busy roads, which greatly increases their risk of being hit by a car. It might seem like an innocent snack, but feeding wildlife does much more harm than good.

Stay on Designated Trails

Trails are there to keep you from getting lost or injured, but they also serve another, equally important purpose: to protect the natural environment around you. In Redwood National Park, trails keep hikers from stepping on fallen logs, which can spread unwanted fungi and tree disease throughout the park. In the desert, veering off the trail to get that perfect snapshot can easily destroy soil crusts that have taken thousands of years to form. These living crusts are crucial to the ecosystem. They prevent erosion, soak up precious water for desert plant life, and can be destroyed with the step of a boot.

Stay Away from the Wildlife

The National Park Service requires visitors to stay at least 300 feet (90 m) from wolves and bears, and 75 feet (23 m) from all other animals. Bison and elk, though not predators, are incredibly large and powerful creatures, and encounters with them can lead to severe injury or even death. This rule should be applied to non-dangerous animals as well since contact with humans can have unintended negative effects on wildlife of all kinds. If you're concerned about an animal, do not touch it. Alert a park ranger instead.

Be Prepared and Know Your Limits

Visitors should try to be as self-sufficient as possible. Always pack enough food, water, and other essentials for the entirety of your adventure in the park. Readiness requirements vary from park to park, so do your research beforehand. Even if you come prepared, remember to be mindful of your limits and abilities: if you're a beginner hiker, those new hiking shoes and that state-of-the-art sleeping bag won't necessarily get you through that grueling hike meant for seasoned alpinists. Staying within your limits is a courtesy to the park rangers who are responsible for a long list of things, your safety being only one. It is also out of respect to your fellow hikers; anyone who stops to help you will almost certainly have to pause or shorten their own adventures to do so.

Leave Things Exactly as You Found Them

The practice of 'leave no trace' means no one should be able to tell you were there when you leave. This involves packing out all of your trash and supplies, but also extends to not making any marks, drawings, or carvings on the rocks or trees. Small changes add up and can gradually destroy a place's beauty. It's also forbidden to take souvenirs out of the park (except the ones you bought in the gift shop, of course). This includes even tiny rocks or feathers. It might seem small to you, but if each of the National Park System's countless visitors took something with them, there would be nothing left to see and it would have devastating effects on local ecosystems.

Eight Lesser-Known Rules

No Loud Shouting. It's very tempting to shout into a canyon or an immense cave to hear your voice echo back. However, this can disturb wildlife habitats, and also mislead park rangers into believing there is an emergency.

Don't Bring Your Own Firewood. That tree you chopped down in your backyard might provide you with free firewood, but it could also spread non-native disease and destructive pests to the park you're visiting. Many parks only allow certified heat-treated firewood, which can be purchased from local vendors. Check your park's firewood rules before your visit.

No Smoking or Vaping. Smoking of all kinds (including e-cigarettes) is prohibited in national parks, except in specifically designated areas. Cigarettes are not only a major source of littering, they can also spark devastating wildfires. Second-hand smoke also negatively impacts the experience of your fellow visitors.

Keep Animals on a Leash. When not in a cage or crate, pets need to be kept on a leash at all times on a max. length of 6 feet (1.8 m). Pets are not allowed in many areas, so it's always a good idea to check the park's rules on pets before you go.

Don't Stack Rocks. Hikers use small stacks of rocks called cairns to mark the correct path when it's not completely clear. You shouldn't make your own stacks in case they are mistaken for cairns, which can be dangerous, or at the very least, very annoying for hikers. You also shouldn't move or take apart existing cairns.

No Drones. Drones can be disturbing to both wildlife and visitors, and malfunctioning drones can litter parks or even cause wildfires. Because of this, flying drones has been prohibited in national parks since 2014. Unless you have written authorization by the superintendent to fly your drone, you can face up to six months in prison and a fine of up to $5,000.

No Metal Detectors for Personal Use. Unless you're a scientist doing pre-authorized research, leave the metal detector at home. The same goes for magnetometers, side-scan sonar, and other metal/mineral-detecting devices.

No skating or skateboarding. Except in designated areas, using roller skates, skateboards, roller skis, etc. is prohibited in all national parks. When in doubt, ask a park ranger.

Acadia

A small group of artists caught the eye of America's
wealthy elite, turning this lone island into one
of the premier tourist destinations in the country.

TOP: A signpost points the way to Cadillac Mountain. RIGHT: The famous peak is not the only attraction on Mount Desert Island: on the southwestern corner visitors will find the Bass Harbor Head Light Station, one of three lighthouses at Acadia.

MAINE

If you ever wanted to see the sunrise before anyone else in the United States, Acadia National Park has got you covered. The park—nestled into the far-flung, rugged coastline of Maine—is not only known for its rocky beaches, coastal forests, and old fishing ports, it's also famous for Cadillac Mountain, the highest point on the Eastern Seaboard. The summit offers stunning views over the Atlantic Ocean and Maine's many small offshore islands. From January 11 through March 6 and from October 7 through November 29, you will be the first to witness the sun on the horizon. (Don't ask. It's complicated.)

Cadillac Mountain is located on Mount Desert Island, which amounts for almost two-thirds of the 77-square-mile

Mount Desert Island is crossed by 45 miles (72 km) of cobblestone carriage roads accessible only to hikers and cyclists. An additional 158 miles (250 km) of hiking trails pass by natural waterways and through spruce forests and river valleys. Each spring a number of these hiking trails are closed to protect the park's resident peregrine falcon come nesting time.

In Acadia, a saying goes, "you can fish with one hand and sample blueberries from a wind-stunted bush with the other."

(199-square-kilometer) park. The island got its name from French explorer Samuel de Champlain, who was the first to describe it in 1604. Since he believed that the relatively high mountains were devoid of vegetation, he called it "Île des Monts Déserts." However, he was not the first to explore it: human traces reach back 12,000 years.

The island's face changed radically in the middle of the 19th century when painters from New York's Hudson River School flocked to the place. Their depictions of the area, when exhibited in Boston, New York, and Philadelphia, caught the attention of people seeking to escape the industrialized cities. Billionaires like John D. Rockefeller, Henry Ford, and the Astor family bought land and transformed the serene islands into a luxury haven.

Within a decade, the once relatively unknown and sparsely populated Mount Desert Island became one of the premier tourist destinations in the country. Some of the new inhabitants also

became wealthy benefactors. Starting in 1901, they bought up and donated extensive tracts of land to the state on the condition that a preserve be established. On February 26, 1919, Congress designated the area a national park. Although the islands remain a costly patch for residents, you don't have to have deep pockets to enjoy its expansive landscape. Mount Desert Island is accessible from the mainland via a short causeway, and the most important landmarks are found along the Park Loop Road.

For cyclists, equestrians, and hikers (or cross-country skiers in winter), there are 45 miles (72 km) of carriage roads, picturesque bridges, tranquil ponds, and waterfalls. When fall foliage peaks in mid-October, the pristine forests become a paradise for leaf peepers and bird-watchers alike. An extensive trail network criss-crosses the park and traverses an impressive landscape formed by ice age glaciers. And if you think you've seen it all, just rent a sea kayak and enjoy some of the most beautiful vistas on the East Coast from a fresh perspective.

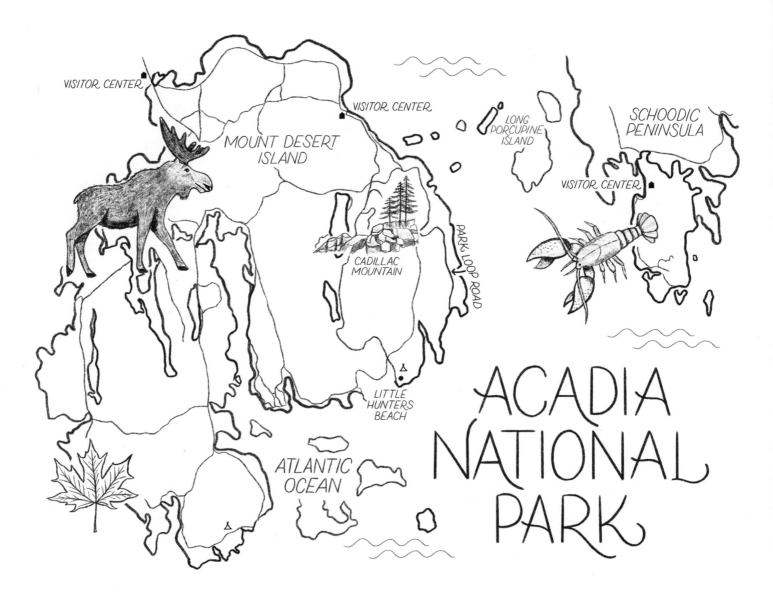

VISITOR CENTER

MOUNT DESERT ISLAND

VISITOR CENTER

LONG PORCUPINE ISLAND

SCHOODIC PENINSULA

VISITOR CENTER

PARK LOOP ROAD

CADILLAC MOUNTAIN

LITTLE HUNTERS BEACH

ATLANTIC OCEAN

ACADIA NATIONAL PARK

Acadia National Park in Maine was the first park east of the Mississippi. Established as Sieur de Monts National Monument on January 16, 1916, Congress designated it as Lafayette National Park on February 26, 1919. Ten years later, on January 19, 1929, the park was renamed Acadia National Park, a name explorer Giovanni Verrazano gave the are in the 16th century after a region in Greece.

SIZE
49,075 acres (77 sq. mi./199 km²)
Size rank among National Parks: 50 of 63

ELEVATION
Highest point: Cadillac Mountain (1,529 ft./465 m)
Lowest point: Atlantic Ocean (sea level)

GEOLOGY
Acadia's history began more than 500 million years ago when immense pressure from the earth's crust turned ocean deposits of mud, sand, and volcanic ash into rock. Later, tectonic forces brought these rock layers to the surface. The landscape bears the unmistakable traces of time: mountains caused by colliding continental plates, molten magma, and huge ice sheets formed the landscape.

FLORA AND FAUNA
This national park is home to lush boreal forests of spruce, fir, hemlock, and pine, and valleys of birch and maple, which provide a home to diverse wildlife. Acadia National Park is home to over 50 species of mammals, including white-tailed deer, coyotes, skunks, and foxes. Seals bask on the rocky shores of its smaller islands, and there's a thriving bald eagle population. There is also an oceanarium on the island which operates one of the rare breeding stations for the famous Maine lobster. In the fall, when the leaves drop, millions of songbirds stop here on their migration routes from Canada to the south. Over 300 species have been spotted here.

CLIMATE AND WEATHER
The coastal climate in Acadia means the weather can change rapidly. Temperatures are mostly mild but can vary wildly,

and rain and wind are possible at any time. Winters are cold, summers warm (with cool nights). Fog often occurs in spring and summer. Due to the influence of the sea, there is snow in winter, but not in large amounts.

CONSERVATION

Acadia National Park was established to preserve the beauty of Maine's mountain-studded coastline. Anticipating the dangers of overdevelopment, a group led by John D. Rockefeller and Charles William Eliot, president of Harvard University, bought up land from 1901 onwards in order to protect it. But it was mainly the tenacity of George B. Dorr (see right) that paved the way to protect the land. Thanks to these dedicated visionaries, the park remains a place of serene beauty. Due to its high popularity, however, Acadia struggles with traffic congestion.

BEFORE YOU GO

The island is divided into an east and west side. The eastern side is very busy, encompassing almost all the tourist hotspots. The west side is quieter and without carriage roads, but hiking trails offer a somewhat less-tamed version of verdant forest, open ridgelines, and rugged peaks. An entrance pass for the park is required, and vehicles must be registered to take the Cadillac Summit Road.

BEST TIMES TO VISIT

September offers mild temperatures and fewer crowds, and fall colors typically peak in October. Most amenities and park roads close during winter.

HIDDEN GEM

Easily accessible but often overlooked, Little Hunters Beach is a secluded pebble beach located just off the Park Loop Road. This small beach is a perfect place for a quiet picnic or meditation. However, due to the strong undertow here, it is not suitable for swimming.

INTERESTING FACTS ABOUT THE PARK

- Although Acadia is one of the smallest national parks in the United States by size, it is routinely in the top 10 when it comes to the number of visitors.
- Much of the park infrastructure was constructed by the Civilian Conservation Corps, an organized job creation scheme for young unemployed people after the Great Depression.
- Packing a rain jacket is never a bad idea: the Maine coast is known for its high annual precipitation, second only to the Pacific Northwest.

George B. Dorr

"FATHER OF ACADIA NATIONAL PARK"

Born the son of affluent Bostonians, George Bucknam Dorr (1853–1944) first visited Mount Desert Island at the age of 15. His parents had decided to buy an oceanfront property at Compass Harbor, just outside downtown Bar Harbor, where Harvard president Charles William Eliot was a summer neighbor. When he was older, Dorr inherited a fortune from his parents. The Harvard graduate never married and focused his energies instead on preserving the beauty of his beloved island. It took him four decades to acquire land (which he donated to the park), build trails, and draw up plans to make the area a national park. Dorr was also a member of two civic conservation groups that both fought to secure federal protection for the land. When he got word in 1913 that one of these groups was at risk of losing its nonprofit status, he traveled from his home in Boston to Augusta, Maine, to personally address the issue. He also made frequent trips to Washington, armed with maps, deeds, and titles, to persuade anyone who would listen to make the area a national park. It took him two years of persistence and tenacity, but it worked: in 1916, President Woodrow Wilson created Sieur de Monts National Monument. It was not the national park status that the trustees had hoped for, but Dorr was determined to get the job done. Three years later, President Wilson signed Lafayette National Park into law. (The name was changed to Acadia in 1929.) In his later years, Dorr—then superintendent of the park—loved to hike and walk the trails of the island; he even swam in Frenchman Bay almost daily, even in the winter. In 1934, during one of these swims, he suffered a heart attack. Though he survived, doctors told him he had six months to live. But Dorr, tenacious as ever, lived for another decade.

New River Gorge

Once filled with coal mines, New River Gorge is now a playground for whitewater rafters, rock climbers, and mountain bikers.

While the name indicates otherwise, New River Gorge is anything but new. While its true age is still debated, some scientists estimate the New River to be up to 325 million years old, making it one of the oldest rivers on earth. The star attraction here is the steep gorge that cuts right into the heart of the Appalachian Mountains, one of the oldest mountain ranges on the planet. Beginning high up in the mountains of North Carolina, the New River crosses Virginia and into the southernmost tip of West Virginia before connecting with the Kanawha River.

The oldest man-made artifacts in the park, Clovis points, were made over 11,000 years ago—a mere blip when measured in river time. These pointed stones were likely used as spearheads for hunting ice age animals like mammoth and mastodon. While

WEST VIRGINIA

the geography of the river and gorge made them hard to navigate, Indigenous communities lived, traveled, and hunted in the surrounding area, and there are 400 documented Indian archeological sites in New River Gorge and the adjacent parks.

The advent of the railroad in the late 1800s not only made it easier to transport people and goods, but it also created an insatiable demand for coal. With its rich veins of coal, New River Gorge became a major supplier of the so-called black gold. More than 50 coal towns popped up along the river. Rusty cables, retired mine sites, and other disintegrating remnants of this period can still be found all over the park.

Today, New River Gorge attracts outdoor adventurers instead of miners. Locally referred to as "the New," it earned national river status in 1978. Dropping 750 feet in 50 miles (230 m in 80 km), the New River features Class III to V rapids, making it a prime spot for whitewater rafting. Climbers flock here too, drawn to the steep walls of sandstone. There are over 1,400 established climbing routes in the park and it offers some of the best rock-climbing opportunities on the Eastern Seaboard.

Even BASE jumpers congregate here, coming for the annual Bridge Day, when dozens of brave souls parachute off the New River Gorge Bridge. At 3,030 feet (923 m) long and 876 feet (264 m) tall, it is the longest-spanning steel arch and the third-highest bridge in the United States. Traversing a stunning and expansive gorge whose tree-covered sides burst with color in the fall, it's one of the most photographed places in the state, and there's a quintessential viewpoint from the Long Point Trail.

While the river may be the focal point of the park, there are also more than 100 miles (160 km) of hiking and mountain biking trails to explore. Thanks to the Boy Scouts, and one of the largest youth service projects ever performed in national park history, the Arrowhead Trails offer mountain bikers 12.8 miles (20.5 km) of incredible singletrack.

The Grandview section of the park offers some of the best views of this majestic and ancient river. If you need a break from hiking and mountain biking, take the 83-mile (134-kilometer) New River Gorge Scenic Drive, which gives visitors a taste of the dramatic landscape from the comfort of their car.

PARK AT A GLANCE

Though logging and coal mining once thrived in the New River Gorge, the New River became a national river in 1978, which fueled restoration and recovery efforts. Four decades later, it was redesignated as New River Gorge National Park on December 27, 2020.

SIZE
72,808 acres (114 sq. mi./265 km²)
Size rank among National Parks: 45 of 63

ELEVATION
Highest point: Swell Mountain (3,291 ft./1,003 m)
Lowest point: New River (900 ft./274 m)

GEOLOGY
Scientists believe that it took the New River somewhere between 3 million and 320 million years to carve out the 1,000-foot- (300-meter-) deep gorge. The process of erosion has exposed several layers of rock formed when sand, mud, and rotting plants compressed over time, forming sandstone, shale, and the resource that West Virginia is most known for: coal.

FLORA AND FAUNA
With 1,400 plant species, New River Gorge has the most diverse flora of any river gorge in the central Appalachians. There are almost 50 species of amphibians here, and the southern Appalachian Mountains contain the most diverse population of salamanders in the world. Migratory birds depend on the New River Gorge for breeding, and the park is also home to endangered species like Indiana bats.

CONSERVATION
Traces of the once-flourishing coal industry can still be found in the park, a reminder of the lasting impact of mining. With its free-flowing river and diverse ecosystems, the area is an important migration corridor for animals and has long been celebrated as a state gem for nature and recreation.

BEFORE YOU GO
There are no developed lodging or camping options in the park, only a handful of first-come, first-serve primitive campgrounds. Just outside the park, there are plenty of options for campgrounds and cabins, and you can also hire guiding companies for river trips here.

BEST TIMES TO VISIT
Late spring before peak rafting season and when wildflowers are in bloom. Guided trips usually start in April, and fall is ideal for spectacular scenic views.

Shenandoah

This scenic mountain range is so wondrous that President Herbert Hoover chose it as his summer retreat.

Only an hour-and-a-half drive from the nation's capital, Shenandoah National Park sits along a 70-mile (112-kilometer) stretch of the Blue Ridge Mountains, some of the oldest on the planet. Part of the Appalachian Mountain Range, these mountains are an iconic part of American history and culture. The national park features a magnificent landscape of mountain streams, waterfalls, and lush hillsides, and is a haven for hikers, with hundreds of miles of hiking trails, including 101 miles (162 km) of the Appalachian Trail. The streams, teeming with native brook trout, are popular with fly fishers, as well as the hundreds of black bears that make the park their home.

The word Shenandoah is thought to have Native American roots, but many know it from the popular folk song "Oh Shenandoah." Many believe the word to mean "Daughter of the Stars," based on a Native American legend in which the morning stars created the beautiful valley by placing the "brightest jewels from their crowns in the river." These gems continue to shimmer today in the twisting Shenandoah River, just west of the park.

VIRGINIA

It was not only the Native Americans who appreciated the region's beauty: by the end of the 1800s, the Skyland Resort in the Blue Ridge Mountains had become a popular vacation destination. In 1924, when the National Park Service was looking to create a park in the famous Shenandoah Valley, the resort's owner, George Pollock, lobbied to make Skyland the center point. As one of Pollock's counterparts noted, "The greatest single feature ... is a possible skyline drive along the mountain top, following a continuous ridge and looking down westerly on the Shenandoah Valley. Few scenic drives in the world could surpass it."

Today the 105-mile (169-kilometer) Skyline Drive is indeed the centerpiece of the park. The scenic road runs north to south along the crest of the Blue Ridge Mountains with plenty of overlooks and stunning views. But, like in other national parks, the creation of this nature refuge came at a human cost. Under the Public Park Condemnation Act, more than 2,000 people were displaced to create the park, many with roots in the mountain region that went back two centuries. To create the illusion of an "untouched" landscape, Civilian Conservation Corps volunteers removed these people's homes along with all evidence of habitation, essentially erasing a vibrant mountain culture. The Corbon Cabin in Nicholson Hollow is now the only intact example of a mountain cabin from the area.

This, however, would not be the end of the park's social struggles. Although national parks in the North were integrated at that time, segregation was still prevalent in the South. In the late 1930s, park officials created a segregated section of Shenandoah for Black visitors and installed "whites only" signs throughout the rest of the park. The facilities were not fully integrated until the 1950s. Visitors to the park will learn that it is defined as much by its history as it is by its landscape.

PARK AT A GLANCE

The gorgeous setting of the Blue Ridge Mountains provides a beautiful backdrop, but the creation of Shenandoah National Park was largely driven by political and economic interests. Although the establishment of the park on December 26, 1935, under President Franklin D. Roosevelt protected this unique mountain setting, it also displaced entire mountain communities.

SIZE
197,438 acres (308 sq. mi./799 km^2)
Size rank among National Parks: 33 of 63

ELEVATION
Highest point: Hawksbill (4,051 ft./1,235 m)
Lowest point: North end of park (535 ft./163 m)

GEOLOGY
An ancient mountain range, the Appalachian Mountains were formed around 470 million years ago. The park's oldest rocks, known as Old Rag Granite and the Pedlar Formation, are over a billion years old, remnants of a time when today's seven continents were still united in the supercontinent Pangea.

FLORA AND FAUNA
Farming and human settlement have caused the disappearance of many native species in the area. Today, the park is a refuge for over 50 mammal species, over 20 reptile and amphibian species, and over 40 fish species. Wild turkeys are the largest of the 200 bird species in the park. There are also over 1,000 native plant species here.

CONSERVATION
President Herbert Hoover was taken with this landscape and established his summer retreat, Rapidan Camp, in the area to take advantage of the secluded scenery and trout fishing. He later donated the property to the national park.

BEFORE YOU GO
Old Rag Mountain is the park's most popular hike. While challenging, it offers spectacular panoramic views. There are two lodges, Big Meadows and Skyland, as well as five campgrounds in the park. The Potomac Appalachian Trail Club manages six backcountry cabins that can be reserved.

BEST TIMES TO VISIT
Its proximity to Washington D.C. means that the park can get crowded, particularly in summer and in fall when the hardwood canopy bursts into color. Spring is quieter and a great time to see the park's abundant wildflower species.

Congaree

With a towering tree canopy that rivals the Amazon, this majestic coastal forest seems like a gateway to a lost world.

Floodwaters from the Congaree and Wateree Rivers contribute to the maze of slow-moving creeks that wind their way through the humid bottomland forests of Congaree National Park, making them a haven for mosquitoes.

SOUTH CAROLINA

Located about 20 miles (32 km) southeast of Columbia, South Carolina, Congaree National Park contains the largest remaining old-growth bottomland hardwood forest in the United States. Although the landscape looks like a swamp, it's actually a floodplain: about 10 times a year, the marshy ground turns into a lake when the area is flooded by the Congaree and Wateree Rivers. Flooding lasts from several days to a month at a time, and the flow velocity is much greater here than what is typically found in a swamp.

Covering just under 43 square miles (111 km²), Congaree National Park is certainly not one of the largest parks in the country. But the lush, moss-covered trees growing in the marshy ground are among the tallest forests in the eastern United States, forming one of the highest natural canopies in the world. Trees and tranquility are two things you'll find in abundance in this park.

Previously, these wetlands were the home of the Congaree Tribe. They subsisted mainly on the fruits of the forest and the fish they hunted in the waters. Their life of harmony with nature ended when European settlers passed through in 1540, looking for gold. Although the prospectors left only 30 years later, they brought death to many Natives by unwittingly importing smallpox. The Native population, having no acquired immunity, was devastated by the disease. The lonely land soon fell to the English crown, which granted landrights in the region until 1776. Then, when South Carolina was admitted to the Union in 1788, it was up to the young state to regulate the ownership of lands.

From 1839 to 1841, dams were built in the northwest and southwest of the marsh. The United States was in dire need of timber, so loggers set their sights on the former Native American territory. Of particular interest were the bald cypress trees that dominated the landscape, prized by loggers for their long, straight trunks. From 1895 to 1905, the Santee River Cypress Lumber Company acquired much of the land, but they just couldn't find a way to navigate the waterways to profitably transport the logs. After 10 years, the company was abandoned.

From then on, the Congaree area was left to its own devices. It was rediscovered only in 1969 when timber prices skyrocketed. Private landowners contemplated plans to resume logging. Luckily, they failed. A citizens' initiative pushed for the protection of the land. In 1974, the area was designated a National Natural Landmark, and by 1976, Congress authorized the establishment of the Congaree Swamp National Monument. A hurricane caused severe damage in 1989, but the numerous fallen logs provided new biotopes. In addition to the fungus that flourished in the hurricane's wake, the number of animal species, especially insects, reptiles, birds, and bats, significantly increased.

It took until 2003 for the area to be designated as a national park. Today, it's one of the youngest in the country. Congaree National Park is a significant sanctuary for plants and animals and offers visitors easy hiking trails and camping opportunities. The best way to admire the majestic trees and numerous birds is by paddling its numerous rivers and creeks. From here, the low-lying floodplains reveal their genuine beauty. If you're more comfortable exploring on foot, there are some 37 miles (60 km) of trails. Some of them push deep into the park's dense western territory, an area that loggers have never touched.

CONGAREE NATIONAL PARK

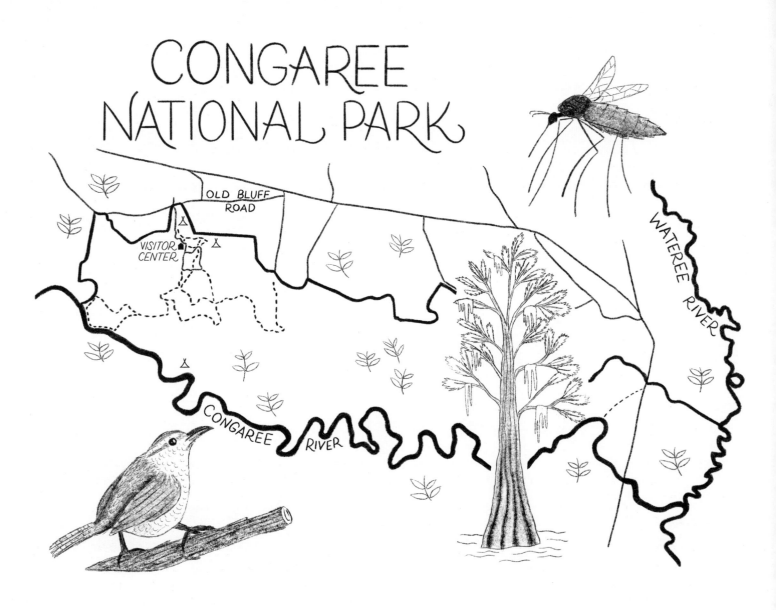

The Congaree River Floodplain was first granted the status of a U.S. national monument in 1976, following a grassroots campaign led by the Sierra Club. Seven years later, the Congaree Swamp National Monument was designated an International Biosphere Reserve, before becoming Congaree National Park on November 10, 2003.

SIZE
26,276 acres (41 sq. mi./106 km²)
Size rank among National Parks: 58 of 63

ELEVATION
Highest point: Old Bluff Road (140 ft./43 m)
Lowest point: Congaree River (80 ft./24 m)

GEOLOGY
The Congaree River Valley is a broad notch that cuts into the Upper Coastal Plain and is filled with river deposits. Numerous old river courses shape the floodplain today. They were formed during the last Ice Age more than 21,000 years ago. The area's topography has been subject to numerous influences: past migrations of the Congaree and Wateree Rivers, historic climate change, geological faults, and the forest itself. Human intervention has also left its mark on the landscape. All of these factors in turn affect the distribution of plant and animal species.

FLORA AND FAUNA
Bald cypress and loblolly pine are the showstoppers at Congaree National Park, but the protected wilderness area is home to many animals, including deer, bobcats, and feral pigs. Congaree's aquatic landscape of rivers, creeks, and lakes are thriving habitats for alligators, snakes, turtles, and a variety of fish. The largest are catfish, pike, and trout perch. Periodic floodwaters sweeping through the bottomland forest carry nutrients and sediments that nourish and rejuvenate the rich ecosystem. The park is an ideal habitat for migrating birds, making it popular with ornithologists. Some rare birds also live in the park, including the red-cockaded woodpecker.

CLIMATE AND WEATHER

Congaree National Park has a humid subtropical climate, resulting in mild winters (though it can dip below freezing at night) and warm, wet summers. High humidity makes the temperature feel much hotter than it actually is, and thunderstorms can pop up unexpectedly.

CONSERVATION

Congaree National Park preserves the largest remnant of old-growth floodplain forest remaining on the continent. In 1969, citizens (supported by the Sierra Club) resisted private landowners' plans to resume logging when timber prices soared. In 1974, the area was designated a Natural National Landmark, and by 1976, Congress authorized the establishment of the Congaree Swamp National Monument.

BEFORE YOU GO

Congaree National Park can be explored on hiking trails or by boat or canoe on the numerous waterways. But be warned: fallen logs are home to spiders, snakes, and wasps. There are two simply designed campgrounds within the preserve but with permission, camping is also possible in the hinterland of the park. Congaree typically floods at least 10 times a year, so make sure to check the forecast.

BEST TIMES TO VISIT

Spring (March to May) is generally the best time to visit Congaree to avoid the sweltering, humid summer temperatures and mosquitos. Fall (September to November) is also a great time to visit to enjoy milder temperatures.

HIDDEN GEM

Check in at the visitor center to see if you can join an "Owl Prowl," a ranger-guided walk at dusk. You will learn how owls have adapted to the ecosystem in Congaree—and might even spot these nocturnal birds in the trees.

INTERESTING FACTS ABOUT THE PARK

- Congaree National Park preserves the largest area of old-growth bottomland hardwood forest left in the United States.
- Despite its former name, Congaree is actually a floodplain, not a swamp. (A floodplain is a low-lying area near a river, covered by water only part of the year, whereas a swamp is permanently covered with water.)
- Escaped slaves often sought refuge in today's park, and moonshiners operated here, as the area was largely inaccessible.
- Congaree's floodplain forest has one of the highest temperate deciduous forest canopies in the world, with an average height of over 100 feet (30 m).

Harry R. E. Hampton

WRITER AND CONSERVATIONIST

If there ever was a man who enjoyed the great outdoors, it was Harry Hampton (1897–1980). He hunted. He fished. He roamed the wilderness. Every other week, he would share his observations in a column called "Woods and Waters." An avid sportsman, the reporter for *The State* newspaper had started the column in 1930 to promote sportsmanship and to urge people to use the state's natural resources wisely. Among the places that Hampton frequented was an area called the Beidler Tract. This part of the Congaree floodplain belonged to Francis Beidler, a timber tycoon, who used it to harvest cypress trees. Beidler also allowed numerous hunt clubs to operate there, one of which Hampton belonged to. Throughout his visits, Harry Hampton noticed that the Beidler Tract was different from the other floodplain forests he knew. The trees were larger, the diversity greater. As he witnessed an increasing amount of Congaree falling to the saw, he started a one-man campaign to preserve the forest. Through his enthusiastic style of writing and his conservation ethics, Hampton had already gained a large following among the state's outdoorsmen and conservationists. Nevertheless, his opinion at the time was unpopular, and numerous forestry groups tried to silence him. But Hampton kept badgering legislators—or anyone else who would listen to him—about the great virtues of the Congaree and why the floodplain should be set aside as a national park. His advocacy didn't go unnoticed, and as younger folks, in particular, came to see the old-growth forest for themselves, they added their voices to the chorus. Hampton's tenacity finally paid off in 1976, when Congaree Swamp National Monument was established. Many of the ancient bald cypress trees that Hampton fought to protect still thrive today.

Everglades

The largest subtropical wilderness left in the country is the only place where you can see both crocodiles and alligators in the wild.

TOP: Everglades' subtropical wetlands provide the ideal habitat for the 16 species of wading birds that have made the park their home. They include herons (pictured), storks, egrets, and spoonbills.

FLORIDA

One of the first journalists to visit the Everglades in 1897 came to the conclusion that the area was a "vast and useless swamp." He wasn't alone in his assertion. Governors, politicians, and industrialists have since declared their desire to (literally) drain the swamp. It took them a while to understand that the Everglades are a diverse and important ecosystem. And contrary to popular belief, the Everglades are not in fact a swamp, rather a slow-flowing river whose current is barely perceptible to the naked eye. This marshland of gigantic proportions floods during the summer months and dries up in the winter. Aptly, the Seminole people call it "Pa-hay-Okee": "river of grass."

Everglades National Park was established in 1947 by President Harry S. Truman. It was the first park to be protected in the United States for its biodiversity and not for its scenic value.

LEFT: Rising 70 feet (21 m) above the park, the Shark Valley Observation Tower is Everglades' tallest point. From here visitors can see as far as 20 miles (32 km) in any direction across a landscape that encompasses such diverse habitats as mangrove swamp, pine-covered rockland, and marl prairie.

"Here are no lofty peaks, no mighty glaciers or rushing streams. Here is land, tranquil in its quiet beauty."

—HARRY S TRUMAN, FORMER PRESIDENT

The park covers just about 20 percent of the total area of the Everglades (over 2,357 square miles, or 6,000 km²), making it the largest tropical wilderness in the United States. The Everglades are fed by the waters of Lake Okeechobee, which move slowly south toward the Gulf of Mexico and Florida Bay. Even though the flow seems eerily calm, the landscape is pulsing with life. Alligators share the wetlands with flamingos, pelicans, and hundreds of other rare and colorful birds.

This delicate ecosystem at the boundary of fresh and saltwater offers a unique landscape. Several trails on elevated wooden boardwalks allow visitors an up-close look at many species of birds and other wildlife; an even better way is boating through the park's vast network of waterways and mangroves. Airboats (also called fan boats, due to the giant fans that propel them forward) are the most common way of getting around, but they're loud—you'll see much more if you take a canoe or kayak trip down one of the many marked waterways. Guides are worth their weight in gold here. The park is home to rare and endangered species such as manatees and the extremely shy Florida panther, and an untrained eye is unlikely to spot them. Be careful when you approach alligators and crocodiles gliding through the water. The Everglades are the only place on earth where you can see both species together in the wild.

As bountiful as the Everglades are, their continued existence is at stake. Large parts of the Everglades are now used for agriculture, and only half of the water from the lake reaches the shore. The wetlands are repeatedly threatened by fire, and pollution is slowly destroying the park's habitats. The number of nesting birds has plummeted in the last decades, and many other species are considered threatened or endangered. Invasive species such as giant Burmese pythons are taking over the land (Miami is one of the capitals of the exotic pet trade), and the rise in sea level, driven by climate change, is threatening the park, due to the salinization of groundwater and the soils above. As a result, the park has been added to UNESCO's List of World Heritage in Danger, along with 52 other endangered World Heritage sites.

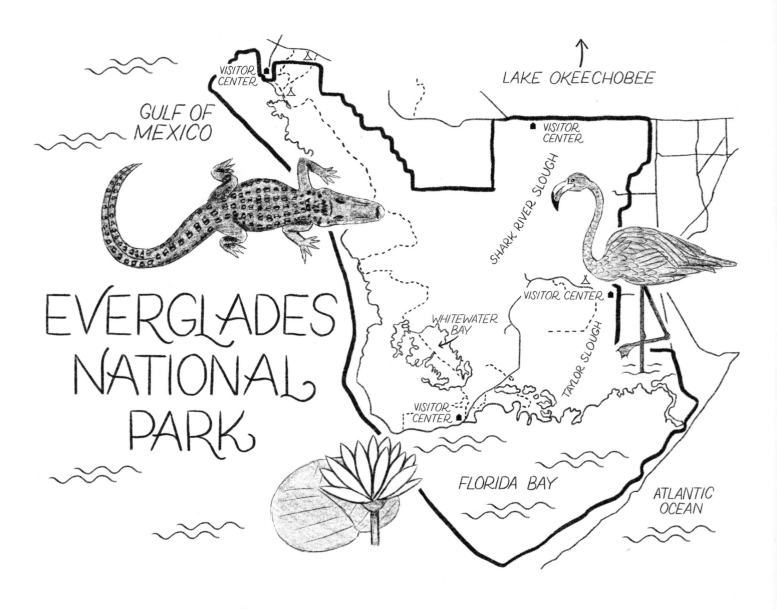

EVERGLADES NATIONAL PARK

GULF OF MEXICO

LAKE OKEECHOBEE

VISITOR CENTER

VISITOR CENTER

SHARK RIVER SLOUGH

WHITEWATER BAY

VISITOR CENTER

TAYLOR SLOUGH

VISITOR CENTER

FLORIDA BAY

ATLANTIC OCEAN

Everglades National Park was authorized in 1934 but not established until over a decade later as a result of difficulties acquiring land. It was declared a national park by President Harry S. Truman on December 6, 1947. The park's area has since been expanded several times. In 1976, UNESCO declared the park an International Biosphere Reserve and in 1979 a World Heritage Site.

SIZE
1,508,976 acres (2,358 sq. mi./6,107 km²)
Size rank among National Parks: 10 of 63

ELEVATION
Highest point: Calusa shell mound (20 ft./6.1 m)
Lowest point: Gulf of Mexico (sea level)

GEOLOGY
The Everglades is a vast, nearly flat seabed that was submerged at the end of the last Ice Age. The bedrock of the park primarily consists of limestone that formed when small marine invertebrates became exposed to the sun as the sea that covered the area receded. The area is fed by freshwater from Lake Okeechobee and weathering, erosion, and the sea continue to shape today's landscape.

FLORA AND FAUNA
With its subtropical wetlands and coastal and marine ecosystems, the Everglades are a sanctuary for many animals. The park is home to the only wild flamingos in the United States. In addition, there are a number of wading birds, including ibis, pelicans, cormorants, and storks. In total, about 400 species of birds, 60 species of amphibians and reptiles, and about 40 species of mammals have been recorded. The Everglades are also the only region on earth where both alligators and crocodiles live. While the alligators avoid salt water, crocodiles live near the coast. The flora is made up of mahogany trees and orchids, bromeliads, bald cypress, and other plants that live on the shore or directly in the water. The Everglades contain the largest continuous stand of protected mangrove forest in the Western Hemisphere.

CLIMATE AND WEATHER

The Everglades have a subtropical and maritime climate with very hot, humid summers with lots of rainfall from May to October and mild, dry winters with intermittent frosty nights. Hurricanes occasionally pass through South Florida and Everglades National Park, primarily during the rainy season.

CONSERVATION

Everglades National Park was established to conserve its natural landscape and prevent further degradation of its land, plants, and animals. About half of the original area of the Everglades is now used for agriculture, and most of the other half is protected by the park and adjacent nature preserves. The water of the Everglades is partly used for the extraction of drinking water for urban areas like Miami, endangering the ecosystems of the Everglades. Due to increasing pollution and decreasing water flow, it has been on the List of World Heritage in Danger since 2010.

BEFORE YOU GO

While the mosquitoes in the region aren't dangerous, they can be a nuisance. Pack tropical clothing and do not forget the mosquito repellent.

BEST TIMES TO VISIT

The winter dry season from December to April offers cooler temperatures, low precipitation, and fewer bugs. It is also the best time to see wildlife in the park when animals congregate in the remaining wetlands.

HIDDEN GEM

Try camping in remote, paddle-in campsites called "chickees"—simple stilt structures with thatched roofs and open sides. A chickee can sleep up to six campers.

INTERESTING FACTS ABOUT THE PARK

- The Everglades are home to the only wild flamingos in the United States. It is also the only region on earth where both crocodiles and alligators live together.
- For centuries, the Calusa people lived in the Everglades. They formed theocratic chiefdoms and worshipped the sun as the supreme deity, lived in adobe houses and subsisted on fish, turtles, plants, and shellfish. European settlers drove them out of the area, but some descendants still live along the northern border of Everglades National Park.
- Oil prospectors and hunters came to the Everglades after the construction of the Tamiami Trail in 1928 and hunted alligators, egrets, and many other species. Large areas of the Everglades were drained, causing further damage to the fragile ecosystem.

Marjory Stoneman Douglas

DEFENDER OF THE EVERGLADES

Marjory Stoneman Douglas (1890–1998) was always ahead of her time. She was not uncomfortable with questioning the status quo, taking up political battles for a whole range of issues. She took a stance against racism. She advocated for women's suffrage. And she fought to protect the fragile ecosystem that is now the Everglades National Park. Born in Minnesota, Douglas came to Florida in her mid-twenties to work as a journalist at what would later become the *Miami Herald*. Back then, less than 5,000 people lived in Miami. As the city's population swelled, reaching 100,000 people in a decade, she called for responsible urban planning, making short work of the myth that the Everglades was nothing more than a useless swamp. She recognized the importance of the vast river system, noting that the Everglades were instrumental in providing fresh water to the entire region. Douglas was a member of the committee that established Everglades National Park in 1947. The same year, her book *Everglades: River of Grass* was published and sold out immediately. While it had a profound impact on Florida's conservation policies, it couldn't stop the widespread environmental damage caused by drainage projects and agriculture. Douglas's biggest fight began when she was already 79 years old. As plans were underway to construct a jetport in the pristine Big Cypress region, she mobilized opposition through her organization, Friends of the Everglades. It was a decades-long battle against corporate and lobbying interests, but she eventually succeeded. Today, the Everglades are a model region for sustainable development thanks to Douglas. She died in Florida in 1998 at the age of 108. Her ashes were scattered in the park's Marjory Stoneman Douglas Wilderness Area.

Biscayne

Once home to a pineapple plantation and later a CIA training ground, this storied park is now a snorkeler's paradise.

Within sight of vibrant, bustling Miami lies Biscayne National Park. With clear blue waters, lush islands, and mangrove-lined shores, this pristine setting teems with wildlife. Unlike most national parks, the majority of Biscayne National Park is found underwater, and the park helps protect the third-largest barrier reef ecosystem in the world. With over 600 types of native fish, the park's waters are a colorful explosion for scuba divers and snorkelers.

The park marks the northern end of the Florida Keys, one of the most famous and most visited archipelagos in the world. The area's stunning natural beauty may have been the reason behind its protected status, but its cultural roots also run deep.

FLORIDA

Human history in the park spans over 10,000 years, with evidence of use by Native peoples on almost every single island. Below the water lie skeletons of ships, and the park's Maritime Heritage Trail charts the location of six different shipwrecks to explore.

Ninety-five percent of the park's almost 173,000 acres (700 km²) are submerged in water, and visitors take full advantage of this. Boat tours are a popular mode of exploration, and with a kayak or canoe, you can make your way through the longest continuous stretch of mangroves on Florida's east coast. Elliott and Boca Chica Keys, perfect base camps for boat exploration, both lie opposite Biscayne Bay.

Elliott Key, formed from a fossilized coral reef like the rest of its counterparts, is the largest island in the park and has seen the most human activity. It was once home to a pineapple plantation, an important crop throughout the Keys, which as a region produced all of the pineapples grown in the United States until around 1884. During the Cold War, Elliott Key became a hub of CIA paramilitary training activity, and Cubans fleeing the Castro regime landed on many islands in the park while seeking sanctuary in the United States.

In the 1960s, as efforts to protect the island grew stronger, local landowners and developers made an attempt to spoil the natural beauty of the island. They bulldozed right down the

middle of Elliott Key, carving out a chunk of land six lanes wide and 7 miles (11 km) long, aptly called "Spite Highway." Protection of the area prevailed, and today, the leftover physical scar through the maritime forest creates the park's main hiking trail.

Once threatened by the risk of commercial development, today Biscayne National Park, an essential habitat for wildlife, faces a different crisis: climate change. The reef is only one of the park's four distinct and biodiverse ecosystems, which also include a mangrove forest, the waters of Biscayne Bay, and the ancient coral limestone keys. As rising sea levels, warming waters, and acidification impact coral reefs around the world, there may be no national park in the country as threatened by climate change as this one.

PARK AT A GLANCE

On October 18, 1968, President Lyndon B. Johnson signed a bill to create Biscayne National Monument, and on June 28, 1980, the area gained its official national park designation.

SIZE
172,971 acres (270 sq. mi./699 km²)
Size rank among National Parks: 35 of 63

ELEVATION
Highest point: Totten Key Point (10 ft./3 m)
Lowest point: Atlantic Ocean (sea level)

GEOLOGY
Around 100,000 years ago during the last Ice Age, sea levels dropped, leaving coral reefs exposed. Over time, these ancient reefs became fossilized, creating the islands now known as the Florida Keys. The park contains the northernmost part of this famed archipelago, and offers a glimpse of how they looked before they were developed.

FLORA AND FAUNA
The park is home to over 20 threatened or endangered species, including Schaus' swallowtail butterflies, manatees, and hawksbill sea turtles. There are over 600 different native fish here, and birds like flamingos, loons, pelicans, and egrets make their home among the mangroves. The warm environment fosters a habitat rich in plant life, including many rare and endangered species.

CONSERVATION
Once threatened by money-making schemes and development interests, the watery wonderland of Biscayne National Park helps to protect one of the most extensive coral reefs on earth, along with the active marine life that thrives in this biologically diverse ecosystem.

BEFORE YOU GO
There is only one mile of paved roadway in the park, and with no bridges, everything beyond the mainland shoreline requires boat access. However, there are guided boat tours and rentals, and the visitor center and Jetty Trail are easily accessible from the mainland.

BEST TIMES TO VISIT
With the subtropical climate comes year-round sunshine and warm water, so there's no real "off-season," and the park is open all year long. However, spring and late fall are good options to avoid sweltering summer temperatures and hurricane season.

Dry Tortugas

A remote set of islands, Dry Tortugas
is home to dozens of coral species
and a 19th-century fort that has never
seen battle.

FLORIDA

In 1513, when Spanish explorer Juan Ponce de León arrived
at the islands off the southwest corner of the Florida Keys,
he saw so many sea turtles that he named the area after them:
"Las Tortugas." While the word "dry" might not seem fitting for
a park that's 99 percent underwater, the description let mariners
know there was no freshwater on the islands.

Situated between the Gulf of Mexico and the Atlantic Ocean,
70 miles (112 km) west of Key West, Dry Tortugas National Park

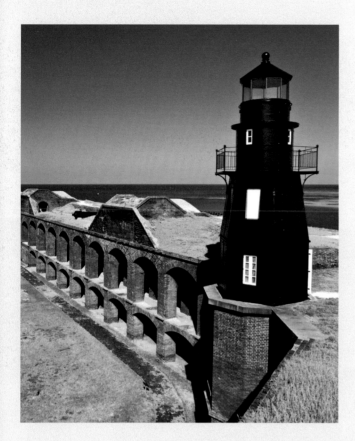

encompasses a seven-island archipelago. Due to its position on the edge of the Florida Straits, a shipping route intensively used since early colonial times, the islands were a highly strategic spot for the United States Navy. To ensure their hold on the region, the navy began construction on Fort Jefferson in 1846.

While never fully finished or fully armed, it's one of the largest 19th-century forts in the United States. Located on Garden Key, the second-largest island in the park, the fort took nearly 30 years and 16 million bricks to complete. Fort Jefferson was later converted to a prison, where its most famous prisoner, Dr. Samuel Mudd, was held after being sentenced to a life behind bars for allegedly conspiring with John Wilkes Booth in the assassination of Abraham Lincoln. (He was pardoned after four years.)

The other six islands include Loggerhead Key, a haven for wildlife and its namesake loggerhead sea turtles, as well as Bush Key, home to the only regular nesting site of sooty terns in the United States. The park's marine ecosystem also provides an essential habitat to more than 30 species of coral. The reef and its shallow waters have long made the area treacherous territory for passing ships. Evidence of this "ship trap" can be seen in the over 200 underwater shipwrecks scattered throughout the park, some dating back to the 1600s.

The clear waters here provide some of the best snorkeling and diving in the United States, with coral reefs teeming with marine life. Just off the coast of Loggerhead Key, divers can visit "Little Africa," a coral formation that uncannily resembles the continent. And just a little further on lies the Windjammer Wreck, a popular shipwreck that can be easily explored by snorkelers and novice divers.

PARK AT A GLANCE

O n January 4, 1935, President Franklin D. Roosevelt designated Dry Tortugas a national monument. It was expanded in 1983 and later became a national park on October 26, 1992.

SIZE
64,701 acres (101 sq. mi./262 km²)
Size rank among National Parks: 35 of 63

ELEVATION
Highest point: Loggerhead Key (10 ft./3 m)
Lowest point: Gulf of Mexico (sea level)

GEOLOGY
Like the rest of the Florida Keys, the islands of Dry Tortugas are made of Key Largo Limestone, a bedrock of fossilized coral reef. Almost all of the coral species contained in this fossilized reef are still found in the area today.

FLORA AND FAUNA
The park has some of the most vibrant coral reef and seagrass communities in the Florida Keys. This, in turn, creates a habitat for marine life such as sea turtles. Dry Tortugas has around 300 species of birds, several types of colorful reef fish like yellow smallmouth and angelfish, and dozens of species of coral including elkhorn and staghorn coral, both threatened species. The park also features a large seabird colony, with sooty terns, brown noddy, and masked booby.

CONSERVATION
Located at the southernmost point of Florida's Coral Reef, North America's only barrier reef, the park is home to nine species of threatened coral. The entire reef is greatly threatened by climate change, and it is also suffering a historic outbreak of stony coral tissue loss disease. First detected in the park in 2021, this infectious, water-borne disease impacts hard coral species, with very high mortality rates for certain kinds of coral. The park closely monitors and treats the infected coral.

BEFORE YOU GO
With its remote location, Dry Tortugas is only accessible by boat or seaplane. Not all of the islands are open to the public, and several closed areas help to protect the local environment and wildlife. There is a primitive campground on Garden Key.

BEST TIMES TO VISIT
Early summer or late fall when there are fewer storms, the water is calmer, and the heat and humidity are less intense.

VIRGIN ISLANDS

Virgin Islands

The grandson of a famous American oil tycoon fought to protect this Caribbean island, conserving its lush mangrove forests, pristine beaches, and coral reefs.

Laurance Spellman Rockefeller was a wealthy man, and as he sailed the Caribbean on his yacht, Dauntless, in 1952, he was struck by the beauty of St. John. The smallest of the three U.S. Virgin Islands—an archipelago that the United States purchased from Denmark in 1927—St. John had no proper roads, no cars, no electricity, not even a dock. Arriving at Caneel Bay, he was so taken with the place that he bought stock in an existing resort on the island. Over the next few years, Rockefeller bought up 5,000 acres (20 km²), eventually donating them to the National Park Service.

Almost two-thirds of the island is a national park today. Known as the "crown jewel of the Caribbean," the island's turquoise waters and idyllic beaches are ranked among the best in the world. Archaeological evidence shows people living on the island as early as 770 BCE. By the time that Christopher Columbus arrived in the New World, it was populated by the Taino people. In 1988, an archaeological excavation at Cinnamon Bay uncovered a Taino temple, and in Reef Bay, visitors can see petroglyphs from the pre-Columbian people.

After Columbus's arrival on St. Croix in 1493, St. John and the surrounding islands had a tumultuous history of colonialism. Sugarcane became an economic force in the region and fueled the Trans-Atlantic slave trade—at one point St. John had 25 active sugar-producing factories. The islands came under Danish rule in the 1600s, and by the late 1800s, after a revolt that led to the abolition of slavery, the Danish West Indies were in economic decline. After much back and forth, the United States purchased the islands from Denmark for $25 million in gold.

Almost half of the park is underwater, and St. John is renowned for its snorkeling. One of the more unique national park trails can be found at Trunk Bay, which features an underwater snorkeling trail. Stretching along the shores of a tiny islet called Trunk Cay, this short trail features underwater plaques that educate snorkelers about the surrounding reef. At Honeymoon Bay, another beach popular with snorkelers, coral species like brain, elkhorn, and pillar corals can be spotted. At Maho Bay sea turtles reign, and you can swim along with green and hawksbill turtles and, on the rare occasion, the less-spotted loggerhead turtle. All three are endangered, and just one part of a fragile island environment continually threatened by climate change. In 2017 the island was severely impacted by category 5 hurricanes, both on land and underwater, and with high temperatures, severe droughts, and rising sea levels, this national park is incredibly vulnerable to the changes wrought by climate change.

PARK AT A GLANCE

Virgin Islands National Park was established on August 2, 1956, under President Dwight D. Eisenhower, and in 1976, it was designated an International Biosphere Reserve by UNESCO.

SIZE
14,737 acres (23 sq. mi./60 km²)
Size rank among National Parks: 60 of 63

ELEVATION
Highest point: Bordeaux Mountain (1,277 ft./389 m)
Lowest point: Atlantic Ocean (sea level)

GEOLOGY
St. John is a volcanic island, and its oldest rocks are from around 100 million years ago. The Virgin Islands sit on the northern edge of the Caribbean plate, and while the islands do not have any active volcanoes, the eastern edge of the plate has 17 of them, located on islands such as Guadeloupe, Martinique, and Saint Lucia.

FLORA AND FAUNA
The park has over 400 tree species, including coastal mangrove and seagrape trees, as well as teyer palm, the only remaining native palm. There are 140 species of birds, 22 species of mammals, and in the water, sea turtles, queen conch, and many fish species make their home in the offshore seagrass beds.

CONSERVATION
A member of the Rockefeller family largely influenced the preservation of the park that visitors see today. When Rockefeller donated the land to become a national park, he kept 170 acres (7 km²) for his Caneel Bay Resort. It became a popular elite getaway, but in 1983, he created a "Retained Use Estate," stipulating that the entire property be turned over to the National Park Service on September 30, 2023. In 2017, the resort property was destroyed by hurricanes.

BEFORE YOU GO
Cars drive on the left side of the road in the Virgin Islands, so it's good to pay extra attention. There are food vendors at Honeymoon Beach, Trunk Bay, and Maho Bay. Honeymoon and Maho also offer kayak and paddleboard rentals, as well as snorkeling gear.

BEST TIMES TO VISIT
April to June when the weather is still warm but peak tourist season has dwindled and crowds are smaller. Temperatures are mild, mid 70s to high 80s °F (20s to 30s °C) and there's very little rainfall.

Great Smoky Mountains

The "Smokies" and their ancient forests are one of the most diverse wilderness regions in the United States. Regrettably, loggers didn't care about that.

The Great Smoky Mountains represent a relatively short stretch of the mighty Appalachian Mountains that dominate America's eastern states. The 2,000+ miles (3,200+ km) Appalachian Scenic Trail—a public footpath—runs right through the park.

TENNESSEE / NORTH CAROLINA

The Great Smoky Mountains owe their name to the magical, blue-gray haze that envelops them in the morning. The mountain range is among the oldest on earth. It even stopped the Ice Age's glaciers on their expansion to the south, resulting in a unique divide between southern and northern flora that can be observed here today. Summits and ridges are crowned with forests that are remarkably rich in life. In addition to the nearly 19,000 documented species of plants and animals, there are tens of thousands that have yet to be recorded. The national park's forest, half of which is in North Carolina and half in Tennessee, is one of the oldest on earth and the largest primeval forest area in the eastern United States.

Many trees here predate European settlement and were even alive when the Cherokee called this region in the southern Appalachians the center of their nation. "Shalonage," they named it: the place of the blue mist. When the first European settlers set up town in the area's sheltered coves and valleys, the Cherokee began to adopt their lifestyle, building homes, churches, schools,

Atop the park's highest peak, Clingmans Dome, a spiralling paved pathway leads to an even higher point—Clingmans Dome Tower—an observation deck with sweeping views of the Smokies and the vast terrain below. Back on the ground scientists have logged some 19,000 of the 80,000–100,000 species of animals and plants they believe are living here.

libraries, mills, and blacksmith shops. Scattered throughout the valley, remnants of these buildings can still be seen today. But when rumors spread that there was gold in the Smoky Mountains, the dream of peaceful coexistence ended. The Cherokee were driven off their farms and imprisoned in camps before being forced into exile in Oklahoma. Some descendants of the refugees now live west and south of the park on reservations.

The settlers admired the trees in the area, but mainly for their economic value. They quickly built up a thriving timber industry. In the early 1900s, timber trading companies began razing the forest for timber. Within 20 years, the natural beauty of the area had almost perished, with two-thirds of the entire forest cut down. In 1923, concerned conservationists and residents banded together to preserve the natural habitat, raising money to save the remaining forest lands. They were supported by the National Park Service and the U.S. Congress. Finally, in 1934, the national park was established through the purchase of 6,000 individual parcels of farmland. Most settlers left the park when the refuge was founded, but some chose to stay and their descendants still live here today.

In summertime, the number of daily visitors to the Great Smoky Mountains can reach 60,000 people on the weekends, and the park welcomes more than 11 million visitors every year, making it the most visited national park in the United States. (That's more than twice as many visitors as the Grand Canyon, which ranks second.) Despite the masses, it's still possible

to find peace and solitude here. The vast majority of visitors follow roads such as the Blue Ridge Parkway, a gorgeous 470-mile (755-kilometer) scenic route along the main ridge of the Appalachian Mountains. Much quieter are the 800 miles (1,300 km) of trails that branch off from the roads, the most scenic being the Balsam Mountain Trail and the Alum Cave Bluffs Trail.

Because of its temperate climate and varied topography, the park is one of the most biologically diverse regions on earth. Rhododendron and mountain laurel grow out of the weathered rocks, and amid the forests and rugged peaks, more than 1,600 species of flowering plants thrive. The wildlife is no less impressive. The Smokies are among the few areas in the eastern United States where black bears live, inhabiting all park elevations. Unlike black bears in other areas, the bears' fur is exclusively black, not brown or cinnamon. The total bear population is estimated at 1,500, which equals approximately 2 bears per square mile (1.5 bears per square kilometer).

GREAT SMOKY MOUNTAINS NATIONAL PARK

VISITOR CENTER

VISITOR CENTER

MOUNT CAMMERER TRAIL

ALUM CAVE BLUFF TRAIL

APPALACHIAN NATIONAL SCENIC TRAIL

BALSAM MOUNTAIN TRAIL

ABRAM'S CREEK

VISITOR CENTER

CLINGMAN'S DOME

VISITOR CENTER

BLUE RIDGE PARKWAY

C overing seemingly endless forest, Great Smoky Mountains is the most visited national park in the United States. It was established as a national park on June 15, 1934. Its extraordinary biodiversity led it to be designated a biosphere reserve in 1976, and the park became a UNESCO World Heritage Site in 1983.

SIZE
522,427 acres (816 sq. mi./2,114 km²)
Size rank among National Parks: 19 of 63

ELEVATION
Highest point: Clingmans Dome (6,643 ft./2,025 m)
Lowest point: Abrams Creek (840 ft./256 m)

GEOLOGY
The Great Smoky Mountains are among the oldest mountains on earth. The range contains some of the highest peaks in the Appalachian Mountains, including Clingmans Dome, the park's highest point. The range was formed about 480 million years ago when the North American and African continental plates collided—the range was likely higher than the Rockies but the soft outer layers of the newly formed mountains soon eroded. Permanent alternations between freeze and thaw produced the fields of rocks that are found at the base of the larger mountains.

FLORA AND FAUNA
The park's forest is one of the oldest on earth. There are eight different types of forests in the region with more than 130 different species of trees and about 4,000 species of plants. As a result of strong altitudinal variations, most of the plants found in the eastern United States can be found in the park. More than 60 different species of mammals live in the park, including white-tailed deer, marmots, and moose. The Smokies are among the few areas in the eastern United States that are home to black bears, which are smaller than their counterparts outside the park.

CLIMATE AND WEATHER

Great Smokies? The name says it all. The park typically has very high humidity and one of the highest levels of precipitation in the United States. It has a mostly cool, humid, continental climate of the kind you'd expect in places further north; temperatures are always a bit cooler here. Summers are warm but nights are cool, while winters are cold with occasional snowfall.

CONSERVATION

The park was established to preserve the last remaining sizable area of southern primeval hardwood forest in the United States. The idea of a national park was first raised in the early 1920s by members of the Appalachian Club, a group of Knoxville residents who had weekend retreats in the region before it became a park. The thriving lumber industry had helped the area become wealthy and prosperous, but the club worried the immense clear-cutting would devastate the forests. Politicians, photographers, journalists, and businessmen, including Appalachian Club member Colonel David C. Chapman, began seriously advocating to establish a national park in the mid-1920s, a campaign that finally succeeded on June 15, 1934, when the park was officially established.

BEFORE YOU GO

On some hikes, you can enjoy beautiful views at sunset, but keep in mind that it gets dark—very dark—in the forest on the return journey. Camping is allowed only in designated campgrounds and for a maximum of three nights. Reservations and obtaining a permit at ranger stations or on the park website are mandatory.

BEST TIMES TO VISIT

March and April offer relatively mild temperatures and fewer crowds. September and October are the best times to catch stunning displays of fall colors but the foliage also draws a crowd. If you can, go on weekdays to avoid the influx of visitors from the surrounding metropolitan areas.

HIDDEN GEM

The strenuous, 12-mile (19-kilometer) hike to the Mount Cammerer lookout tower is worth the effort!

INTERESTING FACTS ABOUT THE PARK

- The park is home to more than 30 different species of salamanders, earning it the moniker "Salamander Capital of the World."
- The glow of fireflies flashing in unison can be witnessed during mating season in the early evening hours of June.

George Masa

PHOTOGRAPHER

Who was George Masa (1881–1933)? Sadly, no one really knows. The Osaka-born photographer arrived in California in 1901 and, for the most part, remains an enigma today. He came to study mining engineering, but his plans soon fell apart. He decided to explore the United States by train instead. In 1915, Masa settled in Asheville, North Carolina. His upbeat attitude helped him land a job as a bellhop and valet at Grove Park Inn, where he quickly worked his way up to being the in-house photographer. He shot the hotel's affluent guests, some of which he kept in touch with. Gradually, Masa's interest shifted from portraiture to mountainous landscapes and wildflowers. Some believe it was his Japanese background that gave him a keen eye for nature and skillful composition; others said he considered the mountains a kind of sacred place. Masa specialized in large-format photography. At his own expense and often working alone, he could be seen trekking through the mountains, armed with his 8×10 box camera, a wooden tripod, and an odometer crafted from an old bicycle wheel, which he used to measure mountain paths in and around the Great Smoky Mountains. The "Ansel Adams of the East" he meticulously cataloged a significant number of peaks, the distances between them, and the names they were given by the local settlers and the Cherokee. He eventually joined forces with local journalist Horace Kephart, who was determined to turn the area into a national park after witnessing firsthand the devastation caused by industrial-scale logging. Their joint effort helped Great Smoky Mountains National Park to become a reality. In 1961, Masa Knob, a 5,685-foot (1,733-meter) peak, was named in his honor.

Cuyahoga Valley

This is the story of a river once so polluted that it caught on fire—and its transformation into a symbol of environmental restoration.

OHIO

A short drive from Cleveland, Ohio, and 15 other cities, Cuyahoga Valley National Park could be considered an urban park. The lush green trees, rolling hills, and winding river, however, invite visitors into a place of recreation and contemplation. People have been in this stretch of river valley between Cleveland and Akron for over 12,000 years. The 85-mile- (137-kilometer-) long Cuyahoga River gets its name from the

Mohawk word *Ka-ih-ogh-ha*, meaning "crooked," and the park encompasses almost a quarter of its winding waters.

In the 20th century, pollution wreaked havoc on the river's ecosystem: by the 1960s the river was filled with industrial waste, due to its proximity to Lake Erie, an important industrial and manufacturing hub at the time. The river is perhaps most famous for the 1969 Cuyahoga River Fire. The flames that surged from its polluted waters were a clear visual symbol of the impacts of pollution and ineffective political policies. While it wasn't the first time the river had caught fire, the event was a galvanizing force for the growing environmental movement, eventually leading Congress to pass the Clean Water Act in 1972.

Thanks to decades of restoration efforts, the river is now on the mend. Once covered in oil slicks and sewage, it is now a designated scenic river that has welcomed back both people and wildlife. Perhaps the most symbolic example of this is the bald eagle nest that park officials recorded in 2007, the first to be found here in 70 years.

Welcoming 2.2 million visitors a year, Cuyahoga Valley is one of the most-visited national parks in the United States. There are over 125 miles (201 km) of trails in the park, and visitors can walk on a boardwalk to see the impressive 60-foot (18-meter) Brandywine Falls. You can also explore the Towpath Trail, following the historic route of the Ohio & Erie Canal. This route was likely part of Ohio's Underground Railroad, a network of secret routes used by enslaved African Americans fleeing the South.

With its wildlife and scenery, the park is an important recreational hub for the region. More than 200 species of birds make the park popular for birding, and the park has earned the distinction of an Important Bird Area from the National Audubon Society.

PARK AT A GLANCE

Cuyahoga Valley National Recreation Area was established in 1974 to preserve the local environment from urban sprawl. It became a national park on October 11, 2000, under Bill Clinton.

SIZE
32,572 acres (51 sq. mi./132 km²)
Size rank among National Parks: 55 of 63

ELEVATION
Highest point: Brush Road (1,164 ft./355 m)
Lowest point: Cuyahoga River (590 ft/180 m)

GEOLOGY
The sandstone in the park was formed by glacial deposits from the last major Ice Age. The river has carved out steep ravines that can drop almost 600 feet (183 m) within just a few miles. The Ritchie Ledges are a striking display of the park's geology, with their massive striated walls of Sharon Conglomerate.

FLORA AND FAUNA
Oak, hickory, beech, and other deciduous trees thrive here alongside evergreens like pine and spruce. There are 943 different plant species in the park, including 90 species of grasses and over 70 species of sedges, as well as 21 state-listed rare plant species. River restoration efforts have helped to make the area welcoming to wildlife, attracting coyotes, white-tailed deer, woodchucks, reptiles, and 54 species of butterflies.

CONSERVATION
Carl B. Stokes was mayor of Cleveland in 1969 when the Cuyahoga River caught fire. The first elected African American mayor of a major U.S. city, his incredible response to the fire helped it gain its status as a symbol of the environmental movement. The national park works to preserve Stokes's legacy, and by protecting the Cuyahoga River, it provides the surrounding urban areas with rural refuge and access to nature.

BEFORE YOU GO
The park is open every day of the year, 24 hours a day, and there's no entrance fee. There are many ways to explore the park's diverse landscape, and one of the most popular is along the easily accessible Towpath Trail.

BEST TIMES TO VISIT
People flock to the park in early spring. Summers can be humid with variable temperatures, so it's good to pack layers. Fall is an excellent opportunity to take in the changing foliage.

Mammoth Cave

Ready to venture deep underground?
This limestone labyrinth features
giant chambers and bizarre formations
with fanciful names like "Pillars
of Hercules" and "Frozen Niagara."

With more than 400 miles (644 km) of underground caverns, Kentucky's Mammoth Cave is the largest known cave system on earth. There haven't been any actual mammoth fossils found here—you can see those three hours north at Big Bone Lick State Park—instead, the park owes its name to the sheer size of its chambers. They're the result of nature's work over the millennia. Slightly acidic rainwater has carved gigantic channels, shafts, and chambers into the limestone layer, creating a five-level cave system that can be observed in guided tours today. Once visitors pass through caves' wide corridors, narrow loopholes, and low crawlways, they are rewarded with breathtaking chambers full of stalactites and stalagmites, underground lakes, and crystal flowers made of gypsum.

The cave's official name is Mammoth-Flint Ridge Cave System because of the ridge under which the caves were formed. Legend has it that a Kentucky homesteader named John Houchin first "discovered" the cave while hunting a bear in 1797. However, to the prehistoric people of the area, large parts of the cave system

were probably known since time immemorial. Archeologists have found torches, sandals, ropes, and pottery here, as well as seven naturally mummified human bodies—evidence that the first human to step deep into the earth through the cave's imposing arch probably arrived some 4,000 years ago.

The first mummies were discovered in the early 19th century by miners who came in search of bat guano to make gunpowder for the War of 1812. Later, as demand for gunpowder declined, the economic value of the cave quickly shifted to tourism. Press reports about the mummies boosted visitor numbers, even after they had long since ceased to exist except in the fanciful stories of cave guides. A railroad was built, and since the land around the cave was not suitable for agriculture, owners of surrounding caves began competing for tourists in the so-called Kentucky Cave Wars.

The national park's creation in 1941 put an end to all the unpleasantries. The park's hilly karst landscape aboveground is mainly covered with hardwood forest. During pioneer times, it was clear-cut except for a few patches. Since the park's establishment, the trees have grown back so thickly that the park is now almost completely covered in forest. It offers refuge to white-tailed deer, foxes, and reintroduced wild turkeys. Because of the park's small size, only a few hiking trails lead to and from the visitor center. They weave past funnel-shaped sinkholes, peaceful swamps, and bubbling springs and can be easily covered in a day. The Green River, which has carved its meandering path deep into the limestone, is great for canoeing or paddle boating, and fishing here is also allowed!

PARK AT A GLANCE

Mammoth Cave was authorized as a national park in 1926 but was only fully established on July 1, 1941. Forty years later, it also became a UNESCO World Heritage Site, and in 1990, it was declared an International Biosphere Reserve.

SIZE
52,830 acres (83 sq. mi./214 km²)
Size rank among National Parks: 48 of 63

ELEVATION
Highest point: Brooks Knob (852 ft./260 m)
Lowest point: Green River (411 ft./125 m)

GEOLOGY
Limestone was deposited in a shelf sea about 340 to 300 million years ago and was later covered by river sand. The labyrinth of shafts and passages was eroded by surface water, which made its way underground from sinkholes in the hilly woodlands of Mammoth Cave, eventually forming a chain of cave chambers on top of each other over five levels.

FLORA AND FAUNA
Like most caves, Mammoth is home to animals without sight such as the blind cave fish, the eyeless crayfish, and the endangered Kentucky cave shrimp—a blind albino shrimp. Of the formerly numerous bats, only a few colonies remain. Aboveground park inhabitants include deer, foxes, rabbits, skunks, tree squirrels, and chipmunks.

CONSERVATION
The park protects the richest known habitat for cave wildlife in the world. The first records of the caves come from Stephen Bishop, an enslaved African American who explored the cave between 1838 and 1850. The caves were first professionally surveyed in 1908, and in 1926, private citizens formed the Mammoth Cave National Park Association to protect the area—donated funds were used to purchase local farms.

BEFORE YOU GO
You are not allowed to explore the caves on your own, but the National Park Service offers several cave tours which can be booked at the visitor center on Mammoth Cave Parkway (reservations are advised during summer, holidays, and spring/fall weekends). A tour is like an underground hike, and difficulty varies greatly, so pick one according to your time and stamina.

BEST TIMES TO VISIT
Since the temperature underground is a constant 54 °F (12 °C) year-round, you might want to consider coming in winter, when there are fewer crowds (but also fewer tours).

Indiana Dunes

Sandy beaches and windswept dunes are the only remnants of a
melted glacier, a stone's throw from one of America's largest cities.

Standing on the sandy shores of Lake Michigan in Indiana
Dunes National Park, you almost feel like you're at the
seaside. Less than an hour from the enormous metropolis of
Chicago, the park stretches along 15 miles (24 km) of sandy
shoreline, welcoming visitors to the beach in all seasons.

The area was once covered by the Laurentide Ice Sheet,
which extended across Canada and much of the northern United
States. When the continental glacier began to melt, it created Lake
Michigan and the other Great Lakes. As it melted, the lake levels
constantly fluctuated, and numerous shorelines were formed in the
process. In the park today, there are four distinct dune systems.

The dunes are an ongoing geologic feature, constantly
shifting and changing. The park's largest "living dune" is Mount

INDIANA

Baldy, which moves 5–10 feet (1.5–3 meters) every year. Human impacts over the last century have caused the 120-foot (36.5-meter) sand dune to move at a faster than normal pace. To counter this, the park invests regularly in restoration projects and restricts access to the summit of the 4,000-year-old dune. The short, paved Calumet Dunes Trail weaves through a dense forest, tracing where the Lake Michigan shoreline once stretched to over 12,000 years ago. For longer adventures, the Glenwood Dunes Trails connect a variety of loops that range in distance from less than a mile to 15 miles (1.5 to 24 km) and can be done on cross-country skis in the winter.

There is much more in this park besides sand, including some of the richest biodiversity in the entire National Park System. The park is filled with swamps, bogs, marshes, prairies, rivers, and forests. Birders come for the abundance of nesting and migratory birds, like kingfishers, tree swallows, and rusty blackbirds. The park also protects a patch of black oak savanna, a richly diverse ecosystem that once spread out over 50 million acres (200,000 km²), from Michigan to Nebraska. Today, there are only about 30,000 acres (121 km²) left, and the park is working to restore about 1,000 acres (4 km²) of this rare habitat. In the process they are also helping species that depend on the habitat, such as the endangered Karner blue butterfly.

Beyond the diverse natural world, visitors will find an architectural oddity in the Century of Progress Historic District, with five buildings that were originally built for the Homes of Tomorrow Exhibition at the 1933 World's Fair in Chicago. During the Depression, the World's Fair theme—the Century of Progress—provided a look towards a promising future. Intrigued by the showcased buildings, local developer Robert Bartlett had some of them barged across Lake Michigan to develop a beach resort. Four of the five houses are modern looking, even by today's standards. The bright-pink Florida Tropical House dazzles visitors with its clean lines and Modernist chic, while the dodecagonal House of Tomorrow, made almost exclusively of glass, has its own airplane hangar—based on the assumption that airplanes would soon be as commonplace as the family car.

PARK AT A GLANCE

The first National Parks Director, Stephen Mather, advocated for Indiana Dunes to be added right after the National Parks System was created in 1916. It wasn't until 1966 that it gained the status of National Lakeshore. A bipartisan effort to redesignate it as a national park was opposed by the Trump administration in 2018, but supporters prevailed, and Indiana Dunes received its national park status on February 15, 2019.

SIZE
15,349 acres (24 sq. mi./62 km²)
Size rank among National Parks: 59 of 63

ELEVATION
Highest point: Mount Baldy (703 ft./214 m)
Lowest point: Lake Michigan (597 ft./1,124 m)

GEOLOGY
Lake Michigan is constantly reshaping the dunes, which were formed around 11,000 years ago. As water levels and weather conditions naturally fluctuate, the beach changes, with a gentler slope in the summer and a narrower, steeper beach in the winter.

FLORA AND FAUNA
Indiana Dunes provides a habitat to more than 1,100 native plant species, more than 350 species of birds, 46 species of mammals, and 60 species of butterflies. Restoration efforts in the park have helped to bring back sandhill cranes and other migratory birds.

CONSERVATION
Its proximity to a major city has made for a long history of struggle between conservation and commerce. Henry Cowles, a botanist from the University of Chicago, helped to kick off a campaign to protect the area in 1899, but as industry boomed in the early 1900s, so did disregard for the environment. The Hoosier Slide, once a 200-foot (61-meter) dune and famous Indiana landmark, was carted away grain by grain to be used for making glass. Today the park helps to protect one of the last remaining oak savannas, as well as 30 percent of Indiana's rare, threatened, and endangered plants.

BEFORE YOU GO
With its close proximity to Chicago, there are plenty of options for accommodations and food. There is one campground in the park, open from April 1 to October 31.

BEST TIMES TO VISIT
Wildflowers are abundant in springtime and it's a good time to watch bird migration. In the winter, there are opportunities for cross-country skiing and snowshoeing.

Isle Royale

For stressed-out city dwellers, this park in northern Michigan—the least visited in the contiguous United States—is the perfect place to get away from it all.

OPPOSITE: Rocky Harbor Lighthouse is one of four lighthouses at Island Royale. In their heyday, they served to spare many vessels from crashing into the craggy rocks flanking what used to be a major shipping lane.

MICHIGAN

Isle Royale lies far from the noise of civilization, floating in the northwest corner of Lake Superior, the world's second-largest freshwater lake. The island, also known as Minong, the name given it by the Ojibwe people, is lushly forested, and in the summer you will find the undergrowth colorfully dotted with wildflowers and berries. Interspersed between the dense forest, you will find lakes, ponds, and marshes. Although Isle Royale is closer to the Canadian shore and Minnesota, it's part of the state of Michigan. It consists of the main island and hundreds of smaller islands, which were formed by the world's largest lava flow and then sculpted by glaciers for millennia; three-quarters of the park is underwater.

Most people come to experience pure wilderness here. However, it's not entirely untouched: history of human habitation and exploitation dates back four millennia when Native Americans started to tap the maple trees for sugar and extract copper from stones, which they then traded. The Ojibwe mainly inhabited the island in summer and, starting in the 19th century, had to share the land with fishermen, loggers, trappers, and even copper prospectors who, like them, were drawn to the island's natural riches. Some of the Ojibwe even served as their guides or worked alongside the newcomers. However, in 1936, a fire destroyed almost

a quarter of the then heavily thinned forest and put an end to the activities of lumberjacks and fishermen, who soon abandoned the island.

Four years later, the national park was created. Of all the parks, it's the least visited outside Alaska—but that's by no means due to a lack of show value, if you consider that it has the highest rate of return visitors. But getting there isn't as easy as hopping in your car. The only way to reach Isle Royale is by boat or by seaplane, and the only way to get around is on foot or by canoe. In other words, Isle Royale offers a more remote wilderness experience than many other parks, but be prepared to put in the effort to discover its beauty. The waterways that connect the numerous islands are a paradise for canoeists and kayakers, and experienced divers can also explore shipwrecks on the bottom of the lake. On land, narrow trails pass through boreal forests, marshlands, and rocky outcrops.

The wildlife is more reclusive here than it is in other places. But don't be surprised if you find a moose quietly feeding nearby. Its ancestors arrived on the island in 1912. Nobody knows if they walked over the ice in winter or swam. Lacking natural enemies, they multiplied rapidly to the detriment of other animals and the environment. By the early 1930s, the moose had cleared the yew stands and undergrowth and began to starve. Caribou, deer, and coyotes previously native to the island also disappeared. Then, in the cold winter of 1948–49, a pack of wolves arrived from the Canadian shore across the frozen lake, and something interesting happened: they gradually re-established an ecological balance. For more than five decades now, researchers have been documenting the activities of the island's wolf and moose populations to better understand the ecology of predation—and what it teaches us about nature—in what is the longest continuous predator/prey study to date.

CANADA

ISLE ROYALE NATIONAL PARK

LAKE SUPERIOR

WINDIGO HARBOR

VISITOR CENTER

MOUNT DESOR

SISKIWIT LAKE

VISITOR CENTER

ROCK HARBOR

Michigan's Isle Royale National Park was established as a national park on April 3, 1940. The park became part of the National Wilderness Preservation System in 1976 to prevent further development; in 1980, it became a UNESCO Biosphere Reserve. In 2019, the park's Minong Traditional Cultural Property was listed on the National Registry of Historic Places, recognizing the cultural history of the island's Native Americans.

SIZE
571,790 acres (893 sq. mi./2,314 km²)
Size rank among National Parks: 18 of 63

ELEVATION
Highest point: Mount Desor (1,394 ft./425 m)
Lowest point: Lake Superior (602 ft./183 m)

GEOLOGY
The formation of Isle Royale began about 1.2 billion years ago when a rift opened the earth's crust, forming the bedrock of the park today. The distinct ridges, valleys, and parallel islands were formed by glaciation. With the retreat of the ice layer about 9,000 years ago, the relief lifted the terrain, and meltwaters created the numerous lakes seen on the islands today.

FLORA AND FAUNA
Because of Isle Royale National Park's rugged and isolated nature, only 19 mammal species live there (among them red foxes, beavers, and ground squirrels), less than half of the number on the surrounding mainland. Peregrine falcons have been nesting on the island since 2012, after the species had been absent for more than half a century. The park's forest mainly consists of spruce, paper birch, and aspen. Isle Royale is also home to 600 species of lichens, more than in any other park.

CLIMATE AND WEATHER
Summers are cool and humid, with temperatures rarely rising above 77 °F (25 °C). Sudden changes in the weather are always to be expected, and nights can get cold, so rain protection and warm clothing are essential. Winters are generally snowy.

CONSERVATION

Albert Stoll Jr., a journalist for *Detroit News,* was one of the first people to campaign for the land's protection after witnessing the commercial exploitation of the island in the 1920s. Because of his efforts, Isle Royale National Park was established by Congress in 1931. The last patch of land was deprivatized in 1940, when the islands became a national park. With the changes in climate, ice bridges, which usually formed in winter and allowed animals like wolves to cross the lake, became increasingly rare. The wolf population subsequently dwindled. To counteract this, wolf relocation projects sometimes fly in the animals to keep the ecosystem in balance.

BEFORE YOU GO

The islands can only be reached via ferry or seaplane and explored on foot or by boat. There are two settlements in the park with visitor centers: Windigo and Rock Harbor. Windigo has a camp store and showers; Rock Harbor boasts a full-service marina with canoe and boat rentals, as well as a camp store, showers, a restaurant offering locally caught whitefish, a lodge, and a campground.

BEST TIMES TO VISIT

Isle Royale is open to visitors from April 16 to October 31. Summertime has the most pleasant temperatures, and you won't encounter many crowds in this park. Most people visit in July and August when blueberries and thimbleberries ripen throughout the park.

HIDDEN GEM

As the least-visited park in the Lower 48, you can reasonably argue that the park is a hidden gem in itself. Experienced paddlers should consider a multiday canoe or kayak trip to several of the park's paddle-in campsites. Visitors with less time or experience may opt for a guided motorboat or paddle trip.

INTERESTING FACTS ABOUT THE PARK

- Isle Royale ("Royal Island" in French) was named in honor of French King Louis XIV, who sent trappers overseas in the 15th century. Indigenous peoples call the island "Minong," which translates to "a good place to get copper."
- According to ancient Ojibwe lore, the lake is home to the feared and respected Mishipeshu, an underwater panther said to prowl the waters surrounding the island.
- Isle Royale is the only national park in the United States that shuts down entirely in winter.
- Isle Royale offers superb views of the *aurora borealis* (Northern Lights), depending on solar activity and magnetic field fluctuations.

David and Heather Gerth

LIGHTHOUSE PRESERVATIONISTS

When David Gerth visited Isle Royale for the first time in 2007, the building facility manager was taken by the island's beauty, solitude, and rich history. A few miles west, on the open waters of Lake Superior within the park's boundaries, he discovered a rundown lighthouse on a small rock outcropping. Learning that there were no ongoing efforts to restore it, he figured it would be a perfect opportunity to give back to the park he loved by sharing his skills and passion for historic structures. In 2008, David Gerth founded the Rock of Ages Lighthouse Preservation Society with the help of his brothers. First, they pushed for the transfer of the lighthouse's ownership from the United States Coast Guard to the national park, then they formed a partnership agreement to restore, maintain, and operate the lighthouse. In 2016, David married Heather Gerth, an ecologist, interpreter, and environmental educator. She soon became the association's Assistant Director. The couple lives near Duluth, Minnesota, with their two children. Every summer, they come out for full-scale restoration work. Every July and August, up to 30 volunteers support them with this enormous task, each staying for a week. When starting out work in the tower, volunteers had to commute each day by boat. After restoring a few floors, they can now stay overnight at the lighthouse as they work. Here the volunteers learn to be flexible and adaptable, working with the materials available, since a quick trip to the hardware store isn't possible. Transportation is subject to the whims of Lake Superior's waves and the notorious Isle Royale fog. Work on the 10-story tower is planned to be finished by 2027. Visitors can then experience life just as lighthouse keepers experienced it 100 years ago, separated from anything that anchors them to modern life.

Voyageurs

In the "Land of 10,000 Lakes," this watery wonderland is the perfect place to observe the *aurora borealis.*

MINNESOTA

In case you're wondering where Minnesota got its unofficial moniker "Land of 10,000 Lakes," just look at Voyageurs National Park, with its four large lakes—Rainy, Kabetogama, Namakan, and Sand Point—and 26 smaller ones, all creating 655 miles (1054 km) of pristine, undeveloped shoreline. Hugging the United States-Canada border, this area is sometimes called the "gift of the glaciers," a reference to the glaciers that carved out its rich tapestry of land and water. The park, dotted with over 500 islands, is an enchanting mixture of steep island cliffs, verdant forests, and rocky shorelines where blueberries and strawberries grow wild.

One-third of the park is covered in water, and most of the land area is made up of the 75,000-acre (304-square-kilometer) Kabetogama Peninsula. Only reachable by boat, the peninsula offers visitors the chance to explore the park's smaller interior lakes. With backcountry campsites and canoe rentals, visitors can paddle, hike, then paddle again to access the park's remotest corners. Voyageurs is also a prime spot for fishing, just as it has been for the Native peoples who have fished these waters for over 10,000 years.

There are 18 different Native American tribes associated with the park, in particular, the Bois Forte Ojibwe and Canadian Ojibwe First Nations. Birchbark canoes were their main mode of transportation, and fishing was an essential source of food, in addition to wild rice, now the official Minnesota state grain. When French-Canadian fur trappers arrived in the area in the late 18th century, they too used these boats. Designed and built by the Ojibwe, who were skilled traders, guides, interpreters, hunters, and trappers, the canoes were 26 feet (8 m) long and designed to hold up to eight men and 3,500 pounds (1,587 kg). At the height of the fur trade, trappers would pile their canoes high with muskrat, deer, moose, and bear pelts, paddling them between Lake Superior and the Lake of the Woods. This waterway eventually became the boundary between the United States and Canada, and the park is named after these voyageurs, or "travelers."

Today it's not just the park's remote waters that visitors come to revel in. Thanks to its northerly location, the *aurora borealis* often lights up the night sky in mesmerizing waves of green and blue. And since the park is designated as an International Dark Sky Park you can also contemplate the Milky Way in all its glory from popular stargazing spots like Voyageurs Forest Overlook and Beaver Pond Overlook. As you look up you may hear a howl piercing the night's stillness, likely like one of Voyageurs' indigenous gray wolves, called the Timber Wolf. Black bears are common too, and they can often be spotted swimming as they "island hop" in search of food.

PARK AT A GLANCE

While the park was established on April 8, 1975, under President Gerald Ford, locals had actually been fighting for its preservation since 1891.

SIZE
218,055 acres (340 sq. mi./882 km²)
Size rank among National Parks: 32 of 63

ELEVATION
Highest point: Mead Wood Road (1,410 ft./430 m)
Lowest point: Rainy Lake (1,108 ft./338 m)

GEOLOGY
The oldest rocks in the park are more than 2.5 billion years old, about half as old as the earth itself. Around 190,000 years ago when the Ice Age began, the area went through at least four periods of glaciation, helping to sculpt the bedrock and carve out the watery landscape the park is known for today.

FLORA AND FAUNA
There are 50 tree and shrub species in the park, as well as over 40 fern and moss species, over 200 grass, sedge, and rush species, and over 400 wildflower species. Moose, bears, and wolves wander the forests, and waterbirds like loons and cormorants can be seen filling up on the park's over 50 species of fish, such as lake sturgeon, walleye, and smallmouth bass.

CONSERVATION
In the late 1800s, wealthy tourists built private summer homes and resorts along the water. Some of these have been maintained and restored by the park. Among these is the Kettle Falls Hotel. Originally built in 1913, it was purchased in 1918 for $1,000 and four barrels of whiskey. It has been known for its home cooking and fine hospitality ever since.

BEFORE YOU GO
The historic Kettle Falls Hotel is the only food and lodging option in the park, and only accessible by boat, like all of the campsites. Because of the threat of invasive species, no personal boats are allowed in the backcountry or interior lakes. Canoes and houseboats are available for rental in the park.

BEST TIMES TO VISIT
Summer is the warmest season, but July and August can be full of black flies and mosquitos. Fall brings fewer visitors and stunning colors, making it an ideal time to visit. The park is open year-round, and winter offers plenty of options for snow-shoeing, cross-country skiing, snowmobiling, and even driving on frozen lakes.

Gateway Arch

The soaring steel arch at the center of America's smallest national park is an architectural feat—and a reminder of the country's complex history.

In the summer of 1804, Meriwether Lewis and William Clark set out from St. Louis, Missouri, along the Missouri River to explore the American West. President Thomas Jefferson had recently signed the Louisiana Purchase Treaty, acquiring a large chunk of land west of the Mississippi River. After nearly doubling the size of the country overnight, Jefferson hired Lewis and Clark to chart this vast western expanse.

The Lewis and Clark Expedition kicked off an era of westward expansion, fueled by the concept of Manifest Destiny and shaping the course of American history. For its role in this significant and pivotal moment, the old St. Louis riverfront was chosen as the site for a national monument in 1935. The Second World War put the memorial project on pause, but it was revived in

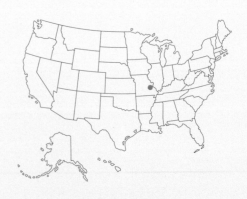

MISSOURI

1947 when Finnish-American architect and modernist icon Eero Saarinen won a competition to design it.

Saarinen's Gateway Arch is undeniably an architectural feat: its bold but elegant arch extends 630 feet (192 m) into the sky, and its foundations reach 60 feet (18 m) below ground. The stainless-steel structure was designed to sway up to 18 inches (45 cm), allowing it to withstand high winds and even earthquakes. The country's tallest monument is as tall as it is wide, and to access the observation deck, visitors must take the built-in tram to the top. Saarinen would unfortunately never see his design realized—he died before construction began—but his audacious design speaks to the spirit of those it was built to honor.

Another essential chapter in American history defines the park, originating in one of the oldest standing buildings in St. Louis, the Old Courthouse. Two blocks from the Gateway Arch, it was here that the enslaved man Dred Scott sued for his freedom, resulting in one of the most important cases in the United States: Dred Scott v. Sandford.

The first two trials of the case were held here, and while the exact courtroom doesn't exist in its original form, the ramifications of the case are solidified in American history. The case dragged on for decades and eventually made it all the way to the U.S. Supreme Court, which delivered the infamous Dredd Scott decision, stating that people of African ancestry were not entitled to citizenship. This enraged abolitionists, fueling the anti-slavery movement and influencing the nomination of Abraham Lincoln to the Republican Party, laying the groundwork for the Civil War.

The Gateway Arch serves as a flashy monument, but it also represents a dark side of American history. Forty square blocks of riverfront property were removed to make space for the arch, gutting a neighborhood with predominantly Black businesses and homes. Under the pretenses of building a memorial, city engineer W.C. Bernard proposed the project as "an enforced slum-clearance program." The public would later learn that the vote to approve city funds for the project was rigged. When it was built, Black workers were excluded from the construction, and in 1964, activist Percy Green scaled the unfinished arch in protest.

The arch's designation as a national park was also tinged with controversy; of America's 63 national parks, Gateway Arch is the only one whose main mission is to showcase and preserve a man-made monument, which critics saw as out of place in a list of national parks whose ethos was to prevent urban development. However, there were positive aspects of the designation too: it brought in funds for a renovation, which allowed the park's museum to tell a more nuanced story of Manifest Destiny—as not just a time of brave discovery and expansion, but also one of oppression and erasure for millions of Native Americans.

PARK AT A GLANCE

The Jefferson National Expansion Memorial was established on December 21, 1935. In 2013, the park broke ground on a $380 million renovation project, making the park much more accessible to St. Louis with 91 acres of green space and a pedestrian bridge over the freeway. These renovations helped to redefine the park, and it was designated as a national park on February 22, 2018.

SIZE
193 acres (.3 sq. mi./.8 km²)
Size rank among National Parks: 63 of 63

ELEVATION
Highest point: Top of the Gateway Arch (1,100 ft./335 m)
Lowest point: St. Louis Riverfront (427 ft./130 m)

GEOLOGY
St. Louis is one of the major cities situated on the Mississippi River, the third-largest watershed in the world. The confluence of the Mississippi and the Missouri River lies just north of town and the park. The Missouri is the longest river in North America.

FLORA AND FAUNA
Sitting between the Mississippi River and downtown St. Louis, the park is home to more wildlife than you might think. Birds are a common urban sight, and 142 different species have been sighted in the park, including the bright-red northern cardinal (the namesake of the local baseball team), mourning doves, and red-winged blackbirds. On their way south for the winter, monarch butterflies also pass through the park.

CONSERVATION
Situated right along the Mississippi riverfront, the park serves as an urban memorial site dedicated to the history of westward expansion and civil rights. The CityArchRiver renovation project, completed in 2018, helped make the park a more integral part of the city's waterfront and revamped the museum to better reflect a nuanced and complex American history.

BEFORE YOU GO
To access the arch, visitors must take a tram built into the structure. You'll need a ticket to ride one of the 5-person capsules to the top, which takes about 10 minutes round-trip.

BEST TIMES TO VISIT
Spring or fall when the park isn't as busy. Summers in St. Louis are hot and muggy, and winter temperatures can dip below freezing.

Hot Springs

In the "Valley of the Vapors," steaming thermal springs flow through old-growth forests and into hundred-year-old bathhouses seemingly frozen in time.

From the steep folds and faults of the Zig Zag mountains along the Ouachita Range emerges the magic of the thermal hot springs. Seated in the lush mountain forests of Arkansas, Hot Springs National Park is a unique destination where promenades of historic buildings lead to foliage veiled in the steam of the springs. In a span of a couple hours, visitors can stroll the historic Central Avenue, otherwise known as Bathhouse Row, and interact with the natural wonders that give the park its name.

The thermal springs have a long history on earth—and below it. After rain falls into the earth's cracks, the water makes a 4,400-year journey through the earth's superheated crust, reaching a depth of about 8,000 feet (2,438 m) before re-emerging, propelled by the forces of heat and pressure. At 143 °F (62 °C),

ARKANSAS

the bubbling, flowing water is naturally potable. In fact, the water was so coveted in the 18th century, that it inspired a truce between rival Indigenous tribes who wanted to enjoy the healing properties of the "Valley of the Vapors." In the 19th century, people traveled from far and wide to drink and bathe in the waters of the valley, believing the pools and creeks could help cure their ailments. Sweating in the heat of the hot spring, visitors were urged to "Quaff the elixir!"

Today, the park service manages an extensive plumbing system that collects 700,000 gallons (2,649,788 liters) of water every day from 33 of the 47 springs so that it can be used for drinking and bathing. Cooled naturally through this system, the water is available at seven thermal spring fountains around Bathhouse Row, where visitors can fill up jugs of the "elixir" to take home. Indoors, Buckstaff Baths and Quapaw Bathhouse offer a chance to bathe in the thermal springs, piped directly from their source. Outdoors, hillside pools at Display Spring and Hot Water Cascade are almost too hot to touch.

The surrounding mountains protect the precious springs, as well as an array of flora and fauna. Visitors can walk along the hot spring's natural course on Tufa Terrace Trail, where they can witness a rare sight: a steaming thermal cascade that flows over a tufa—a kind of mineral deposit left by centuries of buildup from the mineral-rich waters. If you have the time, go for a hike through the old-growth understory of Sunset Trail, the longest trail loop in the park at 17 miles (27.4 km). In the dappled shade of the hundred-year-old oaks and pine, armadillos, foxes, and minks play. And in the leaves of the trees above hide crow-sized woodpeckers and 10 species of bats.

Hikers can also spot rare flora along the Gulpha Gorge Trail, its glades dotted with the purple blooms of the endemic Ouachita blazing star. Meanwhile, outcroppings of sharp Arkansas novaculite rock jut out from the greenery, creating prime viewpoint perches like Balanced Rock at the top of Sugarloaf Mountain. And for a scenic drive through the park, Hot Springs Mountain Tower rewards visitors with panoramic views of the town nestled in the steaming green valley.

PARK AT A GLANCE

Set aside as the first federal reservation in 1832, the protected area around the hot springs predates both the Department of the Interior (established 1849) and the National Park Service (established 1916). On March 4, 1921, Congress designated Hot Springs as the 18th national park, expanding it to 900 acres (3.6 km²).

SIZE
5,554 acres (9 sq. mi./23 km²)
Size rank among National Parks: 62 of 63

ELEVATION
Highest point: Music Mountain (1,405 ft./428 m)
Lowest point: Bull Bayou (415 ft./126 m)

GEOLOGY
The park is nestled in the Ouachita Mountain Range's Zig Zag Mountains, named for its sharp chevron shape. As a result of tectonic plates colliding, the earth's rock layers were tilted upwards, creating the steep terrain. Among the creek valleys and forests are 47 active springs flowing from 400-million-year-old sedimentary rock.

FLORA AND FAUNA
Surrounding the urban promenade is a deciduous forest of oak, hickory, and shortleaf pine, as well as an abundance of grasses. The park is home to 300 acres (1.2 km²) of old-growth forest, with trees that are hundreds of years old. White-tailed deer, black bears, bats, red foxes, salamanders, and toads can be spotted throughout the forest.

CONSERVATION
The park protects the unique natural and cultural resources of the thermal springs that flow from the Zig Zag Mountains. The water systems and rock formations are of special interest to the park, along with the historic preservation of Bathhouse Row's Gilded Age architecture.

BEFORE YOU GO
Visitors are not allowed to soak in thermal springs outdoors. However, for a fee, you can bathe in the thermal spring water at one of two indoor bathhouses: the Buckstaff or the Quapaw. Just a couple miles from town, visitors can camp at Gulpha Gorge Campground for $34 a night (reservation required).

BEST TIMES TO VISIT
Fall offers the mildest temperatures, as well as colorful foliage. Summer is hot and humid, with temperatures at an average of 90°F (32°C) and rising as high as 110°F (43°C).

TEXAS

Big Bend

Known for its starry skies and temple-like rock formations, this lush oasis rises up from a seemingly endless desert.

TOP: In the southeast corner of the park, the Hot Springs trail passes high up above the Rio Grande as it emerges from a deep canyon below and with spectacular views across to the Chisos Mountains rising in the distance.

TEXAS

Big Bend might not flaunt the scenic splendor of its better-known national park siblings; its charm lies rather in the peculiarity of the terrain. From the hot, arid desert, to the wet floodplains of the Rio Grande, to the cool mountain forests, this park is teeming with life. Bears and mountain lions, eagles and hawks, tarantulas and rattlesnakes all coexist here. In fact, the park hosts more types of birds, bats, butterflies, ants, scorpions, and cacti than any other in the United States.

The earliest settlers in the park were from Mexico, arriving in the early 1800s. Soon, others followed, and by 1900, large stretches of the land were being used for sheep, goat, and cattle ranching. However, overgrazing rapidly occurred as a result of such intensive land use. When ore deposits were discovered, settlers flocked to the area to work in the mines or to support the mining operations with work such as smelting or logging.

Besides the vast expanse of desert, Big Bend has a number of geological wonders, including a group of giant boulders—some of them balancing quite precariously. These wonders can be reached by a trail through the Grapevine Hills and the deep-sided Santa Elena Canyon, which has walls shooting straight up from the river, some 1,500-feet (4,60-m) tall.

"Big Bend Park is the untamed, aloof, but never-ugly desert. Some folks say they do not like the desert. I wonder if they remained long enough to know?"

—FREEMAN TILDEN, WRITER

The first efforts to protect the land began in 1930, as the region was increasingly prized for its unique contrasts and beautiful scenery. The national park was established in 1944.

Of the diverse landscapes Big Bend has to offer, the most distinctive is the desert, which covers a staggering 97 percent of the park and extends deep into Mexico, far beyond the borders of the park. At just under 8,000 years old, the Chihuahuan Desert is fairly young. Surrounded on three sides by mountains, rain falls almost exclusively during the summer months. With rain comes life, and the park's numerous century plants (a kind of agave), burst into blossom, enchanting the landscape with their colorful flowers. As enticing as this explosion of life may be, beware: temperatures here can reach upwards of 120 °F (49 °C)—too hot for even the biggest outdoor fanatics, especially since shade is hard to come by.

An overwhelming contrast to the vast desert expanses are Big Bend's craggy mountains and massive canyons etched out of limestone. The Chisos, formed by volcanic activity, form the heart of the park and are home to numerous hiking trails, lodging, and dining establishments. (There's also a hot spring near Rio Grande Village, whose dissolved mineral salts are said to have healing powers.) The slopes become greener and more densely wooded as the altitude increases, reaching an elevation of 2,388 feet (728 m) at Emory Peak, the highest point in the park. Here, visitors are rewarded with spectacular views all the way to Mexico.

It's also a good vantage point to see where Big Bend gets its name: the mighty Rio Grande, lifeline of this otherwise arid region. As it ceaselessly eats its way through the Texan desert and mountain ranges, the river resembles a long, sinuous ribbon. A night cruise on the river, which marks the southern border of the park but also the border to Mexico, offers a tiny, yet spectacular glimpse of what Big Bend National Park's landscape has to offer after sunset.

Because the region around the park is sparsely populated, the night sky here is among the darkest in North America, providing ideal conditions for stargazers and astronomers. In 2022, the park was included in the largest International Dark Sky Reserve ever designated. On particularly clear nights, you can see about 2,000 twinkling stars with the naked eye—up to 10 times more than in a midsize city.

BIG BEND NATIONAL PARK

A s the saying goes, "Everything is bigger in Texas," and, being one of the largest national parks in the United States, Big Bend is no exception. In 1933, efforts to protect the land led to the creation of Texas Canyons State Park. Texas later acquired additional land for the park, and on June 12, 1944, the area was designated as Big Bend National Park.

SIZE
801,163 acres (1,252 sq. mi./3,240 km²)
Size rank among National Parks: 14 of 63

ELEVATION
Highest point: Emory Peak (7,825 ft./2,385 m)
Lowest point: Rio Grande River (1,715 ft./523 m)

GEOLOGY
For millions of years, this geologically complex region was covered by the sea. Tectonic forces slowly raised the sea floor. Then, over countless millennia, sedimentation, erosion, volcanism, and fossilization shaped the area. About 100 million years ago, the region was a large swamp area with lush forests, before it slowly transformed into the arid landscape found here today. Over time, the Rio Grande worked its way deeper and deeper into the rock strata, gradually creating the park's distinctive steep-walled canyons.

FLORA AND FAUNA
Due to the enormous differences in altitude, Big Bend National Park features a diverse array of wildlife and plants, making it the most biodiverse national park in North America. A total of 450 bird species soar through the air here. Black bears live alongside cougars, and the park boasts 56 species of reptiles, 75 species of mammals, and at least 1,200 species of plants. On the slopes of the Chisos Mountains, oak, pine, and juniper forests offer visitors (and wildlife) welcome shade.

CLIMATE AND WEATHER
Big Bend National Park is located in southwest Texas, so the weather is often influenced by the Pacific Ocean, whereas

most of Texas is under the influence of the Gulf of Mexico. Weather conditions can, therefore, be significantly different than other parts of the state. Winter in the Chisos Mountains is cold, with occasional snowfall. In summer, it is noticeably cooler at higher elevations, while in the desert, daytime temperatures often rise above 100 °F (38 °C).

CONSERVATION

Big Bend National Park was established in 1944 to preserve and protect a considerable portion of the Chihuahuan Desert. The park encompasses close to 80 percent of the Chihuahuan Desert and offers a rich biological and geological diversity. Before Big Bend came under the protection of the National Park System, almost all of the trees were cut for timber. Today, the park's ecosystem has been restored to its former glory, and a wealth of plants and animals can be found here.

BEFORE YOU GO

The park lies in one of the most deserted corners of Texas, and the towns located within the park are few and far between. Make sure to bring sufficient food, water, and gasoline. The only accommodations in the national park are the Chisos Mountains Lodge, as well as four campgrounds. Other accommodations for every budget can be found outside the park. In any case, always have your passport and the appropriate papers on you, in case your excursion happens to take you across the Mexican border.

BEST TIMES TO VISIT

Due to extreme temperatures during the summer, it's best to visit Big Bend between November and March when temperatures are warm but not as unbearably high as in summer. There is little shade in the park. Around Thanksgiving week, Christmas, and during spring break, the demand for camping and lodging requires reservations.

HIDDEN GEM

The Upper Burro Mesa Pouroff begins as a meager wash but quickly descends into a steep canyon with hanging gardens and imposing walls. The hike is a mere 3.5 miles (5.6 km) out-and-back but does require some light bouldering.

INTERESTING FACTS ABOUT THE PARK

- Native Americans lived in Big Bend or passed through the area for thousands of years. Pictographs and archeological sites bear evidence of their presence.
- The Civilian Conservation Corps built much of the park's infrastructure by hand in the 1930s.
- Big Bend National Park has the darkest measured skies in the lower 48 states, making it a prime spot for stargazing.

María "Chata" Sada

RESTAURATEUR

When a reporter from the *Dallas Morning News* came to Boquillas, Texas (near today's Rio Grande Village), he wasn't taken with the landscape. Instead, it was the owner of a cherished local store and restaurant that impressed him. Writing that she had the bearing of a queen, he noted that, "Her tortillas were more pungent, someway, her tamales more drippy and a bit more fiery, her chili just a shade tastier than the dishes served on linen and with silver in other establishments." María "Chata" Sada (1884–1973) and her husband, Juan G. Sada, had come from Mexico to the Boquillas area in the 1880s, landing on the Texan side of the Rio Grande in 1906. Building an adobe house with peeled cottonwood logs as beams and supports, Sada turned their place into a welcoming retreat for travelers, where she rented out rooms and cooked tacos on her flat-topped, wood-burning stove. At the time, Boquillas was a long 100-mile (161-kilometer) drive from Marathon, and the Sadas' place marked a welcome end of the road. While her husband operated a silver mine across the river, Sada turned the property into a respite for everyone from law enforcement officers to prospectors to naturalists. She tended to a small plot of land with goats and chickens and irrigated it with water from the river. There was cold beer on hand in a kerosene-powered refrigerator, and she even kept money in a trunk to cash checks for friends. Extending hospitality whenever she could, Sada also took care of many homeless and orphaned children. Known locally as Chata's Place, it became a much-loved institution. In 1957, the restaurant and most other buildings in Boquillas were torn down to make way for the Rio Grande Village development. And while "Chata's Place" no longer exists, her legacy lives on.

Guadalupe Mountains

The terrain here is so harsh and wild that paved roads within the park are literally nonexistent.

Rising out of the arid desert of West Texas, the Guadalupe Mountains reach elevations of more than 8,500 feet (2,591 m) and contain the four tallest peaks in the state. Known as the "Top of Texas," the mountain range is part of the 250-million-year-old Capitan Reef, which was formed in the prehistoric Delaware Sea and eventually pushed to the earth's surface. This whole area of Texas was once covered by water, and the ancient reef is part of the larger fossil-rich Permian Basin, the largest petroleum-producing basin in the United States. The 400-mile- (640-kilometer-) long reef is one of the most well-preserved fossil reefs in the world.

Western Texas can feel like the Wild West, and the park is no different. With no paved roads inside the park, you'll be disappointed if you're looking for a relaxing scenic drive. If you want to discover what this park has to offer, you'll need a good sense of adventure and some serious stamina. The climb to the top of Guadalupe Peak (8,751 ft./2,667 m), the highest point in Texas, attracts seasoned hikers from all over the country. The 8.4-mile (14-kilometer) round-trip hike gains 3,000 feet (914 m) in elevation and is known for being incredibly strenuous. Those who attempt it are rewarded with expansive views of a landscape that millions of years ago would have been covered in water.

There are over 80 miles (129 km) of hiking trails in the park, and most are challenging and require physical fortitude. The ominous-sounding Devil's Hall is one such trail, but those who seize the challenge will get to hike through the trail's namesake hall, a narrow ravine sculpted out of the canyon's eroding limestone. In the 1970s, before the wilderness area was designated as a park, there was much discussion as to whether roads or more amenities should be added to better accommodate visitors. "Go in while you're young," was one conservationist's opinion, and the park was left to exist in its very wild and rugged state.

Many visitors come to the park for McKittrick Canyon, sometimes referred to as "the most beautiful place in Texas." The canyon

is a little less harsh, peppered with desert plants like prickly pear and lechuguilla, an agave species that's only found in the Chihuahuan Desert. Besides providing much-needed shade, the trees that grow here put on a colorful show in the fall. On the west side of the park lie the stark-white Salt Basin Dunes: mounds of white gypsum sand that sit atop the desert floor, framed by the mountains in the background. For sightseers who want a slightly less intense experience, there is El Capitan, which can be seen from the U.S. Highway 62/180. One of the park's most well-known features, this 1,000-foot- (304-meter-) tall limestone cliff glows in stunning hues of pink and orange at sunrise and sunset.

PARK AT A GLANCE

G uadalupe Mountains was established as a national park on September 30th, 1972, the same year that Yellowstone National Park celebrated its centennial.

SIZE
86,416 acres (135 sq. mi./349 km²)
Size rank among National Parks: 50 of 63

ELEVATION
Highest point: Guadalupe Peak (8,751 ft./2,667 m)
Lowest point: Salt Basin Dunes (3,689 ft./1,124 m)

GEOLOGY
A portion of the fossilized Capitan Reef, formed when the area was covered by the sea, was lifted by tectonic forces around 20 million years ago. Erosion of the exposed reef, caused by wind and rain, eventually shaped the Guadalupe Mountains we see today. Surrounded by the Chihuahuan Desert, the Guadalupe Mountains are "sky islands," an isolated mountain range that rises out of the desert landscape.

FLORA AND FAUNA
The desert and mountain landscape are home to more than 1,000 species of plants, including 50 species of cacti. From javelinas to Texas banded geckos, the desert wildlife includes 60 species of mammals and 289 species of birds. There is a high concentration of reptiles, and western diamondback and black-tailed rattlesnakes are common along trails.

CONSERVATION
The land for Guadalupe Mountains National Park was donated by the Pratt Family between 1960 and 1963. William Pratt was hired in 1918 as the first geologist for the Humble Oil Company, which eventually became part of Exxon Mobil. Oil money allowed Pratt to buy ranch property in the area, and he eventually purchased more to include the lower portion and mouth of McKittrick Canyon. After the land was donated, the federal government purchased additional property to create the park.

BEFORE YOU GO
There is no lodging or food in the park, and the nearest town, Dell City, is about 40 miles (60 km) away. Harsh conditions like heat and elevation mean that it's important to carry plenty of water and know your limits.

BEST TIMES TO VISIT
Spring and summer with warm and mild temperatures. High winds are common in fall and winter. The weather can vary greatly depending on elevation, so be prepared.

Carlsbad Caverns

Over millennia, acidic water has dissolved the limestone here into intricate formations, leaving a mysterious underground world—and a sanctuary for bats.

Hidden below a desert landscape lies an exquisite underground cathedral of limestone. Half a million visitors come every year to explore the unparalleled wonders in the Carlsbad Caverns, which is not only a national park but also a UNESCO World Heritage Site. The story of these 120 unique caves began 4 to 6 million years ago when waters rich in hydrogen sulfide seeped into fractures and faults in the limestone. As it mixed with rainwater, it turned into sulfuric acid, dissolving the limestone. This acidic mixture left behind a maze of constantly evolving caverns both large and small.

Dripping water continues to expand and change the majestic speleothems, the cave formations that the park is known for. With names like King's Palace, Hall of the White Giant, and

NEW MEXICO

Whale's Mouth, the formations speak to the park's majesty. The park's namesake cavern is also its most well known, and people have been exploring Carlsbad Cavern since prehistoric times. In the early 1900s, the cavern was utilized for guano mining and was referred to as the "Bat Cave." Later in 1915, a cavern-obsessed cowboy named Jim White paired up with photographer Ray V. Davis to document the cave, and their photos sparked nationwide interest. Decorated with a spectacular array of massive stalagmites, stalactites, columns, flowstone, travertine, and cave "popcorn," this spacious chamber is so stunning that entertainer Will Rogers once called it the "Grand Canyon with a roof over it."

While the guano mining ended a century ago, Carlsbad Cavern is still a refuge for bats and provides a habitat for three species, most famously the Brazilian free-tailed bats whose population has reached an impressive 400,000. The park also offers unique opportunities for scientific research, with many areas of the underground system yet to be explored. In Lechuguilla Cave—open only to research teams—explorers have mapped over 145 miles (233 km) of passages, making it one of the tenth-largest caves in the world.

Part of what makes the park unique is that it preserves a portion of the Capitan Reef, one of the most well-preserved fossil reefs on earth. Created 265 million years ago when an inland sea covered the area, the reef contains marine fossils of ammonites, crinoids, snails, nautiloids, bivalves, brachiopods, and many more. Throughout the caves, visitors have the rare chance to view this fossil reef from the inside.

The underworld of Carlsbad Caverns may be its highlight, but above ground, another world flourishes as well. The park sits in the northern portion of the Chihuahuan Desert. Straddling parts of Mexico and the United States, this is the most biologically diverse desert in the Western Hemisphere and one of the most diverse arid regions in the world. The park offers several desert hiking trails, from the shorter and mostly paved Chihuahuan Desert Nature Trail to the grueling 12-mile (19-kilometer) Guadalupe Ridge Trail.

Under President Coolidge, Carlsbad Caverns was designated a national monument in 1923. On May 14, 1930, Herbert Hoover signed the act that officially made Carlsbad Caverns a national park.

SIZE
46,766 acres (73 sq. mi./189 km²)
Size rank among National Parks: 51 of 63

ELEVATION
Highest point: Guadalupe Ridge (6,368 ft./1,941 m)
Lowest point: Desert lowlands (3,596 ft./1,036 m)

GEOLOGY
Some 250–300 million years ago, an island sea covered the area, and the Capitan Reef grew from its fertile waters. Pushed upwards by tectonic forces, the Capitan Reef created the Guadalupe Mountain range. Underneath, acidic water dissolved the bedrock of limestone, carving out an endless maze of caves and intricate formations.

FLORA AND FAUNA
Carlsbad Caverns sits in the northern portion of the Chihuahuan Desert, which is incredibly biologically diverse. Here you will find 67 species of mammals, including cougars, coyotes, foxes, wolves, bobcats, otters, weasels, badgers, skunks, bats, and shrews. A total of 357 bird species make their home here, and the large colony of Cave Swallows nesting near the cave entrance has been there since the 1960s.

CONSERVATION
Visitors see only a small portion of Carlsbad Cavern, and access to the more secluded caves is strictly controlled and limited to preserve the fragile ecosystem. Even so, the cave ecosystem has seen recent changes, and scientific research is essential to ensure ongoing preservation. The park's future is also at risk from mining interests seeking federal approval for oil and gas drilling in the area.

BEFORE YOU GO
The delicate nature of this underworld expanse means that visitors are strictly monitored. Reservations are required, and there are ranger-led hikes, as well as two trails to explore at your own pace.

BEST TIMES TO VISIT
The park gets about 278 beautiful sunny days a year. The summer, however, can be very hot. Spring and fall are best for milder temperatures. Carlsbad Cavern stays chilly year-round, so bring a light layer for your visit.

White Sands

Home to the oldest known human
footprints in North America, these
blindingly white dunes are so
vast they can be seen from space.

Usually known for its use in plaster and drywall, gypsum is an
incredibly soft mineral. It starts in its crystal form, selenite.
As water seeps in and freezes, it breaks the selenite apart, eventually reducing it to tiny pieces of white sand. And if enough
of those pieces come together, it makes for an impressive sight.
The glittering white dunes of White Sands National Park make
up the largest gypsum dune field in the world, with the highest
dunes reaching 60 feet (18 m) tall. The dune field contains an
incredible 4.5 billion tons of gypsum sand, and is so big astronauts
on the Apollo mission could spot it with the naked eye as they
made their way to the moon.

 The dunes are around 7,000 years old, but the area's history
extends much farther back. Tens of thousands of years ago, the
1,600-square-mile (4,143-square-kilometer) Lake Otero covered
the land. On the lake's shores roamed large ice age animals like
mammoths, ground sloths, ancient camels, and saber-toothed
cats. Their footprints were preserved in the earth, and today,

White Sands National Park has the largest collection of fossilized ice age footprints on the planet. It wasn't just animals who were here either. In 2018, researchers made an impressive discovery: human footprints. Up until then, it was believed that humans arrived on the continent around 13,500 to 16,000 years ago. These new footprints proved to be around 23,000 years old, making them the oldest known human footprints in North America.

The park's ancient roots make it rich fodder for scientific research, but so does its more recent history. The particular environment of the dunes has led to rapid evolutionary changes in the park's animals, prompting researchers to call it a "Desert Galapagos." In just 7,000 years—a mere blip in geological time—several species have entirely changed their coloration to adapt to their surroundings. Three lizard species, the Apache pocket mouse, the White Sands woodrat, and two species of camel crickets all have permanent white coloration to blend in with the environment.

NEW MEXICO

To see this white expanse firsthand, visitors can take Dunes Drive 8 miles (13 km) into the heart of the dune field. There are also five established trails that wander through the dunes, and the most strenuous of these is the Alkali Flat Trail, which leads to the dry lakebed of Lake Otero. Today the only remnant of the ancient lake is Lake Lucero, an ephemeral lake, or playa, that only fills after heavy rain or snowfall in the nearby mountains.

The flat, dry, sandy landscape of the Tularosa Basin hasn't just been accommodating to dunes, it has also been a key location for the United States military and the White Sands Missile Range. Established in response to the bombing of Pearl Harbor, the missile range played an important role in the Manhattan Project, with the first atomic bomb test taking place here in 1945. The desert environment has also been a prime spot for space research. NASA tested the rocket propulsion systems they used in Apollo 11's moon landing on the white, lunar landscape, which has since been featured in dozens of movies over the years.

PARK AT A GLANCE

E stablished as a national monument on January 18, 1933, under President Herbert Hoover, White Sands didn't become a national park until December 20, 2019.

SIZE
148,588 acres (232 sq. mi./601 km²)
Size rank among National Parks: 37 of 63

ELEVATION
Highest point: NE 30, former military installation
(4,116 ft./1,255 m)
Lowest point: Lake Lucero (3,887 ft./1,185 m)

GEOLOGY
The gypsum that makes up the dunes dates back to over 200 million years ago when the area was covered by the shallow Permian Sea. Over time, tectonic plates shifted and collided, forming mountain ranges and creating the ancient Lake Otero in the process. During the last Ice Age, rain and snowmelt carried the gypsum down from the mountains and into the basin. As the lake evaporated, selenite crystals formed, eventually eroding into the tiny white grains of sand that form the dunes today.

FLORA AND FAUNA
The stark and barren landscape may seem inhospitable, but the park is home to over 250 bird species. The desert landscape is even home to a single species of fish, the White Sands pupfish. There are also over 300 plants, 50 mammals, 7 amphibians, and 30 reptiles, including the Sonoran gopher snake, which can grow up to 7 feet (2 m) long.

CONSERVATION
The U.S. military tried for decades to secure land within the national monument for its White Sands Missile Range. When the area was designated as a national park in 2019, the legislation provided the military with 2,826 acres (11 km²) of land within the monument's former boundaries. At the same time, the National Parks Service gained 5,766 acres (23 km²) of land formerly owned by the military.

BEFORE YOU GO
The park only has primitive backcountry campsites, but there are lodging options in nearby towns Alamogordo and Las Cruces. The road into the park is sometimes closed because of missile testing.

BEST TIMES TO VISIT
Crowds clear out in the fall, and the weather is comfortable and sunny, with average temperatures of 60 to 80 °F (18 to 27 °C).

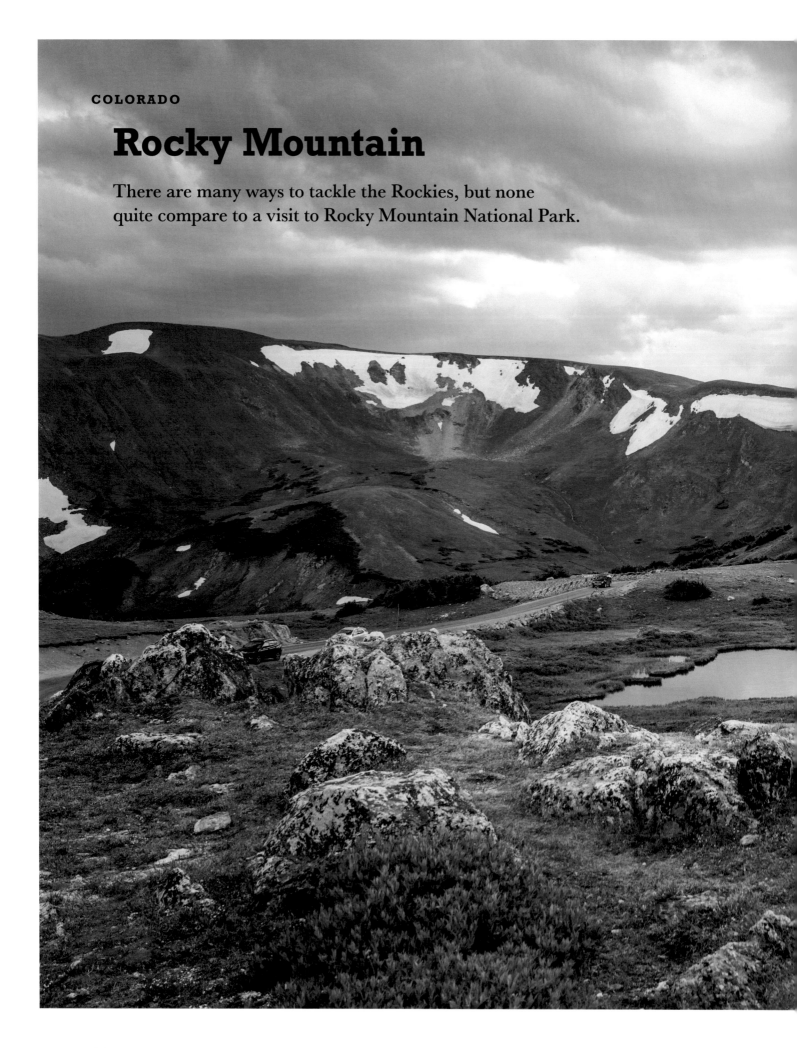

Rocky Mountain

There are many ways to tackle the Rockies, but none
quite compare to a visit to Rocky Mountain National Park.

Rocky Mountain National Park may only have one peak higher than 14,000 feet (4,270 m), but it has some 60 mountains rising 12,000 feet (3,660 m) above the park's meadows, lakes, and forested valleys.

COLORADO

About two hours' drive from Denver, this park delights visitors with some of the most theatrical mountain scenery on the planet, with its endless vistas overlooking the rest of the Rocky Mountains, whose peaks boast a staggering 54 "Four-teeners"—climber lingo for any mountain whose summit scrapes past 14,000 feet (4,267 m). Though the park itself contains only one (Longs Peak), its "smaller" peaks are no less stunning for it. Bearing names like "Chiefs Head," "Isolation," and "Little Matterhorn," the mountains here are a veritable paradise for mountaineers, skiers, and hikers alike.

Nowhere else in the United States is mountain wilderness more accessible than here. And the landscape is still very much untouched—thanks to Enos Mills. The naturalist, born in 1870, is considered the father of Rocky Mountain National Park. At 14,

he moved from Kansas to Colorado in hopes that the crisp mountain air would help him recover from an unidentifiable illness. (It turned out to be a wheat allergy.) At 15, he had already climbed Longs Peak, the "King of the Rockies," where he later established his homestead. Then, at 19, on a beach in California, Mills had a chance encounter with the well-known conservationist John Muir, who encouraged the young man on his quest to dedicate his life to conservation.

Mills grew up just as the country's first national parks were springing up. Inspired by the conservationist zeitgeist, he lobbied to protect a stretch of the Rockies from Longs Peak to Pikes Peak. Fortunately, little gold or other mineral resources were found in the area, and the long winter at high elevations did not provide favorable conditions for agriculture. That helped Enos Mills convince the region's residents to promote the site for tourism. With the First World War in Europe and the rise of the auto-mobile, Americans increasingly turned their attention to tourist attractions in their own country. Mills toured lecture halls, wrote op-eds, and eventually secured financial support. Finally, in 1915, Congress approved the establishment of the national park. Enos Mills built an inn and worked as a tour guide, making the ascent to Longs Peak more than 300 times throughout his life.

TOP: With a population somewhere in the 300 to 400 range, Bighorn sheep have come to symbolise Rocky Mountain. They are just one of 67 species of mammals living in the park, which also include beavers, marmots, and hares.

Today, professional guides continue to follow in his footsteps. Those who enjoy the outdoors can explore the park on a network of more than 350 miles (560 km) of trails along beautifully dappled meadows, rushing streams and waterfalls, and some of the park's 150 lakes (some of which are frozen for most of the year). Whether on foot, horseback, mountain bike, or, in winter, cross-country skis, there are plenty of opportunities to get up close and personal with nature. One of the most popular of these is the Ute Trail, which runs above the tree line almost the entire time and offers unobstructed mountain views. The trail was once used by the Ute and Arapaho Tribes on their way to their summer and winter hunting grounds.

For the less actively inclined, the park is accessible in summer via Trail Ridge Road, one of America's highest (and most scenic) highways. Built by the Civilian Conservation Corps along a former Paleo-Indian trail, it runs halfway through the park from east to west and reaches an elevation of 12,183 feet (3,713 m). Because portions of the road run high above the treeline, it showcases unparalleled mountain vistas filled with glacial moraines and eternal snowfields. Here motorists can explore the sweeping vastness of the alpine tundra, which makes up a third of the park's area. Meadows blanket the slopes like tablecloths, and the animals in the park live largely undisturbed. Especially in the fall, visitors come to catch a glimpse of the park's abundant wildlife, with elk, deer, and bighorn sheep a common sight.

ROCKY MOUNTAIN NATIONAL PARK

Rocky Mountain National Park was established on January 26, 1915, under President Woodrow Wilson, after years of advocacy by naturalist, nature guide, and lodge owner Enos Mills, who was supported by the Sierra Club and the Daughters of the American Revolution. It was designated a UNESCO Biosphere Reserve in 1976.

SIZE
265,461 acres (415 sq. mi./1,074 km²)
Size rank among National Parks: 26 of 63

ELEVATION
Highest point: Longs Peak (14,259 ft./4,346 m)
Lowest point: Big Thompson River (7,630 ft./2,326 m)

GEOLOGY
Over a period of about 130 million years, three major mountain-building phases fundamentally reshaped western North America. During the last of these phases—the Laramide orogeny, from 80 to 40 million years ago—the southern Rocky Mountains took shape as intense plate tectonic activity lifted ancient rock to the surface, creating the rugged landscape they are known for today. Ice age glaciers that rolled over the terrain during the past 2 million years left characteristic traces: trough valleys, moraine hills, and countless firn and glacial lakes.

FLORA AND FAUNA
The harsh mountain tundra of the Rockies is still largely untouched and provides an ideal habitat for several large mammals, including bighorn sheep and elk. Grizzly bears and wolves were mercilessly wiped out in pioneer times; only black bears and cougars are still sighted now and then. The park's distinctive forests are made of aspen, fir, pine, and spruce—interspersed with meadows that bear a beautiful array of flowers in the short high mountain summer.

CLIMATE AND WEATHER
The weather in Rocky Mountain National Park is extreme and unpredictable, especially in the highlands, ranging from

brutally hot summer days to winter snowstorms. At lower elevations, it can drop below freezing at night even after a pleasant summer day. Winters are long (October to May), cold, and snowy.

CONSERVATION

Rocky Mountain National Park was established to preserve the high-elevation ecosystems and wilderness character of the southern Rocky Mountains and to provide access to the park's scenic beauty, wildlife, natural features, and cultural objects. Unfortunately, some arsenic, sodium cyanide, and mercury left over by prospectors extracting gold are still found in the soil. Climate change is also an issue: although the alpine ecosystem seems fit to adapt to climate change due to its high altitudes and ever-changing weather conditions, many of the animal and plant species already live on the edge of their abilities and the slightest change could displace a species from this habitat.

BEFORE YOU GO

Check the weather conditions before you go: afternoon storms are quite common in summer, so be sure to head out early. There's nothing worse than being caught above the tree line in a lightning storm.

BEST TIMES TO VISIT

High-elevation park roads are usually open for a narrow window from May to September, which limits access to most visitors to the summer months. The more adventurous may consider visiting in the colder months to avoid crowds, but they should be prepared for cold temperatures and extreme conditions.

HIDDEN GEM

The East Inlet Trail offers solitude and a variety of terrain, including meadows, forests, rocky ridges, and a waterfall. Experienced hikers can take the trail up to Spirit Lake.

INTERESTING FACTS ABOUT THE PARK

- The source of the famous Colorado River is in Rocky Mountain National Park.
- With a high point at 12,183 ft. (3,713 m) elevation, Trail Ridge Road is the highest continuous paved road in the United States.
- The myriad of wildflowers smell especially intense here because the flowers have a harder time luring their pollinators up to alpine heights.
- The Continental Divide runs through the center of the park: melt and rain water on the west side flows into the Pacific Ocean, while water on the east side of the park flows into the Gulf of Mexico or the Atlantic.

Richard E. Hoffman

CONSERVATIONIST

After a long hike in 1999, Dr. Richard E. Hoffman asked a national park ranger if there was a way he could contribute to improving the trail from Mills Lake to Black Lake, two pristine lakes in Glacier Gorge. Hoffman, a Dallas native, had frequently visited the park since 1959, when his parents sent his brothers and him to summer camp in Estes Park, Colorado. For four consecutive summers, they hiked and backpacked through Rocky Mountain National Park, summiting Longs Peak in 1962 via the Cables Route on the North Face at a time when there still were steel cables in place. From 1976 to 1978, Hoffman served as a general practitioner in Saguache, Colorado, and spent his free weekends climbing mainly in the Sangre de Cristo Range. While completing his clinical and public health training in the eastern half of the country from 1980–85, in early 1986 he decided to return to Colorado to be close to the Rocky Mountains again. With Denver as his home base, he ventured out to climb in the summer months. When he asked how he could help improve the park's trails, the ranger referred him to the Rocky Mountain Nature Association (now Rocky Mountain Conservancy), a nonprofit organization that, among other things, supports the improvement and maintenance of trails in the national park. Over the past 22 years, Hoffman has made philanthropic contributions to improve several trails, including those leading to Mills and Black Lake, to Loch Vale and Sky Pond, to Lake Haiyaha, and for the past two years, the main trail up Longs Peak. He has also contributed to several projects of the Colorado 14ers Initiative, another nonprofit organization that improves trails on tall peaks in other parts of Colorado. "It's been very rewarding for me to be part of the effort," he says, "[It's] a way of giving back for all the thrills and lasting memories that come with being in the mountains."

Mesa Verde

This park offers a glimpse into the remarkable culture of an ancient tribe that built spectacular villages into the steep cliffs of southwest Colorado.

TOP: A large petroglyph panel within the park features symbols and figures carved into the red sandstone by the Ancestral Puebloans. Among them are handprints, spirals and more than 30 animal and human figures.

COLORADO

Mesa Verde is a national park unlike any other. It doesn't preserve pristine wilderness but an archaeological site—and ancient cultural heritage. Towering high above the surrounding desert plain, this densely forested plateau is home to the most beautiful pre-Columbian cliff dwellings in North America, showcasing one of the largest and most important archaeological sites to document ancient Native American culture. They were built more than 700 years ago by the Ancestral Pueblo people. The secretive culture dominated the American Southwest in pre-Columbian times and disappeared more or less without a trace.

As early as 550 CE, people lived in semisubterranean pit houses clustered into small villages. Later the inhabitants of this region began to build dwellings above ground with vertical walls and flat roofs. From this point on, these skilled stonemasons were known as Pueblo people, or "village dwellers." By the 1190s, they

Many of the structures at Cliff Palace (opposite) and Balcony House (below) remain remarkably intact. Within the dwellings, the Ancestral Puebloans built rooms dedicated to rituals and ceremonies. These rooms, known as kivas, were usually round and a number of them can be identified among the ruins.

Mesa Verde was the first park to preserve the works of man, not nature.

had begun building impressive multistory brick and adobe buildings in alcoves and on recessed rock ledges, building whole villages into the cliff walls of the canyon. Irrigation systems helped them grow corn, beans, and squash; men hunted deer, rabbits, and squirrels. Several thousand people were thought to have lived in the area.

But the Ancestral Pueblo people abandoned their extraordinary dwellings only a few decades later, in the span of a generation or two. Researchers are unsure why, but it's possible they left due to long periods of drought. By 1300 CE, the Mesa Verde area was virtually deserted. The sprawling ruins were so remote from any civilization that they weren't discovered until the 16th century when the Navajo happened upon the abandoned villages. Later, in the 1800s, Anglo-Americans started to hear about the wonders of the mesas and began entering on their own. Widespread destruction and looting followed, and to protect against further damage, the national park was created in 1906. The park hosts about 5,000 known archaeological sites (including pit houses, pueblos, masonry towers, and farming structures).

Several of the cliff dwellings are open to visitors. While most of the approximately 600 cliff dwellings in the park only have one to five rooms each, the most famous ones are bigger: the well preserved Spruce Tree House, which could accommodate about 125 people, the smaller Balcony House (40), the Long House (150), and the Step House (27). The largest settlement in the park is

Cliff Palace. Built under a rock overhang, the park's centerpiece structure once accommodated as many as 250 people in more than 200 rooms. The Ancestral Pueblo people built the structure with sandstone blocks and joined them using a mixture of ash, clay, and water as mortar. Wooden beams were used to construct ceilings and doorways.

Cliff Palace, Balcony House, and Long House can only be reached via guided tours, but visitors can explore Spruce Tree House and Step House independently during the summer months. However, to better understand the site's significance, a tour is highly recommended. It feels like a journey through an adventure movie, diving deeper and deeper into the mystical world of an advanced civilization that gained fame for its architecture, agriculture, and art. The engravings etched in the rock here depict human forms and recount stories of a bygone time—spectacular reminders of this mysterious ancient culture.

MESA VERDE NATIONAL PARK

President Theodore Roosevelt established Mesa Verde National Park in southwestern Colorado as one of the first national parks on June 29, 1906. Today, it is considered the most culturally significant national park in the United States, protecting the rich heritage of the Ancestral Pueblo people who lived there from 600 to 1300 CE, and 26 tribes associated with the area. The park was designated a UNESCO World Heritage Site in 1978.

SIZE
52,485 acres (82 sq. mi./212 km²)
Size rank among National Parks: 49 of 63

ELEVATION
Highest point: Park Point Lookout (8,571 ft./2,612 m)
Lowest point: Soda Canyon (6,015 ft./1,833 m)

GEOLOGY
Part of the Colorado Plateau, the "mesa" is actually a cuesta, which is similar to a mesa (an isolated sandstone plateau with steeply sloping cliffs that are topped by a cap of erosion-resistant rocks), but is gently tilted south. This happened when Mesa Verde was uplifted over the last two million years. The rock niches were later formed by stream erosion, which cut deep canyons into the plateau.

FLORA AND FAUNA
The area's plant and animal life has adapted to the barren, desert conditions. The "verde" is mainly made up of small-growing pinyon pines and Utah junipers, while sagebrush grows on the hot and dry canyon floors. The park is home to elk, the most common large animals here. While mountain lions and black bears were once native to the area, they are now rarely seen. The coyotes and bobcats that live in the park tend to avoid people, but snakes (including the venomous prairie rattlesnake) and lizards can be spotted. At dusk, numerous bats emerge, on the hunt for insects.

CLIMATE AND WEATHER
Summers in this semiarid climate are usually hot and dry, but evenings and nights can be quite cool. In July and August, the risk of thunderstorms is very high. Snow can fall as late as

May and as early as October, and while the winter is usually mild, there are occasional snowstorms.

CONSERVATION

Mesa Verde National Park was established in 1906 to "preserve the works of man"—it was the first national park to do so. The area had been empty for more than five centuries when two cowboys looking for stray cattle stumbled upon abandoned cave dwellings in 1888. One of them, Richard Wetherill, dedicated his life to the exploration and excavation of the ruins. A women's group, the Colorado Cliff Dwellings Association, called for the protection of Mesa Verde and raised money to have Balcony House, a complex of 38 rooms built in the 13th century, excavated, and stabilized. As the park wasn't established until 1906, many artifacts from the area are now in museums and private collections around the world, including the British Museum in London.

BEFORE YOU GO

Most of the hikes through Mesa Verde are strenuous because of the high altitude, steep, mostly unpaved trails encompassing stairs and ladders, and the often scorching heat. Although there are no age restrictions, not all hiking trails are suitable for children. Special caution is required because of the danger of falling. If you don't have a head for heights, avoid visiting Balcony House. To avoid long queues for tickets, buy them online or arrive at the visitor center early in the morning. Parts of the park are not accessible during the winter months.

BEST TIMES TO VISIT

To avoid the midsummer crowds, try visiting in May, June, September, or October. Some areas of the park, including the cliff dwellings, are closed from October to May.

HIDDEN GEM

Only about 5 percent of visitors venture onto the mesa above the cliff dwellings. Thirty miles of hiking trails in the park offer an easy opportunity to explore additional cultural and natural sites away from the crowds. If hiking, be sure to stick to the trails to prevent damage to sacred and fragile cultural sites.

INTERESTING FACTS ABOUT THE PARK

- The name Mesa Verde originated with early Spanish explorers who saw the area from a distance and named it accordingly.
- The park administration publishes the most favorable times for photography. From June to September, for example, it's 3:45 to 6:00 p.m.
- For the Ancestral Puebloans, the trees on the mesa were sources of food, building materials, spices, dyes, and medicines.

Jesse L. Nusbaum

FIRST NATIONAL PARK SERVICE ARCHEOLOGIST

Jesse L. Nusbaum (1887–1975) first came to Mesa Verde National Park when he was 20. The site had just been designated as a national park, and one of the most pressing tasks was to obtain an accurate survey of what was out there. Nusbaum fit the job description of a "young and agile man, skilled in photography and interested in archaeology." As a youth, Jess, as he was known to friends and associates, would search for arrowheads and read about the ancient cliff dwellings of ancient Native American cultures in the Southwest. Together with two young archeologists (some later referred to them as the "Three Musketeers of Southwestern archaeology"), the slender, outgoing Nusbaum took scores of photographs documenting cliff dwellings and other Ancestral Puebloan sites in and around the park, providing important data for future archaeological research. Over the coming years, he was asked to lead the excavation, repair, and stabilization of structures like Balcony House—a daring endeavor which involved hauling in supplies on horseback more than 20 miles (32 km) and then returning, months later, in knee-deep snow. Nusbaum drew on the skills his father—a brick mason—taught him, pioneering techniques in a field still in its infancy. The work made him a venerable specialist, and he was even invited to work on the Mayan Ruins in Yucatan. In the meantime, Mesa Verde was plagued by mismanagement. However, this ended when Nusbaum was appointed superintendent in 1921, putting a halt to the ineptitude, theft, and nepotism that had become commonplace in the park. He held the position for 17 years, upgrading facilities, banning grazing, building a museum, and professionalizing the ranger force. At evening campfires, he would personally educate the public about the importance of the site.

Black Canyon of the Gunnison

Water and time have crafted a rugged and dramatic landscape whose geology dates back almost 2 billion years.

Steep cliffs, ancient rock, treacherous descents, and a winding river make the Black Canyon of the Gunnison Colorado's more intimate version of the Grand Canyon. Stretching over just 48 miles (77 km), it is not the longest canyon, but it is one of the narrowest and deepest to be found across the Western United States. At almost 2 billion years old, the rocks here tell a story of earth's earliest days. Sixty million years ago, the ancient metamorphic Precambrian rock was pushed to the surface, only to be covered in volcanic rock 30 million years later. The metamorphic rock lay hidden, until around 2 million years ago when the Gunnison River began flowing in earnest, slowly etching the deep canyon into the landscape we see today.

COLORADO

What remains are steep cliffs of exposed volcanic and meta-morphic rocks, often crisscrossed with shades of pink pegmatite. In fact, the park got its name not from the color of its rock, but from the ever-present shadows in the deep and narrow valley. Some parts of the gorge receive only half an hour of sunlight per day. At its narrowest, the canyon is only 40 feet (12 m) wide. This plunging chasm has always presented an enormous barrier to humans, and here on the ancestral lands of the Ute Indians, the only evidence of human occupation in the area is at the canyon's rim. The first European expeditions through western Colorado in the late 1700s passed it up entirely. The spectacular natural wonder would later get its name from Captain John Williams Gunnison, who led an 1853 survey expedition from St. Louis to San Francisco, his first adventure west of the Mississippi River.

Today you can hike a variety of trails on both the north and south rim, including the Oak Flat Loop trail which allows visitors to explore below the rim without hiking down into the inner canyon—a much more demanding adventure. If you want to venture further, you'll need a wilderness permit and the skill and experience to navigate unmarked wilderness routes. The most popular of these is the Gunnison Route which drops an astound-ing 1,800 feet (549 m) in elevation in just 1.5 miles (2.4 km). On the river below, only expert paddlers should attempt to tackle the treacherous rapids, which are almost unnavigable.

While the harsh landscape may be inhospitable to humans, birds can easily traverse even the deepest canyon, and the park is home to species like the great horned owl, canyon wrens, and peregrine falcons. Colorful wildflowers paint the area, and at the park's highest point in elevation, Warner Point Nature Trail, Pinyon pine and juniper trees flourish. These trees have offered American Indians sustenance, fuel, and medicine for millennia. Gambel oak also grows along the canyon rim, a year-round source of food for mule deer—a reminder that even in the most dramatic and rugged of landscapes, often foreboding to humans, nature is thriving.

PARK AT A GLANCE

On March 2, 1933, President Herbert H. Hoover established the Black Canyon of the Gunnison as a national monument to pre-serve the unique rugged beauty of the canyon. It was officially designated as a national park on October 21, 1999, by President Bill Clinton.

SIZE
30,045 acres (47 sq. mi./121 km²)
Size rank among National Parks: 56 of 63

ELEVATION
Highest point: Signal Hill (8,775 ft./2,675 m)
Lowest point: Canyon bottom (5,400 ft./1,645 m)

GEOLOGY
Gneiss, schist, quartz-monzonite, and granite-pegmatite are all ancient rocks found in the canyon, considered one of the best displays of these rocks in the world. There is a stark difference between the two canyon walls: the south-facing wall is incredibly steep and barren, while the north-facing wall is more sloped and better suited to vegetation.

FLORA AND FAUNA
Scrub oak, pinyon-juniper forests, and sagebrush dominate the canyon rim, with some of the pinyon trees over 700 years old. On the canyon's north-facing slopes are Douglas fir and Colorado blue spruce, while down by the river, deciduous trees reign. The park is home to peregrine falcons and a variety of seasonal raptors, and other wildlife includes river otters, mule deer, bighorn sheep, black bears, bobcats, mountain lions, and elk.

CONSERVATION
While there were other attempts, the first successful expedition of the Black Canyon of the Gunnison was in 1901 by Abraham Lincoln Fellows and William W. Torrence. Fellows became an advocate of protecting the canyon's incredible natural beauty.

BEFORE YOU GO
At 8,000 feet (2.3 km) above sea level, the canyon rim requires visitors to be mindful of the impacts of altitude. For visitors wanting to stay, there's a campground on both the South and North Rim.

BEST TIMES TO VISIT
From late November to April, the North Rim is closed to vehicles, but the South Rim Road remains open to the visitor center. Summer can be both busy and hot, so late spring and early fall are good options if you want a quieter and more comfortable experience.

Great Sand Dunes

Used by NASA to test equipment for Mars landings, these otherworldly sandy dunes form the quietest park in the Lower 48.

In Southern Colorado, wind and water are artists, sculpting the tallest dunes in North America. The Ute people aptly named them "saa waap maa nache," "sand that moves." The dunes date back to when large lakes covered this region of the San Luis Valley. The large ancient Lake Alamosa is believed to have disappeared about 440,000 years ago, leaving behind smaller lakes that eventually dried up and left behind a sand sheet. Formed over the years from that sand sheet, the dunes are part of an ongoing geological process that continues today.

The tallest dunes in the park are Star Dune and Hidden Dune, both rising 741 feet (225 m) tall. It's a good place for explorers who don't like following rules—there aren't any designated trails in the 30 square miles (78 km²) of dune fields, and all of it is up for discovery. While most visitors choose to venture on foot, sand boarding and sand sledding are also popular ways to enjoy the dunes. Although the soft curves of the dunes are inviting, there's a harshness here too—in the summer the surface of the sand can reach up to 150 °F (65 °C), and on a cold winter night, temperatures can reach as low as -20 °F (-29 °C).

Standing at the top of a dune can feel like being on another planet, and the landscape is so otherworldly that NASA has used the dunes to test equipment for Mars landings. In the early

COLORADO

1940s, the U.S. Army tested how jeeps and new camouflage equipment would work in a desert landscape. Others have used the dunes in their work, like Bing Crosby who wrote his hit "The Singing Sands of Alamosa," inspired by the deep ethereal hum that a dune emits when sand slides down its face. A study conducted by the National Park Service showed that Great Sand Dunes is the quietest park in the contiguous United States—so quiet that you can even hear the sand singing.

The sandy dunes might be the focal point and namesake of the park, but there are several important ecosystems that make up this landscape. Wildflowers dot the alpine tundra and, in the southwest of the park, fluctuating groundwater levels leave

a thick crust of alkali deposits called a sabkha. The 14,000-foot (4,300-meter) peaks of the Sangre de Cristo Mountains rise in the background, and snowmelt in the spring gives birth to the seasonal Medano Creek, which flows around the dunes, creating a popular spot for families to splash in the temporary waves.

Pinyon and ancient juniper trees, some as old as 700 years, spread across the drier foothills of the mountains. Evidence of humans in the park dates back 11,000 years, and in Indian Grove, visitors can marvel at the dozens of Ponderosa pines that have been "culturally modified," that is, peeled and harvested for food and medicine by Indigenous people in the 19th century, left today as living artifacts.

PARK AT A GLANCE

To protect the local environment from mining and other human impacts, President Herbert Hoover proclaimed Great Sand Dunes a national monument in 1932. It wasn't until November 22, 2000, under President Bill Clinton, that it finally became a national park.

SIZE
107,346 acres (168 sq. mi./434 km²)
Size rank among National Parks: 24 of 63

ELEVATION
Highest point: Tijeras Peak (13,604 ft./4,146 m)
Lowest point: San Luis Lakes (7,520 ft./2,292 m)

GEOLOGY
Situated in San Juan Valley, Great Sand Dunes National Park is framed by the San Juan Mountains to the west and the Sangre de Cristo Mountains to the east. Over 400,000 years ago, this valley was covered by Lake Armosa, which eventually dried up leaving a sand sheet, the largest component of the Great Sand Dunes system.

FLORA AND FAUNA
With many different ecosystems, including grasslands, wetlands, subalpine forests, and alpine tundra, the park supports a large variety of plants and wildlife. There are over 250 species of birds, including nine species of owls. The park is home to an abundance of mammals, but the Ord's kangaroo rat is the only one who can live its whole life on the dune field.

CONSERVATION
Gold was found in the area in the 1920s, which led not only to gold mining but also sand extraction for cement. This spurred the women of the local Philanthropic Educational Organization who successfully lobbied to protect the dunes and their surroundings. Thanks to the park's remote location and high elevation, it has been designated as an International Dark Sky Park.

BEFORE YOU GO
The park is split into three units. The North and South Units are easily accessible, but the Elkhorn Ranch Unit requires driving on a gravel road. There are no services, restaurants, or lodging in the park, but there are two campgrounds as well as a horse camp.

BEST TIMES TO VISIT
Come in late May or early June if you want to catch the seasonal Medano Creek. The Piñon Flats Campground is open from April 3 to October 31, and all sites require a reservation.

Grand Teton

Considered Yellowstone's "little brother,"
Grand Teton is an alpine hiker's paradise,
replete with ancient forests and glacial lakes.

LEFT: A landmark structure at Teton National Park, the T.A. Moulton Barn is named for Thomas Alma Moulton, who homesteaded here in the first decade of the 20th century, building this barn to shelter his animals.

WYOMING

To many visitors, Grand Teton National Park in western Wyoming is little more than a thoroughfare on their way to the neighboring Yellowstone National Park. An injustice, really, seeing as few landscapes on earth dare to match its spectacular scenery, where the jagged peaks of the Teton mountain range rise high above vast plains and crystal-clear glacial lakes. At 9 to 13 million years old, the Teton Range is one of the youngest in North America, yet it contains some of the continent's oldest rocks. Rumor has it that French trappers called the glacier-carved summits *tétons*, French for breasts, but they're more likely named after "Thíthuŋwaŋ," the name of the Lakota Sioux who inhabited the area long before settlers arrived.

Glacial lakes and waterfalls are among the geological wonders at Grand Teton. Bradley Lake (opposite) is the smallest of six lakes that lie at the foot of the Teton Range with its jagged, snow-covered peaks.

The park encompasses not just the mountains but also Jackson Hole, an adjacent valley, and the Snake River that threads through it. For a long time, this area was a significant hunting ground and place of worship for Native American tribes, who also harvested bulbs and gathered berries in the fertile valley. The first white man known to enter the park area was John Colter, a trapper and trail scout who came in 1805. He was followed by fur traders, explorers, and adventurers. Among them were the legendary Mountain Men—daring loners who hunted beavers for their highly sought-after fur. (Felt hats, made from beaver pelts, were all the rage in the early 1800s.) These men led a life free of attachments in the harsh and dangerous wilderness.

The presence of these settlers made it much more challenging to establish a national park than at Yellowstone. Initially, in 1929, Grand Teton only encompassed the mountain range. Then, John D. Rockefeller Jr. gradually began purchasing thousands of acres of land in Jackson Hole to donate to the existing national park in 1943. (A scenic road was built in his honor.) Further expansion into the lowlands of Jackson Hole took tough wrangling and drawn-out negotiations with landowners, though. This is why you will find some 300 historic buildings in the park, and why some farmers still have grazing rights to this day.

Grand Teton National Park is still a place for the adventurous, especially mountaineers and other outdoor enthusiasts. From leisurely strolls to climbing expeditions and multiday backcountry hikes, anything is possible here. If you're a bit more daring, consider rafting down the whitewater rapids that roar through the valley's gorges. If not, stop by a glacial lake, where on windless days, you can see the scenery flawlessly reflected in the glass-like surface. Grand Teton National Park sees heavy snowfall in colder months, making it a popular destination for cross-country skiers, snowshoers, ice climbers, and ice fishers.

And then there's the wildlife. As part of the greater Yellowstone ecosystem, grizzly bears, moose, and osprey call Grand Teton their home. Additionally, the National Elk Refuge was established in Jackson Hole in 1912. It was founded to protect these animals, which were starving in large numbers during harsh winters, or killed by hunters for their teeth. Today, the pasture and swampland reserve serves as a winter refuge for about 7,500 wapitis. In addition to elk, the park welcomes the largest bison herd in the world, numbering about 800 bison, as it winters here each year.

GRAND TETON NATIONAL PARK

Soon after Yellowstone National Park had been established in 1872, conservationists campaigned to expand its boundaries to include at least the Teton Range. Jackson Hole residents—mostly ranchers—opposed the expansion of Yellowstone and ensuing debates fractured the community. Ultimately, a compromise was reached between ranchers and conservationists in the authorization of Grand Teton National Park on February 26, 1929.

SIZE
310,044 acres (484 sq. mi./1,255 km²)
Size rank among National Parks: 25 of 63

ELEVATION
Highest point: Grand Teton (13,775 ft./4,199 m)
Lowest point: Fish Creek (6,320 ft./1,926 m)

GEOLOGY
The Teton Range is one of North America's youngest mountain ranges. It was formed about five to nine million years ago when two tectonic plates collided—one was pushed downward and formed Jackson Hole, and the other was folded upward and formed the mountain range. Their peaks are comparably jagged, as they have encountered less erosion than older mountain ranges in the country.

FLORA AND FAUNA
Grand Teton's ecosystem has changed little since prehistoric times and provides a unique habitat for many different plant species. On the mountainsides, bears, marmots, and bighorn sheep linger in summer, and wildflowers dot the riverbank. In fall, birch, aspen, and other deciduous trees blaze with color, and the streams abound with migrating fish. The waterways are also home to many water birds, including trumpeter swans, pelicans, and sandhill cranes.

CLIMATE AND WEATHER
Jackson Hole has long, cold winters. The first heavy snowfalls begin in early November and last until April. The cold montane climate accounts for mild summers with cool nights. Occasional thunderstorms can occur but precipitation in summer is moderate. Snow and frost are possible at any time.

CONSERVATION

Grand Teton protects and preserves the extraordinary wildlife, pristine lakes, and alpine terrain of the Teton Range. Its establishment can be attributed to geologist Ferdinand V. Hayden, who was commissioned in 1872 to explore the region of Wyoming that is now Yellowstone National Park. During this expedition he also came to Jackson Hole, and his companions—a painter and a photographer—documented its unique beauty, leading to the designation of the area as Grand Teton National Park in 1929. In 1943, Jackson Hole National Monument was established adjacent to the park. Both areas were merged in 1950. Today, Grand Teton is one of the most heavily visited national parks in the United States.

BEFORE YOU GO

Thousands of climbers visit Grand Teton National Park every year, as permits are not required for alpine mountaineering or summit tours. It makes sense to contact the park for advance information on weather and trail conditions—some areas close for winter, and roads are covered with snow until at least April. Even at the end of July, ice axes are still sometimes needed on mountain trails.

BEST TIMES TO VISIT

September is the best month of the year to visit, with fewer crowds, plenty of wildlife activity, relatively mild temperatures, and fall colors.

HIDDEN GEM

Bring your binoculars, your camera, and your bear spray to the Willow Flats Overlook, which offers excellent wildlife viewing opportunities. The overlook also offers unobstructed views of the Teton Range.

INTERESTING FACTS ABOUT THE PARK

- The Teton Range is the youngest mountain range in the Rockies.
- The mountain range is still uplifted one earthquake at a time along the 40-mile- (64-kilometer-) long Teton fault—on average, the fault moves about 10 feet (3 m) each earthquake.
- Jackson Hole was named for trapper David E. Jackson, who hunted beaver here in the early 19th century. "Hole" was a term used to describe a high mountain valley.
- Occasionally, the first settlers met Indigenous tribes at so-called "rendezvous" in the Teton Range, where they exchanged goods.
- Wolves have been living in the park again since 1999, after migrating from nearby Yellowstone National Park.

Mardy Murie

CONSERVATIONIST

Wilderness advocates often refer to Margaret "Mardy" Murie (1902–2003) as the "Grandmother of the conservation movement." After moving to Alaska at the age of five, she became the first woman to graduate from the Alaska Agricultural College and School of Mines (now the University of Alaska, Fairbanks) in 1924. The same year, she married her husband Olaus Murie, a scientist for the U.S. Bureau of Biological Survey. Both of them loved the land, and the two went on a 550-mile (885 km), 8-month expedition/honeymoon to study caribou. They were an adventuresome duo, and Murie joined her husband on many expeditions, helping to keep meticulous records of specimens and findings. Eventually, his work took them to Jackson, Wyoming, where Olaus was assigned to study elk populations in the Tetons. While they raised three children, Murie continued to assist on research trips, and the two began advocating for environmental causes. Her husband served as president of both the Wilderness Society and the Wildlife Society, and Mardy worked beside him. Their home became a gathering place for fellow conservation leaders. Olaus died in 1963, just a few months before the signing of the Wilderness Act, a piece of legislation that the two had fought tirelessly to enact and which led to the protection of 9.1 million acres (37,000 km²) of federal land. After her husband's death, Mardy continued her conservation efforts, writing letters and articles from her house in the woods and returning to Alaska to help work on the Alaska National Interest Lands Conservation Act of 1980. Mardy sold the Murie Ranch in 1968 to Grand Teton National Park in exchange for a life estate lease. She lived there until she died in 2003, and today her conservation legacy lives on.

Yellowstone

Vast valleys crisscrossed by rivers, bubbling mud pots, mighty geysers, and thundering waterfalls: Yellowstone is a true masterpiece of nature.

Numerous hot springs, mud pots, and fumaroles are bubbling and steaming away across Yellowstone. The park has around 500 geysers in all—that's around half of the world's total.

WYOMING / IDAHO / MONTANA

There's a place where you could get away with murder, and it's right at the edge of Yellowstone. The so-called "Zone of Death" is a 50-square-mile (129-square-kilometer) portion of the park in Idaho, where a criminal could theoretically escape conviction for a crime because of a purported loophole in the constitution. Why? Because the area lacks enough eligible citizens to form a jury. What the park lacks in citizens, it easily makes up for in terms of visitors. More than four million people come to marvel at Yellowstone's crystal-clear lakes, steaming springs, and bubbling mud pots, as well as its imposing canyons, endless grasslands, and thundering waterfalls.

Created in 1872, Yellowstone is the oldest (and probably most well-known) national park in the United States. It is almost entirely located within the state of Wyoming, though parts of it stretch into Idaho and Montana. The enormous caldera in which the park is situated is a remnant of a colossal volcano whose eruption millions of years ago created this unique landscape. Geothermal activity beneath the surface gave rise to a dramatic collection of mountains, rivers, canyons, springs, and geysers.

Many of the hydrothermal features at Yellowstone are powered by a giant super-volcano that lies deep beneath the park. Still active, the last time it erupted was 640,000 years ago. Besides the bison who reside here for part of the year, the park is home to three wildcats—the lynx, the bobcat, and the cougar.

The primary goal of Yellowstone's foundation was not conservation but the creation of a "pleasuring ground for the benefit and enjoyment of the people."

Yellowstone has the world's greatest concentration of hydro-thermal features. As groundwater seeps down the deeply fractured crust, it is heated by the volcano's magma chamber and resurfaces in the form of hot springs or bubbling mud holes. With about 500 geysers, half of the world's active geysers are located in the park. "Old Faithful" is particularly popular with tourists because it spews its water with unusual regularity at intervals of about 60 to 90 minutes.

The area of today's national park has been settled for at least 11,000 years, primarily by the Northern Shoshone. Occasionally, members of prairie-dwelling tribes like the Crow and Blackfoot would come here to hunt, fish, and collect obsidian rock to make cutting tools and weapons. A trapper named John Colter came to the area in 1807 and was likely the first white man to provide a first-hand account of what we now call Yellowstone Park. However, his descriptions of the hydrothermal phenomena were given little credence.

It was not until 1871 that geologist Ferdinand Hayden embarked on a two-year research trip to the area. His 34-member group also included painter Thomas Moran and photographer William Henry Jackson. The pictures they brought back from the expedition impressed the parliamentarians in Washington so much that they passed a law in 1872 to protect the Yellowstone area. But the primary goal of the park's foundation was not con-servation but the creation of "a public park or pleasure grounds for the benefit and enjoyment of the people." Unfortunately, most travelers came for hunting, severely decimating animal herds and displacing all Natives by 1880.

Unable to stop the destruction, the park's managers entrusted the area's management to the U.S. Army shortly after. Since 1894, an absolute ban on hunting has been in place, securing the popula-tion of a number of endangered species, including grizzly bears, wolves, and bison. In the decades before, white settlers had slaughtered bison herds to deprive the Native Americans of their food source. Of the 50 million buffalo that once roamed the Americas, only about 1,000 animals survived. At points, as few as 22 buffalo were counted in the park. Today, nearly 5,000 bison roam Yellowstone National Park again. Though as they migrate north in search of food each winter, hunters are allowed to shoot them. Around 1,500 bison are killed outside the park each year.

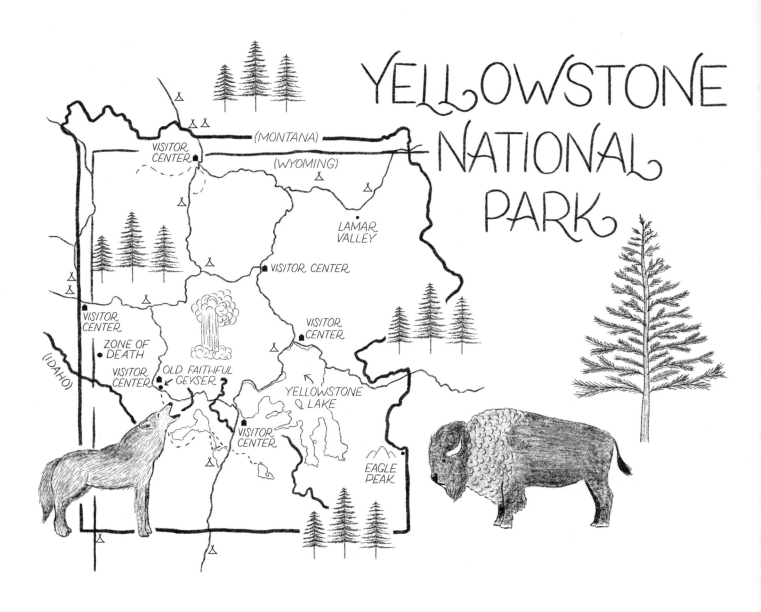

YELLOWSTONE NATIONAL PARK

President Ulysses S. Grant signed the Yellowstone National Park Protection Act into law on March 1, 1872, creating the first national park in the United States. It was named a Biosphere Reserve in 1976 and declared a UNESCO World Heritage Site two years later. The John D. Rockefeller Jr. Memorial Parkway connects Yellowstone with Grand Teton National Park to the south.

SIZE
2,219,791 acres (3,468 sq. mi./8,983 km²)
Size rank among National Parks: 8 of 63

ELEVATION
Highest point: Eagle Peak (11,372 ft./3,466 m)
Lowest point: Reese Creek (5,282 ft./1,610 m)

GEOLOGY
The park is situated in a so-called "hotspot"—a region that has been volcanically and seismically active for tens of millions of years. Today's landscape was formed by a huge active magma chamber underneath the park, which discharged in a violent explosion more than half a million years ago. The chamber's roof collapsed and formed a caldera that was filled with magma again. The overheated underground is the cause of all hydrothermal phenomena in Yellowstone, including the many hot springs, while minerals and algae are responsible for their dazzling colors.

FLORA AND FAUNA
Yellowstone is the core of a larger ecosystem and has established itself as a retreat for rare species of wildlife. The vast forests in the backcountry are home to numerous herds of bison, grizzlies, black bears—and wolf packs, which were reintroduced in 1995 after being completely exterminated in the 1930s. Bighorn sheep and snow goats are found at higher elevations. The park is also home to remarkable plants: researchers found several juniper trees, some as old as 1,500 years, near Mammoth Hot Springs, and an almost 2,000-year-old limber pine (*Pinus flexilis*) in the Absaroka Mountains.

CLIMATE AND WEATHER

The continental climate in Yellowstone National Park is mainly influenced by its location in the Rocky Mountains—which means the weather's rather unpredictable. Nights are cool even after warm, sunny summer days, and temperatures can drop below freezing at night in the mountains. Winters are long and usually very cold, and snowfall is heavy.

CONSERVATION

Yellowstone was set aside to share the wonders and preserve the scenery, cultural heritage, geological features, and wildlife in the park. It first caught the attention of explorers in 1871, who put forward the idea to protect the area from commercial exploitation. In 1872, Congress approved the creation of the first U.S. national park, but there was little protection of animals from hunting. Today, the hunting of mammals and birds is prohibited in all national parks, and the ecosystem in Yellowstone is even healthier overall than it was when Yellowstone first became a park.

BEFORE YOU GO

Yellowstone is open year-round, though from November through May many roads are closed to vehicles. Countless sights are located along the Grand Loop Road, which is connected with the five park access roads.

BEST TIMES TO VISIT

If you are looking for peace and solitude, avoid May to September, which are peak months and can get extremely crowded. April is great for wildlife viewing, while September and October offer reprieve from the crowds with relatively mild temperatures. In winter, except for the road from the north entrance to the northeast entrance, all roads in the park are accessible only by snowmobiles and snow coaches.

HIDDEN GEM

Hike the Lamar Valley Trail for outstanding wildlife viewing and scenery with relatively few people. But don't forget the bear spray!

INTERESTING FACTS ABOUT THE PARK

- The park owes its name to the Yellowstone River, the largest river in the area.
- The lion's share of Yellowstone is located in Wyoming. Only 3 percent is in the state of Montana—and 1 percent in Idaho.
- The Northern Pacific Railway lobbied heavily for the park's founding to boosting tourist traffic to the region.
- The Yellowstone volcano is the largest supervolcano on the American continent and is responsible for about 1,000 to 3,000 earthquakes per year.

Marguerite "Peg" Lindsley

FIRST FEMALE PARK RANGER

Struggling with the "boy's club" atmosphere that reigned over the National Park Service's early days, Horace Albright—then Superintendent of Yellowstone—hired 10 women to join the workforce. One of the most notable new hires was Jane Marguerite Lindsley (1901–1952), a true Yellowstone native. Born and raised in the park, her father served as interim superintendent when the site transitioned from Army oversight to the NPS. Lindsley had an intimate knowledge and a deep appreciation of the area. She started working as a seasonal park ranger in 1921 during her college years alongside two other women, giving educational tours on the park's geology and wildlife. Her plans to become a doctor fell through, so she majored in bacteriology at the University of Pennsylvania. After receiving her graduate degree, she returned to Yellowstone on a second-hand Harley Davidson with a female friend of hers in the sidecar—both disguised as men. In 1925, she became the NPS's first full-time female ranger. Lindsley faced widespread animosity from high-ranking officials who did not deem women fit for the sometimes strenuous and hazardous work. She responded that while she may be qualified for work in the field, "many still think that women's work should be inside, and it is a problem sometimes to satisfy everyone." She proudly wore her pine cone-emblazoned badge, stitched onto a uniform she had designed herself (back then, the NPS didn't have official uniforms for women). The immaculate attire—Stetson hat, jodhpurs, and a belted overcoat, paired with a tie and riding boots—was later adapted by other female rangers. When Horace Albrigth retired in 1933, the NPS once again hardened its stance against women. It wasn't until 1978 that women were allowed to become fully-fledged rangers. Today, they make up a third of the NPS workforce.

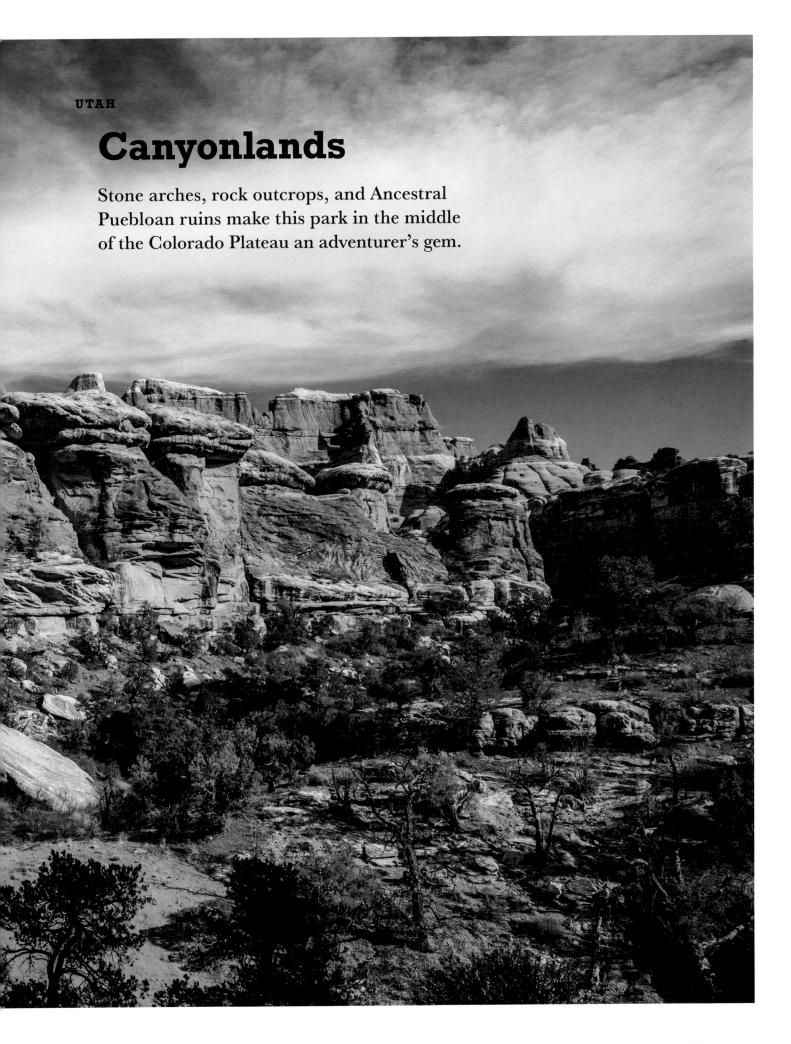

Canyonlands

Stone arches, rock outcrops, and Ancestral
Puebloan ruins make this park in the middle
of the Colorado Plateau an adventurer's gem.

Looking out across the vast Canyonlands from the Colorado Plateau shows how the landscape has been carved by the Green and Colorado Rivers, to reveal layer upon layer of sedimentary rock.

UTAH

When Canyonlands National Park was established in 1964, the remote landscape was largely unknown to the public eye. Only Native Americans and cowboys used to venture into this rugged area, located in southeastern Utah. Canyonlands is a vast wilderness of rock formations and raging rivers. Wind, ice, and water shaped this landscape and created hundreds of colorful canyons, mesas, stone pillars, and arches. This is a park for the adventurous: whether you're backcountry hiking, rafting the white-water rapids, mountain biking, or climbing sandstone towers, the 136,000-acre (550-square-kilometer) Canyonlands National Park won't disappoint.

The national park is located in the middle of the Colorado Plateau, which also includes the Grand Canyon. The land-scape was formed by the Colorado and Green Rivers and their

tributaries, which join in the park and continue south through the multicolored shallows of Cataract Canyon. Over millions of years, the rivers' powerful rapids have carved out deep gorges that divide the Canyonlands into three distinct sections: "Island in the Sky" to the north, "Maze" to the west, and the "Needles District" to the east. All of these areas are more or less untouched deserts, accessible via separate entrances; there are no cross connections.

Visitors who come to see this arid expanse of rock, stone, and stunted juniper bushes will find solitude, peace, and the challenge of being on their own. Although most of Canyonlands is backcountry, the park does offer paved roads to some of the most beautiful viewpoints. Island in the Sky is a broad, flattened plateau with bare canyon walls wedged between the Green and Colorado Rivers. Easy to reach, the park's lookout tower offers spectacular views of the White Rim, a sandstone escarpment some 360 feet (110 m) below the plateau. (Along the White Rim runs the popular White Rim Trail, an unpaved 100-mile (161-kilometer) rock path that can be traveled by off-road vehicles or mountain bikes, subject to approval by the park service.)

The Needles, located in the eponymous district, are jagged, red-and-white-striped pinnacles of rock that jut menacingly into the sky. Geological events have fractured the rocks, and the

TOP: A rock carved with petroglyphs bears witness to the Native Americans who once inhabited these lands. OPPOSITE: Looking through the majestic Mesa Arch of Island in the Sky toward White Rim country.

erosive forces of water, wind, and frost have created the rock formations we see today. The Needles District, with its gently rolling canyons and colorful knolls, is much more secluded and is best reached on foot via rugged hiking trails. The district's namesake pinnacles are accompanied by a variety of other rock formations such as canyons, sinkholes, crevices, and stone arches, with fanciful names such as the Devil's Kitchen, Angel Arch, and Elephant Hill. Unlike in Arches National Park, where many of the sites are accessible by short footpaths or even by car, here points of interest are located in the backcountry and can only be reached by off-road vehicles or long hikes.

The Maze District is the most remote region of the park. In fact, this jumble of canyons and spires is one of the most inaccessible areas in the entire country. There's a reason this area has been described as a "77-square-mile enigma of sandstone." GPS and topographic maps are indispensable here, but visitors will be rewarded with the fantastic sight of the so-called Chocolate Drops—beautiful, towering rock statues. Prehistoric cultures also left their mark on this area. Ghostly, larger-than-life figures painted more than 2,000 years ago adorn the walls of the Great Gallery in Horseshoe Canyon, a separate section of the park northwest of the Maze. (A separate permit is required for this section.)

CANYONLANDS NATIONAL PARK

In 1936, U.S. Secretary of the Interior Harold Ickes proposed an "Escalante National Monument" that would span nearly 7,000 square miles (18,130 km²) of southeastern Utah–but commercial interests and the looming Second World War doomed the project. Two decades later, the superintendent of Arches National Monument, Bates Wilson, lobbied for the creation of a national park in the canyon region. On September 12, 1964, President Lyndon B. Johnson signed the law establishing Canyonlands National Park, which was extended in 1971 to add Horseshoe Canyon.

SIZE
337,598 acres (528 sq. mi./1,366 km²)
Size rank among National Parks: 23

ELEVATION
Highest point: Cathedral Point (7,120 ft./2,170 m)
Lowest point: Colorado River (3,730 ft./1,134 m)

GEOLOGY
Distant mountain ranges such as the ancestral Rockies and the Appalachians are the source of most of the rock found in the park today. Carried here by wind and water, deposits of broken rocks eventually became distinct layers of sedimentary rock. Over the past 17 million years, the vast area has been uplifted by a few thousand feet. The Colorado and Green Rivers began to downcut and are now entrenched in canyons over 2,000 feet (610 m) deep. Because the hardness of the sandstone varies, it weathers at different rates, leading to the formation of fantastic rock sculptures.

FLORA AND FAUNA
The rocky slopes and cliffs of the park are home to many bighorn sheep, although they tend to avoid humans so they're hard to spot—the same goes with most other wildlife in the park. Fifty different species of mammals are native to the area, including mule deer, gray foxes, and bobcats, but you're most likely to spot desert hares and ground squirrels. Trails and paths are great for wildlife viewing, especially in the early-morning hours, during dusk, or in the cooler months. The high plateaus feature sparse desert vegetation typical of Utah, consisting mainly of scattered clumps of grass. Despite that, many birds live in the area.

CLIMATE AND WEATHER

The desert climate of Canyonlands is characterized by hot summers, a pleasant spring and fall, and cold, short winters with nighttime temperatures below freezing. Low humidity moderates the heat in summer, making it a little more bearable. Large temperature fluctuations within a single day are possible at any time.

CONSERVATION

Canyonlands National Park was created to preserve the immense desert wilderness sculpted by the Green and Colorado Rivers and the hundreds of colorful canyons, mesas, buttes, fins, arches, and spires. The first person to advocate for the park's creation was Bates Wilson, the Arches National Monument superintendent (see right). A flight over the confluence of the two rivers in 1961 is said to have sparked Secretary of the Interior Stewart Udall's interest in Wilson's proposal, eventually leading President Lyndon B. Johnson to declare Canyonlands a national park on September 12, 1964.

BEFORE YOU GO

For small children, very old people, or anyone not really fit, most of Canyonlands National Park might not be a good fit. There are two visitor centers, one in the Needles District and one in the Island in the Sky District. There are no hotels, restaurants, or campgrounds in Canyonlands itself.

BEST TIMES TO VISIT

As with many parks in the desert southwest, Canyonlands is best visited in the shoulder months of April, May, September, and October, which offer the best balance of mild temperatures and fewer crowds.

HIDDEN GEM

Be sure to visit a lesser-known corner of the park known as the Needles District. This area has a variety of day-hiking opportunities as well as launching points for longer backcountry adventures. Plus, the scenic drive out to the Needles through the Indian Creek portion of Bears Ears National Monument takes you through a stunning canyon world-famous for rock climbing.

INTERESTING FACTS ABOUT THE PARK

- You can find some of the most remote land remaining in the contiguous United States in Canyonlands.
- The two rivers mainly responsible for shaping the park area are the Colorado River and the Green River. They merge in the heart of the park, at a place called Confluence.
- Canyonlands was the backdrop for the famous last scene of the 1991 Ridley Scott movie *Thelma & Louise*.

Bates E. Wilson

"FATHER OF CANYONLANDS"

The first time Bates Wilson (1912–1983) saw the area that is now Canyonlands National Park was from the window of an airplane. In 1949, after working for years as a foreman in the Civilian Conservation Corps, Wilson arrived in Moab to oversee both Arches and Natural Bridges National Monuments. At the time, few people had ever heard of either place. Wilson not only changed all that, but he also sensed that there was more to this wondrous area. He started exploring the region surrounding the confluence of the Green and Colorado Rivers, an area that he called "the land in between." Wilson spent countless hours charting, exploring, and mapping its unique geology, sometimes accompanied by his son. He not only enjoyed the area's unique wilderness—he fiercely advocated for its protection, too; Wilson took politicians, filmmakers, reporters, congressmen, scientists, and Park Service officials around in his jeep, showing them the land that would later become Canyonlands National Park. Over dinner cooked on a campfire, he persuaded government officials to make the area a national park, a move he dubbed "Dutch oven diplomacy." In 1961, Stewart Udall, the Secretary of the Interior under John F. Kennedy and later Lyndon B. Johnson, joined Wilson on one of these tours. Three years later, on September 12, 1964, Udall signed the bill establishing Canyonlands National Park. Not only did this fulfill Wilson's vision of preserving 250,000 acres (1,012 km²) of jaw-dropping landscape. Bates became the first superintendent of Canyonlands National Park and was known for his hands-on approach, often working alongside seasonal workers and other NPS employees. Due to his tireless advocacy for the park's creation, many refer to him as the "Father of Canyonlands."

Arches

Sculpted by millions of years of erosion, this labyrinth of giant sandstone walls and delicate arches is a dreamland flourishing in the desert.

Each year 1.6 million travelers make their pilgrimage to Arches National Park to witness its otherworldly beauty. This surreal desert landscape is home to over 2,000 natural stone arches and hundreds of soaring pinnacles shaped by nature's perfect architectural ingredients: wind, water, stone, pressure, erosion, and time. Over the course of 65 million years, these unrelenting forces have shaped the vibrant orange and red Entrada sandstone into a massive, natural sculpture garden. Despite the harsh conditions that created this landscape masterpiece, Arches is home to 483 drought-resistant plant species, 52 species of mammals, and 186 species of birds, including bald eagles, Mexican spotted owls, peregrine falcons, and great blue herons. The park is also a second home for avid climbers, stargazers, mountain bikers, and rafters, who come to channel their passions in the mesmerizing desert surroundings.

The main attraction for visitors is hiking through the park with a camera ready to photograph the spectacular red rock

formations. The iconic red sandstone contains iron oxide, which creates lustrous and vibrant colors that shift as the sun moves across the sky. Every corner of the park is picturesque, but the top site that travelers flock to year after year is the majestic Delicate Arch. The world's most famous natural stone arch stands at 52 feet (16 m) tall, atop an electric-orange bluff. The hike to the arch is three miles round-trip and takes an average of three hours. Bring plenty of water, and, if you plan to take in the changing colors at sunset, be sure to pack a flashlight for your return voyage.

The ethereal shapes of the park's collection of arches, fins, windows, spires, and balanced-rock formations only add to the surreal and sacred quality of visiting the park. And every hike in Arches National Park pulls you deeper into the dream. There are mountains with carved-out windows revealing blue skies, stone

UTAH

PARK AT A GLANCE

On April 12th, 1929, President Hoover designated 4,520 acres of now protected land as the Arches National Monument. In the decades that followed, the land remained undeveloped. On November 12, 1971, Arches was declared a national park.

SIZE
76,678.98 acres (120 sq. mi./311 km²)
Size rank among National Parks: 44 of 63

ELEVATION
Highest point: Elephant Butte (5,653 ft./1,723 m)
Lowest point: Visitor Center (4,085 ft./1,245 m)

GEOLOGY
Over 65 million years of erosion, rain, flooding, and earthquakes have sculpted the area's red sandstone into the iconic pinnacles, windows, bridges, and arches we see today. The park's various rock formations highlight the millions of years of geologic progression that shaped the stunning red rock sculptures.

FLORA AND FAUNA
Bighorn sheep, kit foxes, and mule deer rule over the land, while the skies come to life with over 186 bird species including peregrine falcons, great blue herons, eagles, and many more. Despite low rainfall and extreme temperatures, 483 resilient plant species also manage to flourish in the high desert.

CONSERVATION
Arches National Park is dedicated to protecting and preserving the area's spectacular collection of geologic features and to furthering education surrounding the history, science, and culture related to this beautiful natural landscape.

BEFORE YOU GO
Arches National Park has no lodges or general stores, so purchase any food, beverages, and supplies you might need in Moab before entering the park. The best time to witness the hypnotic color-changing effects of Delicate Arch is at sunset. For travelers with limited time, Balanced Rock, Park Avenue, and Devil's Garden are popular sites that are accessible just off the main park road.

BEST TIMES TO VISIT
Mid-spring/early fall when temperatures are mild. These more temperate months are, however, more crowded. Summer is the off-season for visitors as temperatures regularly reach 90–100 °F (32–38 °C) and can also reach extremes of 114 °F (46 °C).

towers that chatter and gossip, and red rock monoliths that defy reality with their impossible balancing acts. These are the mad visions of nature as the architect. And these marvels have names befitting their magic: Devil's Garden, Fiery Furnace, and the Tower of Babel are just a few. There's even a Park Avenue here, its prehistoric skyline rivaling even New York City's most ambitious skyscrapers.

Adding to the dreamlike character of Arches is its ever-changing landscape. The same wind and water that sculpted these magnificent forms are also causing the park to erode. Since the park opened in 1971, 43 arches have collapsed. And yet, just as the old forms decay, new ones emerge, as the process of erosion continues each day. Nature the architect never stops creating new wonders in the splendor of Arches National Park.

Capitol Reef

This remote landscape is a geological marvel, with millions of years of history on dazzling display.

Over 1,000 years ago, humans took to the red rock walls of what is now Capitol Reef to depict their lives, etching stories into the hard surface. This ancient artwork of the Fremont people, whose oral traditions associate them with the Hopi, Zuni, and Paiute, has survived to this day. And this collection of petroglyphs is just one of the many glimpses into the past at Capitol Reef National Park.

An even older story is on display here, one that spans about 270 million years of geological history. Over millions of years, almost 10,000 feet (3,038 m) of richly layered sedimentary rock built up as vast quantities of sand and mud accumulated on the bed of the ancient sea that once covered this region. Eventually, this rock was pushed to the earth's surface forming the Capitol Reef Waterpocket Fold. This "wrinkle" in the earth stretches for almost 100 miles (161 km) and is filled with cliffs, canyons, natural bridges, and arches. The ongoing process of erosion here provides visitors with an eye-catching cross section of 19 different rock formations. The Waterpocket Fold is the largest exposed monocline in North America.

The strikingly different strata of Capitol Reef tell all kinds of stories about the area's past, from rivers and swamps to ancient oceans. Fossils remain in these layers, like the 100-million-year-old oysters preserved in the Dakota Sandstone. The park's formations were also the inspiration for its name: the rounded white tops of Navajo Sandstone resemble the domes of capitol buildings, and the rocky cliffs that define the park have created a barrier, much like an ocean reef. At the north end of the park in the Cathedral District (accessible only by dirt road) the otherworldly desert landscape is peppered with enormous rock monoliths with names like the Temple of the Sun and Temple of the Moon.

There are signs of more recent history too, like the orchards planted by the Latter-Day Saints who began settling in the area in the late 1800s. In the historic town of Fruita, almost 2,000 fruit

UTAH

PARK AT A GLANCE

President Franklin D. Roosevelt established Capitol Reef as a national monument in 1937. It was officially designated a national park under President Richard Nixon on December 18, 1971.

SIZE
241,904 acres (378 sq. mi./979 km²)
Size rank among National Parks: 29 of 63

ELEVATION
Highest point: Thousand Lake Mountain (11,306 ft./3,446 m)
Lowest point: Halls Creek (3,880 ft./1,183 m)

GEOLOGY
The Waterpocket Fold offers an almost complete set of Mesozoic-era sedimentary rock, its layers created over millions of years and eventually pushed to the earth's surface. Between 35 and 75 million years ago, the Laramide Orogeny is believed to have reactivated a buried fault line, allowing the layers to rise up, creating the monocline that that park is known for today.

FLORA AND FAUNA
There are over 840 plant species in the park, and many of them have very particular and defined areas in which they can survive, dependent on things like soil, elevation, and specific geologic formations. There are more than 40 rare and endemic plant species in the park, with six of them listed as threatened or endangered.

CONSERVATION
The park protects both cultural treasures and a diversity of habitats. Capitol Reef's varied terrain creates distinct microclimates throughout the park, harboring various desert species that require very particular conditions to thrive. Like other wilderness areas in Utah, this distinct area is continuously threatened by encroaching oil and gas interests and fossil fuel extraction.

BEFORE YOU GO
The Fruita Rural Historic District provides access to both the orchards and the Capitol Reef petroglyphs, just off Highway 24. The southern district of the park is more remote but is the best place to explore the notable Waterpocket Fold.

BEST TIMES TO VISIT
Spring and fall, as they offer more mild temperatures. The park only gets about 7.91 inches (20.1 cm) of rain every year, but the summer monsoon season between July and September brings the risk of dangerous flash floods.

trees continue to grow today, and many are open for harvest, with designated signs welcoming visitors to pick their apples, apricots, plums, and cherries. Once you fill your basket, just stop by the self-pay station, with proceeds supporting the preservation of the historical agricultural area.

Due to its remote location in south-central Utah, Capitol Reef is also designated as an International Dark Sky Park, offering refuge to nocturnal desert animals like ringtails, kangaroo rats, night snakes, and owls. The park's night skies are also a prime habitat for its 16 species of bats. Animals and humans are both increasingly impacted by the effects of light pollution, and while artificial light has made it difficult to view a truly dark night sky, Capitol Reef is one of the best places in the West to see the star-studded night in all its glory.

Bryce Canyon

Sculpted by nature over millions of years, red and orange spires—believed by Native Americans to be punished spirits—pierce the vast skies of this park.

An ethereal landscape filled with red rocks and slender spires draws more than 2 million visitors a year to Bryce Canyon. The tall spires, called hoodoos, mark the sprawling expanse, their red and orange hues intensifying and softening with the rising and falling of the sun. The park is known for these unique rock formations and is home to the greatest number of them on earth. If nature here is a sculptor, then ice is her chisel: water that seeps into cracks in the hoodoos expands when it freezes, gradually eroding the geological wonders. This process is fueled by Bryce Canyon's conditions, where for more than 170 nights of the year, temperatures hit both below and above freezing.

UTAH

The area has long held an important role for many Native American tribes like the Hopi and the Paiute people, who have been on this land since 1200 CE. According to Paiute creation stories, the hoodoos are the result of a punishment from Coyote. The To-when-an-ung-wa, the Legend People that existed before humans, were overly indulgent and didn't respect the land, and as a consequence, Coyote turned them to stone, resulting in the name Angka-ku-wass-a-wits, meaning "red-painted faces."

The unique natural beauty of these stones has enraptured many and is a large part of why the park was created. J.W. Humphrey, a U.S. Forest Service Supervisor, was a driving force in making Bryce Canyon a national park. Upon arriving at what is now Sunset Point, he remarked: "You can perhaps imagine my surprise at the indescribable beauty that greeted us, and it was sundown before I could be dragged from the canyon view. You may be sure that I went back the next morning to see the canyon once more, and to plan in my mind how this attraction could be made accessible to the public."

He carried out his promise, and in 1916, he managed to get $50 (about $1,290 in today's economy) to improve the road and make the rim accessible to automobiles, quite literally paving the way for the area to become a national park. Today, visitors come to see the stunning hoodoos, which can rise to 150 feet (46 m) tall. Ogling them from all angles is made easy by an interconnected

system of trails. Hikers can mix and match all kinds of trails, from easy to strenuous, and popular routes include Fairyland Loop, Navajo Loop Trail, and Peekaboo Loop Trail. While nature's architect reigns in the red rocks, the park also features epic structures of the man-made variety, with the iconic Bryce Canyon Lodge, built in 1925.

Like all of nature, Bryce Canyon is evolving, but at a quicker pace than other places, giving visitors a profound sense of time and change. The story of the hoodoos is one that is ever diminishing, eroding at a rate of 2–4 feet (60–120 cm) every 100 years. Nature continues to shape the landscape, offering visitors the chance to see a park that someday will no longer look the same.

PARK AT A GLANCE

Bryce Canyon was established as a national monument in 1923 by President Warren G. Harding. It was officially designated a national park by Congress on February 25, 1928.

SIZE
35,835 acres (56 sq. mi./145 km²)
Size rank among National Parks: 52 of 63

ELEVATION
Highest point: Rainbow Point (9,115 ft./2,778 m)
Lowest point: Yellow Creek (6,620 ft./2,018 m)

GEOLOGY
Despite its name, Bryce Canyon isn't a true canyon but rather an eroded escarpment of the Paunsaugunt Plateau, created by a geological uplift 10 to 20 million years ago. The multiple layers of rock—limestone, dolostone, siltstone, and sandstone—were pushed to the surface and the unique landscape and conditions helped to create the park's famed hoodoos.

FLORA AND FAUNA
Utah is one of only six states in the United States where ancient bristlecone pine, one of the oldest organisms on earth, can be found. The park has three distinct climatic zones: spruce/fir forest, ponderosa pine forest, and pinyon/juniper forest. These zones help to cultivate a robust biodiversity and are home to all kinds of wildlife, including mule deer, Utah prairie dogs, chipmunks, golden-mantled ground squirrels, Steller's jays, wild turkeys, and mountain short-horned lizards.

CONSERVATION
While the area has been an important site for Native Americans for thousands of years, the park was named after a Mormon pioneer, Ebenezer Bryce. He was responsible for constructing a timber road into the Bryce Amphitheater. This led the locals to call it "Bryce's Canyon" and the locals' name stuck.

BEFORE YOU GO
Bryce Canyon has often been a popular alternative to Zion, and its teeming crowds. However, there's a free park shuttle to help alleviate congestion, and it offers easy access to many trailheads.

BEST TIMES TO VISIT
An incredibly busy park, Bryce Canyon is best during the off-season. The park is open year-round and is busiest between May and September. There may be temporary road closures in winter depending on conditions, so it's a good idea to check ahead.

Zion

A dramatic landscape of canyons, cliffs, and mesas make this park a premier destination for climbing and canyoneering.

With its miles of spectacular rugged canyon country awash with fast-flowing rivers and waterfalls, Zion National Park is a popular destination for big-wall mountain climbers and canyoneers.

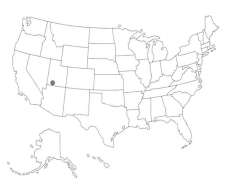

UTAH

When Mormon settlers arrived at what is now Zion National Park in the early 1860s, they gave it an ancient Hebrew name: Zion—"place of refuge." Until then, the area had been known as Mukuntuweap, or "straight canyon," among the Paiute Tribes who defied the harsh conditions in this land for centuries. The Mormons got to know the nomadic hunter-gatherers as friendly and knowledgeable people. They were valuable guides, too: In 1858, some Paiute helped guide a young Mormon named Nephi Johnson on his quest to find suitable farmland for his fellow settlers.

Contrary to what Johnson reported back, the area around the canyon was not particularly well-suited for agricultural use. The river often flooded its banks, and the soil wasn't exactly productive. Nevertheless, more and more farmers settled. One of them, Isaac Behunin, built a one-room log cabin on the east side of the Virgin River. He cleared some land and planted an orchard with tobacco, sugar cane, and corn. In the presence of friends, he proclaimed: "A man can worship God among these great cathedrals as well as he can in any man-made church; this is Zion."

While Zion National Park has incredible geologic formations—in the Narrows, for example, where the Virgin River has carved the rocks over millions of years—this is not purely canyon territory. In fact, the park boasts four ecosystems that range from desert and riverside to pinyon-juniper and conifer forest, and more than 1,000 native species of plants grow here.

Mormons escaping religious persecution arrived here in the Mid-1800s. "These are the Temples of God," they said: "This is Zion."

Farming ceased here in the early 1900s, and the area became an increasingly popular destination for nature lovers. Inconspicuous at first, the beauty of the terrain reveals itself best when you lace up your boots and immerse yourself. Zion's high plateaus, mazes of narrow, deep sandstone canyons, and impressive freestanding arches were formed when the ancient Virgin River cut its way through the rock, leaving behind a rich landscape shimmering in different hues of cream, pink, and red. In 1919, the area was declared a national park.

Zion National Park comprises two independent sections. The most famous of these is Zion Canyon in the south, the main draw for most of the park's 3 million annual visitors. The canyon is about 15 miles (25 km) long and narrows upstream from a valley into a spectacular gorge some 2,000 to 3,000 feet (600 to 900 m) deep. It is one of the premier destinations for canyoneering in the country. A separate entrance in the northwest corner leads to the Kolob Canyons, named for the star Kolob,

described in Mormon scripture as the star nearest the Throne of God. While larger than Zion, the Kolob Canyons are much more cumbersome to reach. But solitude, wilderness, and empty trails are well worth the strain. (Plus, it's usually 10 degrees cooler there than in Zion Canyon.)

Along with Yosemite National Park, Zion National Park is one of the most famous spots for climbing in the United States. With hundreds of climbing routes here, climbers can find everything from short bouldering to multiday tours. Unlike the granite of Yosemite Valley, however, the sandstone of Zion National Park is very fragile, and it's crucial to follow existing routes. Meanwhile, believers will take comfort in knowing God is everywhere here: almost every dome and pinnacle owes its name to the Supreme Being—from Angels Landing (arguably one of the most beautiful hikes in the country) to the Three Patriarchs, the Great Organ, Temple of Sinawava, or the Altar of Sacrifice.

ZION NATIONAL PARK

HORSE RANCH MOUNTAIN

VISITOR CENTER

KOLOB CANYONS

TEMPLE OF SINAWAVA

ANGELS LANDING

THE GREAT ORGAN

THE THREE PATRIARCHS

ALTAR OF SACRIFICE

VISITOR CENTER

VIRGIN RIVER

A flood of expedition reports, paintings, and photographs led President William Howard Taft to designate the region around Zion Canyon in Utah as Mukuntuweap National Monument in 1909. Nine years later this was renamed Zion, and on November 19, 1919, the park was enlarged and established as Zion National Park. The Kolob Canyons area was incorporated into the park in 1956.

SIZE
146,597 acres (229 sq. mi./593 km²)
Size rank among National Parks: 36 of 63

ELEVATION
Highest point: Horse Ranch Mountain (8,726 ft./2,660 m)
Lowest point: Coalpits Wash (3,666 ft./1,117 m)

GEOLOGY
The park area is part of the Colorado Plateau, a huge sedimentary cover that has been uplifted several thousand feet and extends from northern Mexico far up into Utah and Colorado. The nine visible rock layers of Zion National Park are part of the Grand Staircase, a rock formation that stretches from Bryce Canyon to the Grand Canyon like stairs. The lower layer of rock in Bryce Canyon is the uppermost layer in Zion, and the lower layer in Zion is the uppermost layer in the Grand Canyon. Sediment-heavy rivers started the erosion process responsible for Zion's dramatic rock formations.

FLORA AND FAUNA
As the park is located at the intersection of the Colorado Plateau, Great Basin, and Mojave Desert, there is remarkable biodiversity amid the green riverbanks, barren plateaus, and dense forests. Bighorn sheep often climb the sandstone slopes and rattlesnakes and tarantulas can be found in the desert climate of the canyons. Chipmunks can be encountered almost everywhere.

CLIMATE AND WEATHER
Zion National Park has a cold steppe climate. Summers are dry, but storms and thunderstorms can occur. Days are hot

(with temperatures rising up to 97 °F/36 °C in July) and nights are mild to cool, but even in late fall, nights in the valleys are mild. Winters are cold, with little snowfall.

CONSERVATION
The park was established to protect the rich biodiversity in Zion Canyon. The John Wesley Powell expedition explored the canyon between 1869 and 1872, after they had explored the Grand Canyon. Drawings and photographs moved President William Howard Taft to declare the area a national monument in 1909, and all agricultural use was prohibited. In 1919, the canyon was declared a national park, and the protected area was substantially enlarged. In 1956, Kolob Canyons, with its vertiginous cliffs of red Navajo sandstone, was added to the area.

BEFORE YOU GO
The park consists of two sections, the little-visited Kolob Canyons in the northwest and Zion Canyon in the southeast. (It's not possible to visit both in a day.) Within the canyon, temperature and humidity can reach extreme levels as early as spring, so be sure to carry more than enough water with you on every hike. The visitor center is located north of the small town of Springdale, along the so-called Scenic Drive, where you can find most of the hiking trails. The name is a bit misleading though—you are not allowed to drive your own car on the road from March to October. There is a free shuttle bus service.

BEST TIMES TO VISIT
Summers in Zion are typically very hot and very crowded. In fall, the leaves in Zion Canyon shine beautifully and water levels make the Narrows more accessible. Winter offers the best time for solitude.

HIDDEN GEM
Most visitors to Zion National Park flock to Zion Canyon. Visit the wilderness area of the Kolob Canyons away from the bustling Zion Canyon area.

INTERESTING FACTS ABOUT THE PARK
- The Paiute have a strong spiritual connection to the rocks, rivers, and springs in Zion Canyon and see themselves as caretakers of the area.
- Together with its headwaters, Virgin River runs a gradient of nearly 7,500 feet (2,286 m), one of the steepest in North America.
- Zion is famous for its unique hanging gardens of trees, ferns, wildflowers, and mosses that form over the banks.
- Much of the park infrastructure was built by the Civilian Conservation Corps.

Frederick Samuel Dellenbaugh

ARTIST AND TOPOGRAPHER

Three decades after accompanying John Wesley Powell on his second expedition down the Colorado River, Frederick Samuel Dellenbaugh (1853–1935) found his way back to Springdale. In the summer of 1903, he made several forays into Zion Canyon, whose towering cliffs he had previously only spotted from a distance. Trained as an artist in Munich and Paris, Dellenbaugh produced a series of oil paintings depicting Zion Canyon in vivid colors, something photography could not convey at the time. When he showcased his work at the St. Louis World's Fair the year after, he created quite a stir. Spectators were awe-struck, but his work fell on incredulous eyes: people assumed the towering, red-hued rocks had sprung from the artist's imagination. The same year, Dellenbaugh published "A New Valley of Wonders," a 17-page spread in *Scribner's Magazine*, accompanied by photographs. "One hardly knows just how to think of it," he wrote. "Never before has such a naked mountain of rock entered into our minds! Without a shred of disguise, its transcendent form rises preeminent. There is almost nothing to compare to it." Dellenbaugh's painting and writing prompted many to explore the canyon. It also helped persuade President William Howard Taft to proclaim Zion Canyon as Mukuntuweap National Monument in 1909. (A decade later, Congress changed the name to Zion National Park.) In 2006, the Zion National Park Foundation purchased one of Dellenbaugh's paintings and donated it to the park's museum collection. A rare depiction of the park in the time before it became a national monument, the painting shows green crops where roads and park buildings exist today, while Zion Canyon, rendered in hazy pastel hues, floats in the background.

Saguaro

These cacti, some more than a century old, are an icon of the Wild West.

When asked to draw a cactus, most people would draw a tall, spiny trunk with outstretched arms like a giant saguaro (*Carnegiea gigantea*). Visually, these cacti are everywhere, from T-shirts to movies to art museums. Saguaros have become a recognizable symbol of the American West. But their actual habitat is quite small, found only in parts of the Sonoran Desert. It goes without saying that these majestic cacti, whose white blossoms are the Arizona state flower, are the main feature of Saguaro National Park.

Unlike many parks, Saguaro National Park has a fairly urban location, and the city of Tucson is nestled in between the park's Rincon Mountain District to the east and the Tucson Mountain District to the west. City dwellers can reach the park in less than half an hour, and even in town, there's a 30-foot- (9-meter-) tall neon saguaro sign in homage to the symbolic cactus.

ARIZONA

The cacti are bursting with symbolism and beauty, but as a keystone species, they also serve an essential role in the desert ecosystem. The saguaros provide food and shelter for all kinds of animals. They have also long served a role for the local Tohono O'odham people—the "Desert People"—whose creation stories involve the cactus. The Tohono O'odham continue to harvest ripe saguaro fruit in the early summer, and their word for the cactus is hashan but they often referred to it as O'odham, or "people," proof of their deep reciprocal relationship with the plant.

Saguaros are stalwarts of the desert, and the oldest ones live for 150 to 175 years, with some as old as 200. The cacti need that time—it can take over a decade to grow just one inch (2.5 cm)—but when they reach maturity after a century, they tower above the desert floor, measuring about 40 feet (12 m) tall. The tallest saguaro in the park collapsed in 1986, but while it was still living, it reached a height of 78 feet (23 m). If you're looking for the tallest cactus in the park now, you may be searching for a while. There's no longer one particular saguaro singled out as the tallest, but the Rincon Mountain District has older and taller cacti than on the west side, and the 3.8-mile (6.1-kilometer) Loma Verde Loop is a good place for spotting them.

Besides the famous saguaro cacti, there are lots of other things for hikers to see on the 150 miles (241 km) of trails in the park. It's common to spot owls in the cliff above the wash on the Freeman Homestead Trail, and the Garwood Trail passes through the kind of cactus forest that the park was established to protect.

To ensure that protection, the park relies on the help of citizen scientists to map and measure the giant cacti. These citizen scientists are also particularly helpful in studying Gila monsters (*Heloderma suspectum*), a native species in the Sonoran Desert. Exceptionally rare to see, they are one of the only venomous lizards in the world, and since 2008, the park has relied on visitors to send in photos whenever they spot one. Every decade, the park calls on volunteers and supporters to perform a citizen science census. For the 2020 census, over 500 volunteers clocked over 3,500 hours and collected data on more than 23,000 saguaros.

PARK AT A GLANCE

Made iconic by silent Western movies, the push to protect the saguaro and its landscape began in the 1920s. In 1933, Herbert Hoover declared the area a national monument. Additional lands were added over time, and on October 14, 1994, it was upgraded to Saguaro National Park.

SIZE
91,445 acres (143 sq. mi./370 km²)
Size rank among National Parks: 41 of 63

ELEVATION
Highest point: Mica Mountain (8,666 ft./2,641 m)
Lowest point: Sanders Road (2,180 ft./664 m)

GEOLOGY
The western part of the park sits in the Tucson Mountains, mostly the eroded remains of a 15-mile- (24-kilometer-) long volcanic caldera formed by a volcanic eruption 70 to 75 million years ago. There is a rich mining history in the park, and there are 149 mining excavations in the area.

FLORA AND FAUNA
The saguaro cactus is an essential part of the desert habitat. When the cacti bloom in early summer, birds, bats, and honeybees depend on the flowers for their nectar. Meanwhile, pack rats and jackrabbits eat the water-rich flesh, and birds make holes in the trunks and limbs for nests. The park is home to distinct desert species like the Gila monster, desert tortoises, and six species of rattlesnakes.

CONSERVATION
The parklands were originally established to protect the saguaro and the unspoiled desert landscape. Extreme weather conditions caused by climate change have had a significant impact on the saguaro, which require particular conditions to survive. Since the 1990s, younger saguaros have struggled to stay alive, a situation attributed to drought and higher temperatures.

BEFORE YOU GO
There are hike-in campsites, but no car camping in the park, and no concession stands or restaurants. On the east side of the park, bicycles are allowed on some trails.

BEST TIMES TO VISIT
Summers are hot, so peak season is January to March. Visitors who want to hike and explore in a more tranquil setting should opt for fall. To catch the saguaro in bloom, you'll need to come May through the first week of June.

Petrified Forest

The Painted Desert of John Steinbeck's *Grapes of Wrath* is full of trees turned to stone, shimmering in rainbow hues.

ARIZONA

I magine a lush forest full of flowing rivers and streams, where enormous coniferous trees grow, shading the giant ferns and horsetails that grow below. A place where reptiles and amphibians make the verdant landscape their home. This is the forest preserved in Petrified Forest National Park. Over 200 million years old, trees that once stood as tall as 20-story buildings are today laid flat, transformed into chunks of nearly pure quartz. Over millennia, the cells of their bark and wood were replaced with different minerals, like manganese and iron. They shimmer now

in rainbow-colored layers, from purple amethyst to yellow citrine to smoky quartz.

Scattered across the park, today's "forests" are actually old log jams, created as trees died and ended up in the river, getting quickly covered with sediment. Appearing as if someone had felled the trees with a chainsaw and sliced them into chunks, these groupings like Crystal Forest and Jasper Forest are what the park is known for. There are several trails for exploring these ancient forests of brittle quartz. Long Logs is one of the largest concentrations of petrified wood in the park, and the short Giant Logs Loop takes visitors through the largest and most colorful logs in the park, including "Old Faithful," a petrified tree whose base is almost 10 feet (3 m) wide.

Besides wood, the park preserves a variety of fossils from the Triassic period, often referred to as the "dawn of the dinosaurs." Containing one of the most continuous sections of Triassic-age rocks anywhere in the world, the park offers rich opportunities for paleontologists, and the park has an ongoing summer paleontology internship program. In 2020, interns in the program discovered *Skybalonyx skapter,* a new specie of drepanosaur, a kind of burrowing reptile that lived about 220 million years ago. The sedimentary layers of the Blue Mesa area of the park have been particularly fruitful for fossil discovery, and on the Blue Mesa Trail visitors can walk through the badland hills, their stratified layers showcasing a palette of blue, purple, gray, and peach.

With over 13,000 years of human history reflected here, archeological research is also an important aspect of the park. Over 800 archeological and historic sites are found within its boundaries, including Newspaper Rock, which is covered in more than 650 different petroglyphs made by Ancestral Puebloans 650 to 2,000 years ago. Throughout that history, the park's namesake resource has been of great use. Paleoindians at the end of the last Ice Age used it to carve sharp points to hunt mammoth and bison with, and later, the Puebloans would use petrified wood to build shelter. Agate House, a Puebloan dwelling that was excavated and reconstructed in the 1930s, is an excellent example of these petrified wood structures, one of many in the park.

PARK AT A GLANCE

The Arizona Territory legislature petitioned Congress to turn the area into a national park in 1895. However, Petrified Forest didn't officially gain its national park status until December 9, 1962, under President John F. Kennedy.

SIZE
221,390 acres (345 sq. mi/896 km²)
Size rank among National Parks: 31 of 63

ELEVATION
Highest point: Pilot Rock (6,235 ft./1,900 m)
Lowest point: Puerco River (5,307 ft/1,618 m)

GEOLOGY
Deposited over 200 million years ago, the Chinle Formation creates the colored layers and mesas of the Painted Desert. The barren but stunning landscape was the backdrop of the film *Grapes of Wrath,* based on the classic John Steinbeck novel.

FLORA AND FAUNA
The park is home to 16 different species of lizards and snakes. Many animals in the park are crepuscular, active at dawn and dusk, like bobcats, pronghorn, and badgers. Grasslands are an important part of the ecosystem and include rice grass, which can live to be over 100 years old.

CONSERVATION
Petrified wood was documented in the area in the 1850s, and tourists and commercial interests soon followed. Locals quickly saw the need to protect the unique local resource. The original national monument was set up to ensure that the petrified forest stayed intact. Thanks to these efforts, it's now illegal to take any petrified wood from the park, but some people still can't resist. Sometimes, a guilty conscience ensues, and the park regularly receives rocks mailed back with letters of apology.

BEFORE YOU GO
Unlike all the other national parks, Petrified Forest is not open 24 hours a day, and the gates are closed at night to help prevent the theft of fossilized wood. This is the only national park to have a section of Historic Route 66 in it. There are no developed campgrounds in the park.

BEST TIMES TO VISIT
Spring can have cold nights but mild and comfortable days, and May offers the best chance for wildflowers. Summer is busy, and the monsoon season is from July to September.

Grand Canyon

One of the greatest natural wonders on earth bears
silent witness to two billion years of geological history.

Numerous trails crisscross the landscape on both the North Rim and the South Rim, all of them with stopping points offering breathtaking views across the ancient landscape; the park's oldest rocks are almost two million years old.

ARIZONA

Teddy Roosevelt once called the Grand Canyon the one place every American should see, and, if you go by the numbers, people seem to take him at his word. Grand Canyon National Park in northwestern Arizona is one of the most visited (and arguably one of the most famous) nature preserves on the planet. It encompasses a 277-mile (446-kilometer) stretch of the Colorado River, which has carved its way through layers of shale, granite, limestone, and sandstone over millions of years to create a canyon of gigantic proportions.

Contrary to popular belief, it is not the largest in the world (that record is held by the Yarlung Tsangpo Grand Canyon in the Himalayas), but the breathtaking vistas offer visitors an astounding sense of how the earth has changed since its formation—and the sheer amount of time over which these changes occurred.

No other place on earth has a record of geologic events as extensive and profound as here. The riverbed is surrounded by the oldest exposed rock on our planet, dating back to when the earth's crust began to solidify, around two billion years ago. The overall color of the canyon is red, but it consists of rock formations of considerably different ages. Each stratum has a distinctive hue, ranging from yellow to gray to green to pink and changing with the light. The vast majority of visitors soak up the view from the southern flank of the canyon.

A road runs along the South Rim for several miles, giving views of the Colorado River in some places. (Daredevils explore the area on rafting tours, which last from 7 to 30 days.) The North Rim is much quieter and less developed. It is 1,000 feet (300 m) higher, and its alpine environment is more reminiscent of a drive through the Alps than a trip through Arizona. The North and South Rim are only 10 miles (16 km) apart as the crow flies, but with no bridges to connect the two, the drive from one rim to the other takes at least 4 hours.

Humans have lived in the area for 13,000 years. Much of the land within the park is still tribal land, and six main tribes call the Grand Canyon home. Their ancestors subsisted on farming and hunting in the canyon, and the canyon also played an important role in their religious rites. European explorers came

TOP: Mary Colter's Desert View Watchtower at the eastern end of the South Rim. OPPOSITE: With its bands of colored rock, the canyon itself is 18 miles (29 km) wide and 1 mile (1.6 km) deep.

in 1540 but left aghast, as the canyon represented an obstacle on the way to the promising West. Even in 1857, explorer Joseph Ives noted that "the region is, of course, altogether valueless … After entering it, there is nothing to do but leave. Ours has been the first, and will doubtless be the last, party of whites to visit this profitless locality."

He was obviously wrong. A few decades later, the first tourists arrived in the wake of ore miners, who charged them tolls to navigate their harrowing and dangerous trails. (Today, only experienced hikers should venture down into the canyon on foot.) When President Roosevelt declared the Grand Canyon a national monument in 1908, and the National Park Service set up on the South Rim in 1908, the canyon walls were full of mine shafts and mule trails, and there were over 300 deeded mining claims for copper, asbestos, lead, and uranium.

In 1903, Roosevelt, who often visited the area, gave a (now-famous) speech at the Grand Canyon, where he made his wishes clear: "I hope you will not have a building of any kind, not a summer cottage, a hotel, or anything else, to mar the wonderful grandeur, the sublimity, the great loneliness and beauty of the canyon," he said. On February 26, 1919, Congress passed "An Act to Establish the Grand Canyon National Park in the State of Arizona." The date is associated today with the beginning of the conservation movement in the United States.

GRAND CANYON NATIONAL PARK

Future president Benjamin Harrison repeatedly tried to establish the Grand Canyon as a national park in the late 19th century, but it wasn't until Theodore Roosevelt's presidency that the Grand Canyon National Monument was founded in 1908. The Grand Canyon National Park Act was signed on February 26, 1919, by President Woodrow Wilson. The park's area was greatly enlarged in 1975, and four years later, the Arizona park was designated a UNESCO World Heritage Site.

SIZE
1,218,375 acres (1,904 sq. mi./4,931 km²)
Size rank among National Parks: 10 of 63

ELEVATION
Highest point: North Rim Lookout Tower (9,165 ft./2,793 m)
Lowest point: Lake Mead (1,173 ft./358 m)

GEOLOGY
The acronym "DUDE" is a handy mnemonic for explaining how the Grand Canyon formed: deposition, uplift, down cutting, and erosion. About two billion years ago, the rocks of the inner gorge were deposited in warm shelf seas and covered by layers of sedimentary rock. The whole region rose up between 70 and 30 million years ago (creating the Colorado Plateau), before the Colorado River began carving its way downward about six million years ago, gradually widening the canyon and exposing two billion years of geological history.

FLORA AND FAUNA
As a result of its sheer size and considerable differences in altitude, five climate zones exist in the park. The wildlife has adapted to these zones: Mule deer, coyotes, and cougars live in the dense aspen, spruce, and fir forests of higher elevations; lizards, rattlesnakes, and small rodents such as the kangaroo rat—a mouse-sized animal that hops on its hind legs—roam the bush vegetation of the lower elevations. Although it gets hotter and more hostile the further you descend into the canyon, the Colorado River provides an oasis for beavers, herons, and rainbow trout; willows and cottonwoods line the waterways. The canyon region is also home to raptors including bald eagles and peregrine falcons.

CLIMATE AND WEATHER

Desert summers are hot, dusty, and sometimes unbearable, with frequent showers in the afternoons. From November to March, temperatures are regularly below freezing. At the North Rim, temperatures are usually lower compared to the South Rim, and snow is likely there in winter.

CONSERVATION

Grand Canyon National Park protects the natural and cultural resources and ecological and physical processes of the Grand Canyon along with its scenic and scientific values. It became more widely known John Wesley Powell's 1869 geographic expedition. Ten years later, the first accommodations for tourists sprang up on the South Rim. The park was created in 1919, and the North Rim developed in the 1920s. Electric companies had tried to make use of the river's hydroelectric potential since the turn of the 20th century. In the 1960s, plans to build dams in the Grand Canyon were halted after a grassroots campaign led by the Sierra Club.

BEFORE YOU GO

Especially in summer, it is much hotter in the canyon than on the edges. Altitude and heat demand a lot from your body, so hiking into the valley is a hazardous undertaking and should only be attempted by those in good physical condition. Even experienced hikers shouldn't plan for a return journey in one day. Headgear and sun spray are crucial, as you're exposed to the sun almost non-stop. Bring plenty of food and water—otherwise, you'll be one of several hundred tourists who have to be rescued every year. Overnight stays are possible at the historic Phantom Ranch nestled within the canyon.

BEST TIMES TO VISIT

Opt for the shoulder seasons to avoid crowds and extreme temperatures. October, November, March, and April have generally mild weather and fewer crowds. The North Rim is only open from late May to early October.

HIDDEN GEM

For those equipped with a four-wheel-drive vehicle and an adventurous spirit, the Toroweap Overlook offers extreme solitude and stunning scenery from the North Rim.

INTERESTING FACTS ABOUT THE PARK

- Geologist John Wesley Powell's 1869 expedition was the first U.S. government sponsored passage through the Grand Canyon by boat.
- The canyon's characteristic red color originates from iron minerals in the rock layers reacting with oxygen in the atmosphere.

Mary Elizabeth Jane Colter

ARCHITECT AND DECORATOR

The South Rim of Grand Canyon National Park not only boasts spectacular views of nature, it's also home to some of the only remaining works of the master architect and interior designer Mary Colter (1869–1958). A chain-smoking perfectionist, she is responsible for a handful of structures that took inspiration from the landscape around them and presciently blended modern and Native American architecture. Born in Pittsburgh, Colter grew up in Minnesota, Colorado, and Texas, before attending art school in California. At 32, the Fred Harvey Company offered her a job to decorate Santa Fe's new Alvarado Hotel. After a few years, Colter became the company's chief architect and decorator, tirelessly defending her vision in a predominantly male domain. Over the course of 30 years, she conceived a series of hotels, shops, and rest areas along major railway routes. But her most well-known projects are four building complexes on the southern rim of the Grand Canyon: the 1905 Hopi House, shaped like a Hopi pueblo; Hermit's Rest, a 1914 building whose exposed beams, rustic stone walls, and soot-blackened fireplace create the illusion it was built (and lived in) by a local mountain man; Lookout Studio Observatory, a rough boulder structure from 1914 that looks like a natural rock formation growing out of a precipice; and the Desert View Watchtower at the eastern end of the South Rim (1932), which mimics an Ancestral Puebloan watchtower and even features paintings of Native American designs. By employing Indigenous builders, demanding the use of on-site materials, and incorporating references to Native American arts and crafts, she shaped American visions of the Southwest.

Theodore Roosevelt

In honor of an American symbol of conservation, this park celebrates a man whose legacy is full of complexities.

I n 1883, at the age of 24, Theodore Roosevelt arrived in the Badlands of North Dakota, enchanted by romantic visions of the West and ready to hunt bison. The trip would help change the course of American history, planting the seed for the conservation policies that would later define his presidency. The park, named in honor of the nature-loving president, is a place where bison still roam and where the buttes of the Badlands pepper the landscape, marking the end of the Great Plains.

Roosevelt was born into a life of wealth and privilege in New York City, but he had been fascinated by nature from a young age, exploring near his home and collecting animal

NORTH DAKOTA

specimens to document in his journal. He struggled with asthma and bad eyesight, and his father encouraged him to exercise to build up his strength. He followed his father's advice and, along the way, became enamored with the stories of Western frontiersmen like Davy Crockett. For his 1883 trip to North Dakota, he hired a guide, and when the guide insisted on returning to town, Roosevelt stayed out by himself. It took him 10 days to kill the bison that he had come for, and by the time he left North Dakota, he had invested in a ranch.

When he was back in New York City, in 1884, his wife, Alice Lee, gave birth to their daughter Alice. Two days later, both his wife and mother died on the same day. Grief-stricken, he sought solace in North Dakota and his "home ranch," a landscape now preserved in the park's Elkhorn Ranch Unit. The Harvard graduate eventually returned to the big city and a life in politics, but his time in the outdoors had left a lasting impression, one that led to a lifelong commitment to conservation. In 1906 he signed into law the American Antiquities Act, and during his presidency protected around 230 million acres (930,000 km²) of public land.

The park is an homage to a man who laid the groundwork for federal conservation policies and grew the National Park System. It is an often-celebrated history but a highly conflicted one: Roosevelt was a symbol of conservation and land protection, but he was also highly prejudiced toward the people who called these lands home. "The most vicious cowboy has more moral principle than the average Indian," he said in an 1886 speech. His vision for vast tracts of protected wilderness didn't include the Native Americans who had been stewards of these lands for millennia.

However complicated the president's legacy may be, it's clear that the park has carried out his wish to preserve the natural beauty of pristine landscapes. Today, the Wind Canyon Trail affords visitors gorgeous views of the winding Little Missouri River, and bison, now deemed the National Mammal, continue to roam its grounds. The colorful layers of the North Dakota Badlands, softened by the mixed-grass prairies below, set the stage for visitors to contemplate the complexities of the conservationist president and what the legacy of "America's Best Idea" really means.

PARK AT A GLANCE

The Recreation Demonstration Area was established in 1935 to honor President Theodore Roosevelt. The area eventually became Theodore Roosevelt National Park under President Jimmy Carter on November 19, 1978.

SIZE
70,446 acres (110 sq. mi./28 km²)
Size rank among National Parks: 45 of 63

ELEVATION
Highest point: Peck Hill (2,865 ft./873 m)
Lowest point: Little Missouri River (2,240 ft./682 m)

GEOLOGY
The Little Missouri Badlands began to take form 65 million years ago when sediment and volcanic ash settled and slowly turned into sandstone, siltstone, mudstone, and bentonite clay. Around two million years ago, enormous ice sheets covered the area. As they melted, the Little Missouri River was formed, which sculpted the sediment, revealing the present-day Badlands.

FLORA AND FAUNA
It's common to spot bison, elk, mule deer, wild horses, bighorn sheep, and prairie dogs. There are more than 185 species of birds in the park. The floodplains and grasslands of the park provide an important habitat to more than 400 species of plants, and on the prairie, you can witness a dazzling display of wildflowers in late spring and early summer.

CONSERVATION
The ancestors of American bison have been traced back 400,000 years, and for centuries, the local Native Americans coexisted with the animal. However, the arrival of white hunters and traders almost decimated the population. By the turn of the 20th century, there were less than 300 wild bison. Federal legislation had to be put in place to ensure their survival. In 1956, bison were reintroduced to the park where they continue to roam today.

BEFORE YOU GO
The North and South Units of the park are easily accessible, but the Elkhorn Ranch Unit requires driving on a gravel road. There are no services, restaurants, or lodging in the park, but there are two campgrounds and a horse camp.

BEST TIMES TO VISIT
Its remote location means that summer is a little less crowded than in other parks. It's also when all park programs are in full swing, and the wildflowers are in bloom.

Badlands

Ruthlessly ravaged by wind and water, this otherworldly wonderland boasts rock formations in earthy hues.

SOUTH DAKOTA

Rising from the vast prairies of South Dakota, the Badlands are nothing if not striking. Visitors find themselves awestruck by the park's theatrically bizarre topography of buttes and ridges, bare peaks, and sharply eroded pinnacles. It is a feast for visitors' eyes, but for millennia, this stretch of land offered nothing but drought and death to humans. Since the lack of water and the extreme temperatures made it hard to traverse, the Oglala Lakota people dubbed this harsh and seemingly inhospitable landscape mako sica: "bad lands." But it's not all dust and rocks. In fact, the clay soil nurtures the largest undisturbed mixed-grass prairie in the United States, which provides a home to hundreds of species of mammals, reptiles, birds, and insects.

The rock formations may be devoid of most vegetation, but they're a treasure trove for paleontologists (and fossil fans). The Badlands once lay at the bottom of an ancient sea. Over millions of years, it became a subtropical forest and later an open savanna. Some 75 million years ago, powerful currents and rivers started the erosion process, creating rock stratifications in rusty, gray, yellow, and purple shades. Each of the delicately banded colors represents a different layer of sediment. There are three-toed horses, camels, and ancient rhinos among the fossil remains found here. Prehistoric bones are still being uncovered today, even by visitors—a seven-year-old recently discovered the skull of a saber-toothed cat—but beware: collecting fossils (or anything else, for that matter) is illegal.

When hiking the Badlands or following the Badlands Loop Road or the Sage Creek Rim Road, there's plenty of wildlife to take in. Five large ungulate species roam the park's boundaries, with mule deer and white-tailed deer being the most common. In 1963, 50 bison were reintroduced to the wild. The herd has since grown to over 1,000 animals, which can be seen throughout the park. They play an important role in the ecosystem, as prairie dogs like to burrow in lands that the bison have grazed. The prairie dog colonies (called "towns") also attract predators such as silver badgers, bobcats, coyotes, and large birds, as well as the nocturnal black-footed ferret, one of the most endangered mammals in the world.

For thousands of years, Indigenous tribes used the Badlands as hunting grounds. The Oglala Sioux Tribe—the Lakota people—have lived here since time immemorial. In 1868, the United States assured them that the land would forever be theirs; only 21 years later, the United States broke that treaty and confiscated their land. As a ceremony against settlers, members of the Sioux Tribe performed "Ghost Dances" on the Stronghold Table in the late 19th century. The dances ended with the Wounded Knee Massacre in 1890, when 300 Lakota people were killed by United States Cavalry officers. Today, the Stronghold District in the southern part of the park—revered as a ceremonial sacred site—is jointly managed with the Oglala Lakota Tribe.

PARK AT A GLANCE

*T*he Badlands were designated as a national monument in 1939 and got upgraded to a national park on November 10, 1978. Despite the park's unappealing name, it welcomes around a million visitors annually. (When the park was first proposed in 1922, the much cheerier name, "Wonderland National Park," was suggested.) The park's rugged beauty has been used as a backdrop for several blockbusters, including Dances with Wolves and Armageddon.

SIZE
242,756 acres (379 sq. mi./982 km²)
Size rank among National Parks: 28 of 63

ELEVATION
Highest point: Red Shirt Table (3,340 ft./1,018 m)
Lowest point: Sage Creek (2,460 ft./750 m)

GEOLOGY
The erosion process of the Badlands began roughly 500,000 years ago. It continues today, at the rate of about one inch per year. Geologists estimate that in 500,000 years, the Badlands will have vanished completely.

FLORA AND FAUNA
From tiny shrews to giant bison, the Badlands National Park is home to over 329 animal species. In addition, 400 plant species thrive in the mixed-grass prairie, dotted with colorful patches of wildflowers.

CONSERVATION
The park strives to preserve the ecosystem and the natural scenery of the Badlands, which includes a substantial remnant of native prairie land. It also hosts one of the world's richest fossil beds, allowing scientists to study the evolution of mammal species such as horses, rhinos, and saber-toothed cats.

BEFORE YOU GO
Badlands National Park has two campgrounds for overnight visits: Cedar Pass and Sage Creek Campgrounds. Cedar Pass Lodge offers overnight accommodations and a restaurant. The one-mile (1.6-kilometer) Door Trail and the half-mile (.8-kilometer) Window Trail boast magnificent views over the weathered landscape.

BEST TIMES TO VISIT
Late summer/early fall when temperatures are mild and crowds are gone. In late summer, the Fossil Preparation Lab in the Ben Reifel Visitor Center shows paleontologists at work.

Wind Cave

The birthplace of the Lakota people, this underground cave system breathes air to the world above in one of the country's oldest national parks.

Stand next to a small 10-inch (25-centimeter) hole in the rocks near the ground in Wind Cave National Park, and you might feel a burst of air coming from the world below. This is Maka Oniye, or "breathing earth." In the Lakota oral tradition, this sacred site is a portal to the spirit world below, and the place where their ancestors and bison first emerged from.

It's also the place where a gust of air reportedly blew Jesse Bingham's hat off in 1881, leading him and his brother Tom to bring friends back to see the oddity. When they returned, the air current had changed and when they placed a hat over the hole, it was immediately sucked inside. That same year, Charlie Crary of Custer squeezed his body through the very same hole. Wind Cave's first known explorer, Crary carried only a candle for light and string to mark his route.

SOUTH DAKOTA

This small hole in the earth leads to an entire underground world, a complex system of 150 miles (241 km) of caves (that we know of), some of it over 300 million years old. One of the first extensive accounts of the cave came from Alvin McDonald, a teenager who had accompanied his father to South Dakota in 1890. J.D. McDonald, the boy's father, had been hired by South Dakota Mining Company to manage the mining claim they had placed on the cave. While his father tried, unsuccessfully, to set up a mine in the cave, Alvin spent hours in the cave, taking extensive notes in his journal. After a nine-hour trip in the cave in 1891, he wrote, "Have given up the idea of finding the end of Wind Cave." Researchers still haven't found the end, and studies of the airflow through the entrances show that it's possible only 10 percent of the cave has been explored.

Established in 1903, it's one of the nation's oldest national parks, but with only around 125,000 visitors a year, it's not as well known as its iconic cousins established around the same time. This underground world, though, is more than deserving of attention. Besides the cave breathing—a phenomenon caused by differences in barometric pressure between the outside and subterranean worlds—Wind Cave is famous for its boxwork, a mineral structure with a distinct honeycomb pattern that covers many of the cave's walls and ceilings. There is more boxwork in Wind Cave National Park than in all the other caves in the world combined. Other mineral formations (known to geologists as speleothems) decorate the cave, from small, rounded clusters of calcite called "cave popcorn" to dogtooth spar with its gleaming, spike-shaped crystals. Visitors can still see the original hole that led to the cave's discovery, although a wider, more accessible hole was made in the 1890s.

Above ground, there's no shortage of things to see either. Iconic wildlife like bison and pronghorn roam the prairie much as they did hundreds of years ago. South Dakota's state flower, the pasque flower, is one of the first of many wildflowers to bloom, and over 30 miles (48 km) of trail take visitors through mixed-grass prairie and forests of ponderosa pine. Located in the southern portion of the Black Hills, this area is warmer and drier than to the north and is sometimes referred to as South Dakota's "banana belt."

PARK AT A GLANCE

Wind Cave was designated a national park on January 3, 1903, under President Theodore Roosevelt, 13 years before the National Park Service was officially established.

SIZE
148,588 acres (232 sq. mi/601 km²)
Size rank among National Parks: 37 of 63

ELEVATION
Highest point: Rankin Ridge Fire Tower (5,013 ft./1,527 m)
Lowest point: Beaver Creek (3,559 ft./1,084 m)

GEOLOGY
The first cave passageways started to form around 320 million years ago as the ancient oceans retreated. With the oceans gone, freshwater, seeped underground, causing the limestone in the ground to dissolve. Around 40 to 60 million years ago, the Black Hills uplift opened fractures in the limestone allowing the cave system to expand. As water sat in the limestone, it continued to help the erosion process, turning small cracks into larger passageways, and sculpting the complex system of caves visitors see today.

FLORA AND FAUNA
The Black Hills are home to over 200 species of birds and larger animals like bison, elk, and pronghorn. Black-footed ferrets, one of the rarest mammals in North America, also make their home here. Ponderosa pines dominate the landscape, but there's also an abundance of juniper shrubs, maple trees, and paper birch.

CONSERVATION
While Wind Cave was originally established as a national park for the wonders of the cave, it also became an important conservation site above ground. Identified as a prime place to restore the wild population of bison, Congress established the 4,000-acre (16-square-kilometer) Wind Cave Game Preserve in 1912. A year later, the American Bison Society sent 14 bison from the New York Zoological Gardens (now the Bronx Zoo) to Wind Cave. The bison continue to roam free today.

BEFORE YOU GO
There are no services or lodging in the park, but the Elk Mountain campground is open year-round. It can get cold in the cave so a jacket or long sleeves are recommended.

BEST TIMES TO VISIT
Fall with its mild weather and fewer visitors. The region can get especially busy in August during the Sturgis Motorcycle Rally.

Glacier

The park's glaciers, veritable giants of ice and snow, are 7,000 years old. They may be gone by 2030.

Mountain goats are among the many species that are quite at home in this rugged terrain. Others include mountain lions, grizzly bears, and beavers. Ospreys and eagles are among the park's more than 250 hundred species of birds.

MONTANA

There's hardly a place in the United States where the climate catastrophe (and humanity's failings) have become as daunting as in Glacier National Park in Montana. The park, located on the eastern flank of the Rocky Mountains, near the Canadian border, encompasses 1,583 square miles (4,101 km²) and was home to 150 active glaciers as recently as the early 1900s. The vast majority of these 7,000-year-old giants have vanished in recent decades, and the remaining 26 are steadily declining. Scientists estimate that the last holdouts will be gone by 2030.

What remains after the great melt is a park whose landscape was gradually carved out by glaciers millions of years ago. Its majestic peaks have earned it the nickname "Crown of the Continent," and rightly so. Countless streams tumble over

Besides the Going-to-the-Sun Road, which crosses the Glacier National Park from east to west, visitors have more than 700 miles (1,100 km) of trails to follow when exploring this glacial landscape, complete with boardwalks across rivers and streams. Naturally, there are also boating activities on many of the park's lakes.

vertically abraded rock faces and flow through dense coniferous forests and flower-filled meadows. Ice tongues have given way to azure mountain lakes running across the main ridge of the mountains. Of the 750 lakes fed by waterfalls and rushing mountain streams, less than a fifth even have a name.

For a long time, the park was the realm of the Salish and later the Blackfoot Tribes. When fur and bison hunters arrived in the late 18th century, many Native Americans were killed by disease and war, and the bison were largely extirpated. Things got even worse in the late 1880s, when prospectors came in search of valuable mineral deposits in the region's mountains. The pressure on the Blackfoot people became so great that they sold their territory for $1.5 million on the condition that they could continue to use it. They retreated into the mountains and later into Canada. Today, their descendants live on a reservation.

The national park was created in 1910. The Great Northern Railway, whose rail line ran along the park's southern border, built countless hotels and small lodges throughout the area, most of which were accessible only by hiking or horseback. This changed in 1932 with the creation of the Going-to-the-Sun Road, a 50-mile (80-kilometer) road that winds in dizzying switchbacks through the park's many terrains. This engineering marvel is considered one of the most beautiful scenic roads on earth, climbing mountain passes and passing picturesque lakes, whose surfaces reflect the peaks of the surrounding granite giants.

As beautiful as this park is by car, the true nature of the park reveals itself only to hikers and climbers. It is not without reason that Glacier National Park is considered the birthplace

of mountaineering in North America. The park is one of the few areas that humans have hardly touched. This seemingly endless expanse of undisturbed land produces a diversity of plant and animal life which can be observed along more than 620 miles (1,000 km) of trails and paths. Some are even approved for mountain bikes or horseback rides.

Glacier Park is one of the largest and most intact ecosystems in North America. Where avalanches carve paths through the forests in winter and flower meadows bloom in spring, grizzly bears, bald eagles, and mountain lions have found their home alongside elk and woodland caribou. The gradual disappearance of the glaciers threatens not only their habitat; Montana's water supply and agriculture industry rely on the glaciers. Milder winters, earlier snowmelt, and hotter summer temperatures also contribute to more frequent and longer-lasting wildfires. Since the mid-1980s, a quarter of the total area of the national park has burned.

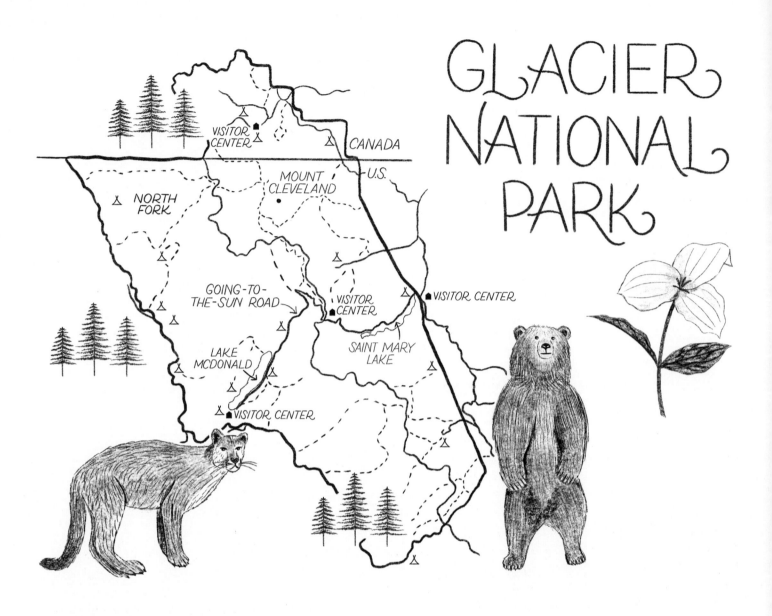

GLACIER NATIONAL PARK

Glacier National Park was established on May 11, 1910. Two decades later, a historic agreement merged Glacier with the adjacent Waterton Lakes National Park in Canada, under the name Waterton-Glacier International Peace Park–the world's first transboundary nature reserve. Glacier National Park was declared a Biosphere Reserve in 1976, and in 1995, the joint park received UNESCO World Heritage status.

SIZE
1,012,837 acres (1,583 sq. mi./4,100 km²)
Size rank among National Parks: 12

ELEVATION
Highest point: Mount Cleveland (10,468 ft./3,190 m)
Lowest point: Flathead River (3,150 ft./960 m)

GEOLOGY
In the lowest layers, the rock in Glacier National Park is over one billion years old. Mud, sand, gravel, and lime were deposited here and the deeper sediments solidified into stone under the weight of overlying layers. From time to time, magma reached the earth's surface. Ice age glaciations have put the final touch on this landscape, giving birth to wide valleys with high, steep rock faces and over 200 lakes.

FLORA AND FAUNA
Located at the crossroads of different biological communities, Glacier National Park features a wide array of plants and animals that do not normally live together; nowhere else do species of the Pacific Coast and the Great Plains get as close. Bears and mountain lions roam the dense woods in the western valleys, while mountain goats and bighorn sheep inhabit the higher elevations. Streams and lakes are home to beavers, muskrats, and water-loving birds. Wildflower meadows support elk, coyotes, and hawks. More than 250 bird species call the park home.

CLIMATE AND WEATHER
Glacier National Park straddles the Continental Divide of the Rocky Mountains, dividing the park into two climatic regions.

Warm, moist Pacific air moves in from the west and brings moderate temperatures and heavy precipitation. At the Continental Divide, it clashes with cold and dry air from the Arctic, leading to extreme temperature fluctuations, strong winds, and blizzards in the east. Summers are generally warm but nights are cool, and winters are mild. Snowfall is possible al any timc, ospecially in areas above the tree line.

CONSERVATION

Glacier National Park preserves a pristine landscape of forests, alpine meadows and lakes, and rich biodiversity. Because of its long history of research and its remoteness from civilization, the park serves as a reference area for the study of climate history and global warming. But its glaciers are under threat: because milder winters provide more rain than new snow in the mid-mountain areas and summer months are becoming hotter and drier—the number of days with temperatures above 90 °F (32 °C) has tripled in the past 100 years—the snowpack gets thinner and exposes the dark blue glacial ice, which in turn absorbs more heat and speeds up melting.

BEFORE YOU GO

It may sound odd, but make sure to get the park right when arranging your visit in advance; this Park is in Montana—but there's a Glacier National Park in Canada and a Glacier Bay National Park in Alaska. Visitor centers at Glacier are open on a rotating basis throughout the year but may close at short notice on certain dates (depending on the weather).

BEST TIMES TO VISIT

While the park is open year-round, the entire route of the Going-to-the-Sun Road is only open seasonally, depending on snowfall and weather conditions. It's usually open from late June to September/October. May and June offer opportunities for cycling while the road is still closed to vehicles, and also good conditions for whitewater rafting.

HIDDEN GEM

The North Fork area of the park offers solitude and incredible scenery for those with four-wheel or all-wheel drive vehicles.

INTERESTING FACTS ABOUT THE PARK

- The Triple Divide Peak feeds water into three oceans: the Pacific, Atlantic, and Arctic.
- Indigenous people called these northern U.S. Rockies the "Backbone of the World."
- Parks Project sponsors the Native America Speaks program, which is the longest running Indigenous speaker series in the National Park Service.

Mariah Gladstone

EDUCATOR AND ADVOCATE

Mariah Gladstone, Piikuni (Blackfeet) and Tsalagi (Cherokee), grew up in Northwest Montana near Glacier National Park. From a very young age, she has educated visitors to Glacier National Park in the Native America Speaks program, the longest-running Indigenous speaker series in the National Parks. She is also known for her interpretive performances in American Indian Sign Language (AISL). AISL has great cultural significance for many Native Americans, since it acted as a common language for several tribes, allowing them to communicate despite their linguistic differences. When she was three years old, Gladstone's father and grandfather tilled a garden for her, in which she learned to grow many plants—thus sparking a lifelong passion for food. Gladstone has turned that essential connection to place and food into a career focused on cultural revitalization and Indigenous foods. Gladstone started Indigikitchen, an educational platform that teaches people about Indigenous foods and allows them to share recipes both online and in community spaces. Food isn't just about physical sustenance, as Gladstone has said, "There's a spiritual aspect when Native peoples eat foods of their ancestors. It recognizes the wisdom of our elders and strengthens our ties to Mother Earth." Armed with a master's in environmental science, her approach is both academic and ancestral, and she has done cooking demonstrations for the Smithsonian's National Museum of the American Indian and testified before a Senate committee on The Farm Bill. This advocacy work has earned her recognition as one of the 25 Under 25 Leaders in Indian Country. She's also been named a Culture of Health Leader through the Robert Wood Johnson Foundation, a MIT Solve Indigenous Communities Fellow, and a Luce Indigenous Knowledge Fellow.

North Cascades

Adventure awaits in the rugged wilderness of the "American Alps."

Just three hours from Seattle, a hiker's paradise awaits in the vast and pristine wilderness. North Cascades National Park is a raw, imposing landscape that is home to rugged mountain peaks, the largest collection of glaciers in the contiguous United States, and beautiful forests with more flora biodiversity than any American national park. The park is almost entirely made up of protected wilderness, with very few roads or man-made structures. To help preserve the landscape, campers must enter the park on foot, horseback, or by boat, helping to keep pollution low and prevent vehicles from harming the delicate ecosystems. But don't let this deter you: once you've made it into the park, there are countless opportunities for exploration and adventure.

Covering just over 504,000 acres (2,040 km²), the park's immense scale and diverse terrain make for some of the most ideal mountain country in North America, attracting hikers, backpackers, climbers, and campers of all experience levels. There are nearly 400 miles (644 km) of mountain and meadow hiking trails, ranging from leisurely strolls to expert climbs up daunting mountains. Some areas of the park are so difficult to access that only the most intrepid adventurers can reach them; the park's more arduous ascents have fitting and foreboding names like Torment-Forbidden Traverse and Desolation Peak.

The most popular day hike is the Cascades Pass trail, offering stunning panoramic views of the impressive Eldorado and Magic Peaks. And up Horseshoe Basin, hikers pass clusters of waterfalls cascading from melting glaciers. There are multiday excursions like the climb to the quartz summit of Eldorado Peak. Another, Mount Shuksan, is the famed "Crown Jewel of the North Cascades." At 9,131 feet (2,783 m), climbers must cross glaciers, follow jagged ridges, and scale tall basalt cliffs. Those who successfully reach the summit are rewarded with a sublime view of the valleys below and Mount Triumph, Despair, and Terror beyond. The park is also home to over 200,000 acres (809 km²) of old-growth forest, whose horizon is punctuated by imposing, glacier-topped peaks. Over millions of years, the glacial ice

WASHINGTON

PARK AT A GLANCE

Through a congressional act that also established the adjacent Ross Lake and Lake Chelan National Recreation Areas, the more than 500,000 acres (2,023 km²) of the North Cascades became a national park on October 2, 1968.

SIZE
504,654 acres (789 sq. mi./2,043 km²)
Size rank among National Parks: 20 of 63

ELEVATION
Highest point: Goode Mountain (9,206 ft./2,806 m)
Lowest point: Skagit River (400 ft./122 m)

GEOLOGY
Featuring over 300 glaciers and 300 lakes and dozens of major tributaries, the park's landscape, especially the towering metamorphic rock of its mountains, is shaped by this abundance of ice and water. In the 8,800 feet (2,682 m) that separate the park's tallest point from its lowest, you will find a myriad of dynamic habitats.

FLORA AND FAUNA
From lowland forests of hemlocks and firs to alpine ecosystems teeming with hummingbirds, marmots, and coyotes, the park is home to a wide range of animals. The park also protects many rare species, like the wolverine and grizzly bear, as well as over 1,600 vascular plant species and a kingdom of fungi so vast that it still remains uncounted.

CONSERVATION
The park preserves a unique volcanic geology, which offers both recreational and scientific opportunities. Hydrothermal and volcanic features in the park might offer insight into what life on Mars once would have looked like, and NASA runs an astrobiology student intern program in partnership with the park.

BEFORE YOU GO
Although the park requires no entrance fee or parking passes, all camping requires a backcountry permit. The backcountry distinction here is crucial: there is no vehicular access to most campsites, requiring visitors to enter the park on foot, horseback, or by boat. However, lodging can be found in the adjacent recreational areas.

BEST TIMES TO VISIT
Mid-June and late-September, with most trail snow melted by mid-July. Due to wintery conditions, the park's visitor and information centers close in September or October.

sculpted these mountains, creating the dramatic, craggy peaks that helped earn its nickname, the "American Alps." The glaciers also helped form the park's abundance of lakes and rivers, which are perfect for kayaking and whitewater rafting. Aquatically minded visitors can even stay in a floating cabin at the Ross Lake Resort.

If camping's not your thing, the scenic drive down the North Cascades highway offers a different way to glimpse the park's incredible beauty. This route showcases the park's stately peaks, glacial crowns, and, in fall, the blazing yellow of golden larches amidst a backdrop of lush evergreens—all just a few hours' drive from the city.

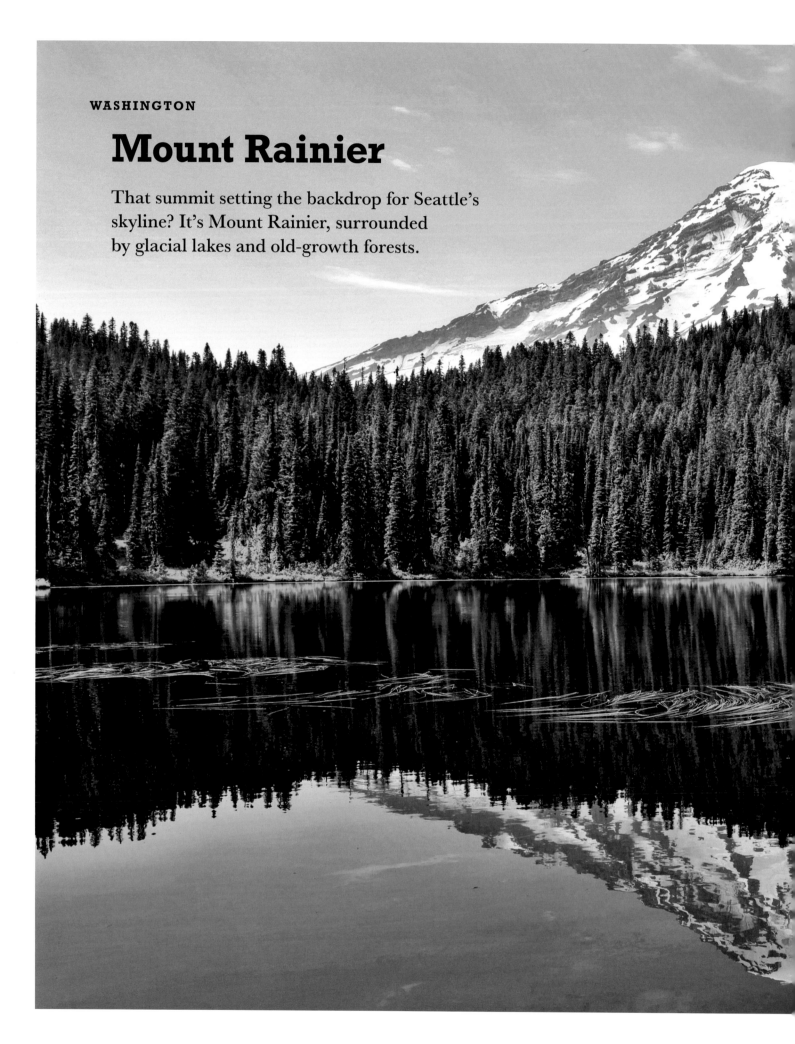

WASHINGTON

Mount Rainier

That summit setting the backdrop for Seattle's skyline? It's Mount Rainier, surrounded by glacial lakes and old-growth forests.

TOP: A western redcedar tree rises up from the boardwalk on the Grove of the Patriarchs Trail, a 1.1-mile (1.8-km) looped hike through forest land on boardwalks, bridges, and dirt tracks.

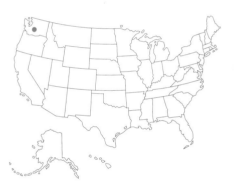

WASHINGTON

In 1879, when mountaineers Hazard Stevens and Philemon Beecher Van Trump ventured out to conquer the summit of Mount Rainier—a dormant stratovolcano some 100 miles (160 km) southeast of Seattle—they ignored the pleas of their Native American guides who tried to deter them from their potentially deadly endeavor. To the tribespeople, the ice-covered crater of Takoma—the Puyallup tribe's name for the mountain—was a sacred and dreaded place. More than two dozen glaciers and patches of permanent ice descend the flanks of the volcano. Its climate can be brutal. But the two pioneers went up anyway. Ill-prepared for the cold, Stevens and Van Trump almost died in the crater, spending the night hunkered down in a cavern warming themselves on the corrosive sulfur evaporating from the ground.

The two men made it down alive, and as more and more settlers came to the Northwest, Mount Rainier became one of the country's premier destinations for excursionists. (Van Trump himself climbed the mountain at least five more times.) Due to its climate and soil conditions, the park area is exceptionally fertile and lush, with peaceful mountain lakes, rushing torrents, and thundering waterfalls. As the snow thaws each year, mountain

Clear glacial waters are a common sight at Mount Rainier. Home to the most glaciated peak in the lower 48 states, the park has at least 150 waterfalls, some plunging depths of more than 300 feet (90 m). Among the many wildflowers that grow in the park's subalpine meadows, is the vibrant *Castilleja miniata,* commonly known as scarlet paintbrush.

"The mountain receives our expressions and becomes part of us; we imprint our memories upon it and trust it without dearest divisions of our lives."

—BRUCE BARCOTT, WRITER

meadows transform the volcano's slopes into lush carpets of flowers. Native Americans had spent the summer months in these fertile and cool foothills for thousands of years. While the women gathered berries and herbs and hunted small animals and birds, the men pursued game and fished.

With the arrival of settlers came the deforestation, cattle farming, and mining that had already ravaged much of the American West. The early onset of mass tourism only added to the considerable damage that had been going on in the region for decades. With the help of Van Trump and other conservationists, John Muir campaigned to preserve the old-growth forest that covers the foothills of Mount Rainier. Congress eventually agreed, but only after being assured that nowhere in the park was suitable for farming or mining. The creation of the national park in 1899 stopped the destruction, at least within small

boundaries. (All efforts to enlarge the park area have since failed.) Thanks to these efforts, the region around the volcano remains a virtually untouched wilderness today. The park is crisscrossed by various hiking trails of varying lengths and difficulties. They bear names like "Wonderland Trail," the first trail in the park that fully encircled Mount Rainier. It winds through low-lying forests, flower-strewn valleys, and mountainous regions. (You might even spot a black bear or cougar along the way.) It's safe to say that many routes lead to Paradise here—an apt name for a place famed for its magnificent views of the panorama. Paradise is one of the most popular destinations in Mount Rainier National Park. Receiving on average 643 inches (16.3 m) of snow a year, it is also the park's top destination for winter sports, with options for sledding, skiing, snowboarding, guided snowshoe walks, or even winter camping—brrr!

MOUNT RAINIER NATIONAL PARK

SEATTLE (100 MILES)

VISITOR CENTER

WHITE RIVER ENTRANCE

MOUNT RAINIER

WONDERLAND TRAIL

VAN TRUMP PARK

PARADISE PARK

COMET FALLS

VISITOR CENTER

NISQUALLY ENTRANCE

STEVENS CANYON ENTRANCE

VISITOR CENTER

Mount Rainier was the fourth national park to be established in the United States, passing Congress legislation on March 2, 1899. Ninety years later, in 1988, large portions of the park were given greater protection by being designated as wilderness. In 1997, the park was recognized as a National Historic Landmark for its General Plan, which is exemplary for further national park development.

SIZE
236,381 acres (369 sq. mi./956 km²)
Size rank among National Parks: 30 of 63

ELEVATION
Highest point: Mount Rainier (14,409 ft./4,392 m)
Lowest point: Ohanapecosh River (1,600 ft./488 m)

GEOLOGY
Mount Rainier began forming about 500,000 years ago and had its last major eruptions 5,000 and 2,000 years ago. During one of the last eruptions, part of the cone's summit was probably blasted away. During the eruption the glaciers of the mountain melted, and the rock material was buried under the debris and mudflow. Today activity is limited to hot vapors from the crater of a new cone.

FLORA AND FAUNA
The park encompasses a wide range of vegetation zones because of its different elevations. The area surrounding Mount Rainier is covered by dense virgin forest, while the lower elevation and rainier northwest is covered by rain forest. During warmer months, wildflowers cover the alpine meadows. The park is home to at least 50 different species of mammals, including mule deer, snow goats (a sight in themselves!), and elk. The largest birds—often seen circling the park—are golden eagles; the smallest are hummingbirds, which have adapted perfectly to this harsh landscape.

CLIMATE AND WEATHER
The park sees abundant rainfall throughout the year. That's good for nature, but bad for views: Mount Rainier is often shrouded in clouds for weeks at a time, and equally long

periods of rain are not uncommon. Winters are cold and very snowy (elevation considerably affects temperatures).

CONSERVATION
Mount Rainier National Park preserves the majestic, eponymous volcano, along with its natural and cultural resources. It became a destination for excursionists soon after European settlement in the Northwest. The advance of agriculture, forestry, and mining led to efforts to preserve the mountain and its scenic surroundings in 1899, following a long campaign by John Muir and other conservationists. The park's 1920s General Plan represented a major advancement in the management of scenic and recreational lands. More than 97 percent of the park is wilderness, and Mount Rainier's glaciers are an important source of water for the region.

BEFORE YOU GO
Park roads run halfway around the mountain to the south and east, with spur roads leading to the main attractions and visitor centers. Plan for at least two days because of the distances. Lodging includes the historic Paradise Inn, a hotel built in 1916 and one of the most renowned of the U.S. national park lodges. The weather can throw a wrench into plans, as surprise snow or heavy rains can cause road and trail closures.

BEST TIMES TO VISIT
July, August, and September provide the greatest accessibility to the park—roads will be open and most trails free of snow. Experienced winter travelers can enjoy solitude in the park during the spring and late fall, but be prepared for extreme conditions and heavy snowfall.

HIDDEN GEM
While many people visit the stunning Comet Falls, much fewer continue hiking past the falls to Van Trump Park, a gorgeous meadow with sweeping views of Mount Rainier. Relax in Van Trump Park or continue another mile to Mildred Point for a superb view of the mountain.

INTERESTING FACTS ABOUT THE PARK
- Mount Rainier is the most glaciated peak in the contiguous United States. The park itself contains 25 major glaciers.
- In 1792, English navigator Captain George Vancouver was the first European to sight the "very remarkable high round mountain" and named it after his friend, Admiral Peter Rainier. The Puyallup people continue to advocate for the mountain to be renamed to its indigenous name: Tacoma.
- The park contains four historic fire lookout towers, perched on summits around the park.

Craig Romano

HIKING GUIDEBOOK AUTHOR

Craig Romano is—quite literally—a trailblazer. Growing up in rural New Hampshire, he had no choice but to love the outdoors, Romano jokes "because there was nothing else to do." The former Boy Scout has traveled to Argentina, Sicily, and South Korea and explored far-flung places like the wilderness of Alaska. He's worked as a hiking guide in the Pyrenees, as a backcountry ranger in New Hampshire's White Mountains, and at several ski resorts in New England. But no place quite struck him like Washington. The Evergreen state, he says, is home to some of the most beautiful places he has ever seen. And Romano's mission is to hike them all. Calling Washington home since 1989, the avid hiker, runner, and cyclist logged about 30,000 trail miles (48,280 km), from Cape Flattery in the northwest to Puffer Butte in the southeast; and from Cape Disappointment in the southwest to the Salmo-Priest Wilderness in the northeast. Romano particularly loves the state's national parks—from North Cascades ("You don't see anyone."), to Olympic ("Still my favorite."), and Mount Rainier ("I'm in awe every single time."). Since 2005, Romano has written more than 25 hiking guides for the Northwest, quitting his teaching and part-time waiter job to become a full-time author. He has written books like *Backpacking Washington, Day Hiking North Cascades,* and *Urban Trails Vancouver, WA.* And in 2016, he had the honor of writing the updated edition of *100 Classic Hikes in Washington,* putting his own spin on a beloved classic. The iconic guidebook was first published in 1998 by Harvey Manning and Ira Spring, and the two hiking advocates—along with naturalist John Muir and philosopher Henry David Thoreau—were Romano's heroes when he first moved to Washington. Oh, and what to hike at Rainier? Romano says: the Sourdough Ridge trail.

Olympic

Gleaming glaciers, fairy-tale forests, and secluded beaches: the landscape here is so diverse it could easily be mistaken for three separate parks.

The park has around 73 miles (117 km) of coastline on the west coast of the Olympic Peninsula. In some places rugged cliffs rise from the waves below; elsewhere visitors can find sandy or rocky beaches to explore.

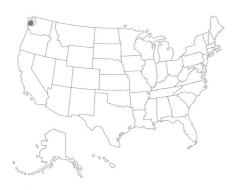

WASHINGTON

Olympic National Park, which covers about half of the eponymous peninsula in the northwesternmost tip of Washington state, is one of the most fascinating places in the United States. Surrounded on three sides by water, the park is home to a variety of unique plants and animals that have evolved in relative isolation. A refuge for numerous endemic species, it is one of the most significant wilderness areas in the country. There are few places in the world where you can find three distinct ecosystems in such close proximity: the long and wild coastline, the dense thickets of temperate rain forest, and the towering, glacier-capped peaks of the Olympic Mountains.

Encircling the park is the Olympic Peninsula Loop. Short roads lead to trailheads around its perimeter, guiding visitors into the lush rain forests that cover the mountain foothills. The humid Pacific air releases its moisture over the western slopes, allowing one of the last temperate rain forests on earth to grow. Some trees are so old they sprouted before the arrival of human

This park is named for the mythological Mount Olympus of ancient Greece, a stunning wilderness worthy of gods. Among the animal inhabitants of this U.S. version you can expect to find salmon, beavers, eagles, and elk.

Olympic's rainforests are overgrown with giant ferns, mosses and fungi. Together, they create a hazy, almost fairytale-like atmosphere.

civilization; some are as tall as small skyscrapers. The ancient Douglas firs, Sitka spruce, and western hemlock are covered with moss and epiphytes, creating a hazy, almost fairy tale-like atmosphere; the soft, musty, earthy-smelling forest floor is densely overgrown with giant ferns, mosses, and fungi.

President Cleveland declared these woods a forest reserve in 1897 to protect them from rampant logging. While it spared the trees, it didn't save the elk, which hunters slaughtered by the thousands. Killed for their canine teeth—vestigial tusks which could be sold as ivory—their population had dropped to fewer than 20,000 by 1900. Therefore, in 1909, President Theodore Roosevelt, an avid big-game hunter but also a renowned conservationist, designated a portion of the Reserve as Mount Olympus National Monument. But the withdrawal of such large tracts of the forest was controversial, and the reserve's area was cut in half within a year.

Stephen Mather, then director of the National Park Service, and his successor Horace Albright, waged a 23-year battle to establish a national park on the Olympic Peninsula. Finally, Franklin Roosevelt signed the legislation establishing the Olympic National Park in 1938. Fifteen years later, the park was expanded to include a narrow strip of densely wooded shoreline along the Pacific Coast. Here the trunks of felled trees— snatched by the mighty wind—line the beach, and bald eagles and ospreys lurk in the treetops or glide above the water, hunting for fish. They have shared this area with Native tribes, which have lived along the fertile and fish-rich coastline for millennia. While the cold Pacific here is hardly suitable for a beach vacation, its striking cliffs and coastal tide pools are a stunning sight. Particularly memorable are the gray whales that pass close to the coast in large pods on their fall migration from the Arctic to the Gulf of California.

OLYMPIC NATIONAL PARK

L *ocated on the Olympic Peninsula in the western part of Washington State and originally established as a national monument in 1909, Olympic was designated a national park on June 29, 1938. It was classified as a UNESCO Biosphere Reserve in 1976 and was declared a World Heritage Site in 1981.*

SIZE
922,650 acres (1,442 sq. mi./3,734 km²)
Size rank among National Parks: 13 of 63

ELEVATION
Highest point: Mount Olympus (7,962 ft./2,427 m)
Lowest point: Pacific Ocean (sea level)

GEOLOGY
The history of the Olympic Mountains is closely related to plate tectonic processes off the U.S. West Coast. Born in the sea, the basalts and sedimentary rocks of the Olympic Mountains were laid down 18 to 57 million years ago offshore. When the upper basalt layers of the ocean floor collided with the continental shelf, they uplifted, folded, bent, overthrust, and eroded, forming the jagged peaks that stun visitors today.

FLORA AND FAUNA
Olympic National Park is one of the most diverse and varied national parks in the United States, with flower-filled mountain meadows, vast lavender fields, and deep green rain forests. The fauna is as varied, with the park's signature Roosevelt elk, but also black bears, lynxes, and mountain beavers (*Aplodontia rufa*)—primitive rodents that aren't actually related to the beaver. Off the coast, you can spot whales, sea lions, and dolphins, and the park is also rich in waterfowl and shorebirds. The few mountain lions that make the park their home live very reclusive lives; the chances of encountering one of these shy big cats are extremely slim.

CLIMATE AND WEATHER
Olympic has a temperate maritime climate. The west side of the park holds annual precipitation records—unsurprisingly,

Mount Olympus is often shrouded in clouds. Winters are mild and summers pleasant, with cool nights and somewhat lower precipitation. In spring, it is usually humid, mild, and often windy. The east side is significantly drier, and temperatures vary greatly.

CONSERVATION
Olympic National Park was founded to preserve the large wilderness containing the finest sample of primeval forest in the United States, to provide a suitable winter range and permanent protection for the herds of native Roosevelt elk and other wildlife, and to preserve the pristine Pacific coastline. The creation of the park had been preceded by a 23-year struggle by two former NPS directors against the U.S. Congress, which was at the time composed of a majority of utilitarians who had little sympathy for protecting economically viable land.

BEFORE YOU GO
The relative proximity to big cities such as Seattle and Portland makes Olympic a popular destination for weekend getaways or overnight stays, but the sheer size of the national park limits what you can see and do in one day. If you "only" want to drive a complete loop around the peninsula, that's already 329 miles (531 km), and doesn't even include all the destinations on the side roads. Ideally, plan at least three days for a visit to see the different areas.

BEST TIMES TO VISIT
It rains almost every day in the winter months, so Olympic is best visited from May to September if you want to stay dry. Spring is the best time to encounter elk near the park's rain forests, while May and June are the ideal times to spot black bears in the river valleys. Since it usually doesn't start snowing until October, you can still visit the high country of Olympic National Park in the fall.

HIDDEN GEM
Be sure to check out the Quinault Valley, a less-visited corner of the park with a scenic drive, several short hikes, and a visitor center. The Valley also serves as a trailhead for longer backpacking trips.

INTERESTING FACTS ABOUT THE PARK
- Olympic National Park is home to the rainiest point in the contiguous United States.
- At the heart of the forest lies Mount Olympus, which gives the park its name.
- The nearby town of Forks became famous as the setting and filming location for the *Twilight* film series, prompting the Olympic Peninsula to become a pilgrimage site for fans.

Robert Elofson
TRIBAL ELDER AND RIVER RESTORATION DIRECTOR

The Elwha River, a coastal stream running through the temperate rain forest of Olympic National Park, has been the site of an ecological restoration project that is unprecedented in size and scope. Over the course of four years—from 2011 to 2014—dams were demolished in the largest dam removal project in U.S. history. The dams prevented several species of salmon and steelhead from reaching their spawning grounds and devastated the tribal community. Members of the Lower Elwha Klallam Tribe had long called for the removal of the dams—the Elwha River has been their lifeline for generations. Robert Elofson is a tribal elder who spearheaded the project, serving as the tribe's Elwha River Restoration Director for 15 years. "Just sitting there waiting for someone else to do it doesn't help anyone," he says. The dam removal has allowed summer steelhead, bull trout, and king salmon to reclaim habitat that was long inaccessible (the number of spawning salmon has increased from about 3,000 to over one million since restoring the original water regime). It also gave a second heyday to the traditional Dungeness crab fishery; the animals returned to Freshwater Bay when washed-in sediment transformed the pebbly area back into a sandy beach with tidal channels. For the Salish people, whose tribes live all around the Salish Sea on the Olympic Peninsula, the river rebirth brings back a life of traditions. Many feel a spiritual connection to the environment, to the sea and its waterways, and salmon and other migratory fish play a major role in their traditions. Elofson, who studied physics and biology, wants humankind to be more considerate of nature—"not just slowing down our negative impact on the Salish Sea, but improving upon it."

Crater Lake

Sitting in a dormant volcano, Crater Lake is not only revered for its brilliant deep-blue hue—it's also one of the deepest lakes in the world.

TOP: Crater Lake sees 44 feet (13 m) of snowfall a year, and is roamed by foxes, bears, and coyotes, among other animals. OPPOSITE: Crater Lake Lodge, one of two accommodation options in the park.

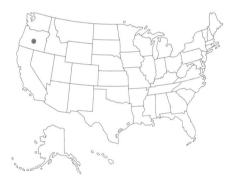

OREGON

If there's one state which certainly doesn't lack jaw-dropping landscapes, it's Oregon. In fact, there are so many forests, mountains, lakes, and rivers to explore that one trip will hardly do the Beaver State justice. It might come as a surprise, though, that Oregon only has one national park. To be fair, it's a magnificent one, with views so breathtaking they are hard to come by anywhere else in the world. Its name? Crater Lake National Park.

The park lies in the snow-covered Cascade Mountains in the southern part of the state. Numerous volcanoes shaped the landscape of the present mountain range. The highest peak is Mount Scott. At 8,929 feet (2,721 m), the climb up is not for wimps, but the view from the top is truly phenomenal: a diorama of rolling hills, evergreen forests, and towering cliffs encompassing the giant Crater Lake, which boasts a diameter of nearly 6 miles (9.7 km).

Crater Lake has been a sacred site to the Native American tribes in the region for thousands of years. Klamath and Umpqua oral traditions suggest that humans witnessed the eruption that created the lake some 7,700 years ago. However, the lake was not "discovered" by Western settlers until relatively recently, when gold prospector John Wesley Hillman came to the area in 1853. Instead of gold, Hillman and his crew found one of the most stunning geological treasures in the world.

Crater Lake is the remnant of a volcano, Mount Mazama. When it erupted and subsequently collapsed, lava sealed the floor of the geological structure and formed the lake's basin. With a maximum depth of 1,943 feet (592 m), it is the deepest lake in the United States and the ninth deepest in the world. The lake is fed only by snow and rain; there are no in- or outflows. Because the water is so pure and contains no sediment, algae, or pesticides, it absorbs all colors of the spectrum except blue.

Novelist Alexander Theroux called the lake "almost intolerable in its beauty," noting that the deep blue "can swamp with emotion the flickering power of analysis." The brilliant color stands in stark contrast with the ochre and rust hues of the surrounding cliffs it reflects. It can be best observed from the 33-mile (53-kilometer) Rim Road alongside the rim or from one of the many hiking trails around the crater.

TOP: A precarious-looking observation post with a deck overhanging the lake. OPPOSITE: Phantom Island seen from the Sun Notch Trail, a looped walk on which a short section follows the rim of the crater.

"Here all the ingenuity of nature seems to have been exerted to the fullest capacity, to build one grand, awe-inspiring temple."

—WILLIAM GLADSTONE STEEL

If you want to take a dip in the freezing waters, you have to tackle the Cleetwood Cove Trail, which descends about a mile and a half (2.4 km) to the only shoreline open to swimmers. (Open depending on the weather.) Those who dare can dive into the crystal clear water from the 20-foot (6-meter) rock ledge, a ritual for many brave swimmers these days. The waters are among the purest—if not the purest—in North America.

Fishing is also an option: in 1941, humans introduced rainbow trout and kokanee salmon into the formerly fishless lake. You can also take a boat to the two islands in the lake: the larger, Wizard Island, is a volcanic cone near the western edge that rises 750 feet (289 m) above the water's surface. The smaller Phantom Ship Island is a bizarrely shaped structure in the south. So fitting for this land of wonders, it is practically invisible in fog and low light and often appears or disappears as if from nowhere.

CRATER LAKE NATIONAL PARK

Crater Lake National Park is one of the oldest national parks in the country—and the only one in Oregon. Its designation came after extensive lobbying from William Gladstone Steel, who devoted his life to Crater Lake and even organized a U.S. Geological Survey expedition in 1886. Crater Lake was established as a national park under President Theodore Roosevelt on May 22, 1902.

SIZE
183,224 acres (286 sq. mi./742 km²)
Size rank among National Parks: 34 of 63

ELEVATION
Highest point: Mount Scott (8,929 ft./2,722 m)
Lowest point: Southwest corner of the park
(3,990 ft./1,216 m)

GEOLOGY
Mount Mazama started forming about half a million years ago. It grew episodically through many overlapping volcanoes, each of which was probably active for a comparatively brief period. It had a height of around 12,000 feet (3,700 m) and was only intermittently active until its dramatic eruption 7,700 years ago. In just a few hours or days, the roof of Mazama's magma chamber collapsed and formed a caldera that now holds Crater Lake, a process that probably took more than two centuries. It's possible that Mount Mazama might erupt again in the future.

FLORA AND FAUNA
Numerous species of animals—deer, black bears, porcupines, chipmunks, wild boars, coyotes—roam the forests of the park, which consist predominantly of pine and fir trees. Much less life is seen in and around the lake. Although fish are not native to the lake, various fish were introduced between 1888 and 1941. The only surviving species are rainbow trout and kokanee salmon. While the lake itself provides little habitat for birds (it's simply too deep and too pure), over 200 different species live in the park area. Particularly in summer, there is an abundance of songbirds.

CLIMATE AND WEATHER

Crater Lake is one of the snowiest inhabited regions in the United States. Winters are very long and dominated by blizzards, high winds, extreme cold, and low visibility. The snow usually only melts in July, and from then until mid-September, it is generally milder with little precipitation.

CONSERVATION

Crater Lake National Park preserves Crater Lake, scenic landscapes, volcanic features, and the unique ecological and cultural heritage of the site. Its designation was spearheaded by William Gladstone Steel (see right), who became the park's first concessionaire in 1907. It wasn't easy to convince Congress, as many Americans didn't yet have cars and some congresspeople feared it would drain the treasury. Even after the establishment of the park, Steel pushed for infrastructure development—he had the Army Corps of Engineers build the first rim road around the lake, commissioned the construction of the Crater Lake Lodge in 1915, and even wanted to build a bridge to Wizard Island.

BEFORE YOU GO

While Crater Lake National Park is open year-round, many activities available in the park are seasonal. Many of the roads and facilities close in winter, either with the first big snowstorm in October or on November 1st—whichever comes first. In winter, there is no possibility to refuel in the park, and Rim Drive is closed. Skiing, however, is allowed on marked slopes and trails. There are also ranger-guided snowshoe walks between November and April.

BEST TIMES TO VISIT

Huge amounts of snow fall in the park—an average of 42 feet (13 m) annually—so the season is short; most of the park is only accessible during the months of July, August, and September.

HIDDEN GEM

Two Saturdays a year, Rim Drive is closed to vehicle traffic but open to bicycles. For cyclists, this is an excellent opportunity to enjoy the park without having to share the road with vehicles.

INTERESTING FACTS ABOUT THE PARK

- The lake contains 4.6 trillion gallons of water (that's 21 trillion liters).
- People lived in what is now Crater Lake National Park as early as 8,000 to 12,000 years ago, possibly witnessing the collapse of Mount Mazama. The site became a sacred place for many tribes including the Klamath people.

William Gladstone Steel

"FATHER OF CRATER LAKE"

When he was eating lunch at school, 15-year-old William Steel (1854–1934) took a closer look at the newspaper he had wrapped his meal in. "Among [the articles]," he later remembered, "was a description of a sunken lake that had been discovered in Oregon. In all my life I never read an article that took the intense hold on me than that one did, and then and there [I] determined to go to Oregon and to visit that lake and to go down to the water." Two years later, in 1872, the Kansas farm boy came one step closer to his dream, when his parents moved to Portland, Oregon. To his surprise, it took Steel seven years to figure out where it was. Steel first set eyes on the sapphire-blue waters and towering cliffs in 1885, when he was 31. It would change his life forever. Despite having no connections, no wealthy friends, or any influence, the USPS delivery man almost single-handedly started a campaign to protect the lake and make it accessible. He befriended businessmen and politicians, guiding them around the area on nature hikes and campfire lectures. Lobbyists from the lumber, sheep, and cattle ranching industries bitterly complained he was trying to ruin them. Unimpressed, Steel kept pushing for 17 years. His lobbying caught the attention of Gifford Pinchot, director of the U.S. Forest Service. With Pinchot's endorsement, Steel got direct access to Theodore Roosevelt, rebuffing his critics and paving the way to protect Oregon's crown jewel. On May 22, 1902, Theodore Roosevelt signed the bill making Crater Lake a national park. Unlike John Muir, however, Steel receives hardly any recognition today. In a eulogy after his death, a friend wrote: "He left no perishable fortune, but he did leave an imperishable monument."

Redwood

Majestic redwoods, among the largest and oldest living things on earth, aren't the only attraction in this park on the California coast.

Besides its infamous redwoods, this park has a diverse range of habitats that include oak woodlands, prairielands, and some 40 miles (64 km) of California coastline with sandy beaches and clifftop trails.

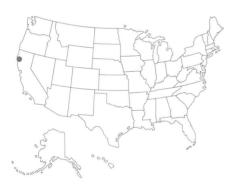

CALIFORNIA

Rising 379.7 feet (115.72 m) into the sky, "Hyperion" is considered the tallest living tree on earth. You're likely to feel dwarfed next to it: the giant coast redwood (*Sequoia sempervirens*) is five stories taller than the Statue of Liberty. It was discovered in 2006 by naturalists Chris Atkins and Michael Taylor in a remote valley of Redwood National Park. Preliminary measurements were done with professional laser equipment until Botanist Stephen C. Sillett used a more accurate measure: he climbed to the top and dropped a tape to the ground.

Although the tree's exact location remains a secret, it's not the only giant that keeps visitors flocking to Redwood National Park. The park is just one of a series of protected areas along the Pacific Coast in northern California, which safeguards nearly

Six of the world's tallest 10 trees can be found in Redwoods National Park. Besides Hyperion, there is Helios, Nugget, Icarus, Laurelin, and Orion. Most of them have names taken from ancient Greek mythology.

half of the world's coastal redwoods. The Pacific's humid climate, abundant rainfall, mild winters, and ideal soil conditions contribute to the extraordinary growth of these ancient trees, which live up to 2,000 years. Besides the redwood forests, the parks also include many miles of pristine coastline with tide pools and sandy beaches, as well as rivers and prairie—not to mention an imposing fern canyon.

For thousands of years, these lands have been inhabited by Native Americans of Asian descent. Among them are the Yurok people, who use the hard and weather-resistant redwood timber to build their shelters and long canoes, which they use to navigate the area's rivers. The Yurok consider redwoods their "eternal spirits." Nature is an essential part of their life. They weave elaborate baskets from roots, fern shoots, and grasses. For millennia, they have gathered plants and fruits and used fires to burn down the undergrowth in deciduous forests so that they could better gather acorns and other tree fruits.

Things got ugly after gold was discovered in the mid-1800s, first outside and later inside today's park boundaries, as miners kept pushing deeper and deeper into the forest. As settlers encroached on native lands, conflicts inevitably arose. The settlers, claiming that the Yurok Tribe was violating their property claims, decided to raid their villages. They murdered, pillaged, and raped the natives, whose numbers had already dwindled due to a smallpox epidemic. The last Native peoples were deported to a reservation in 1855. But the destruction of the forest had only begun.

Most prospectors found little to nothing to mine and soon turned to a new source of income: the red gold of the forest. The tremendous population growth on the West Coast had led to an enormous demand for lumber, and coastal redwoods were highly sought after since their wood is particularly weather-resistant and not susceptible to fungi. In 1902, an average redwood covered the material needs of 22 houses, making them highly attractive to loggers. After the Second World War, bulldozers carved roads into the hillsides, and heavy trucks hauled the logs to the sawmill. Entire groves and rainforests were clear-cut.

The call to protect the redwoods was raised as early as 1872 when Yellowstone National Park was established. It wasn't until after the turn of the century, when San Francisco had to be rebuilt following a major earthquake, that people began to see just how few redwoods remained. The "Save the Redwoods League" managed to secure the designation of three state parks between 1923 and 1929. Over the next fifty years, the association worked to transfer even more land from private ownership to national or state ownership, and in 1968, President Lyndon B. Johnson signed the charter for the new Redwood National Park. By then, 95 percent of the old-growth forest had already been irreversibly lost.

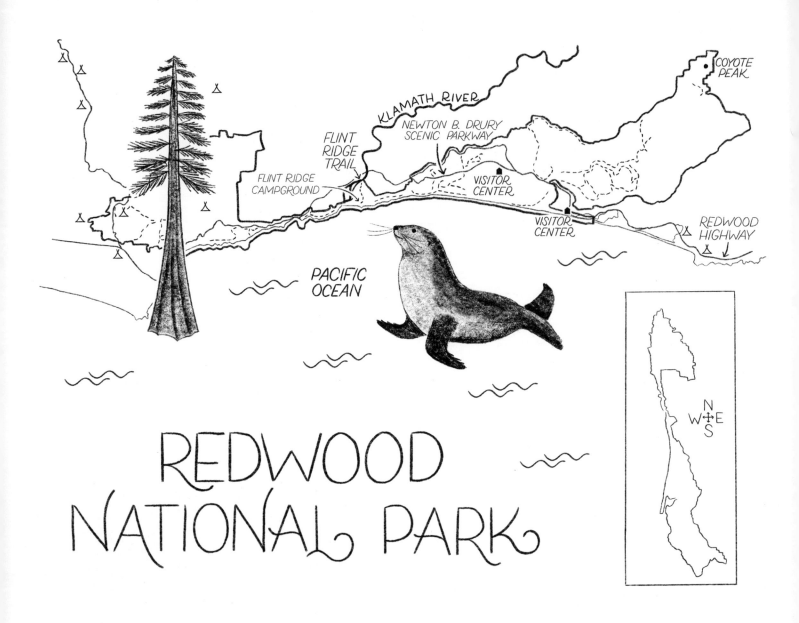

REDWOOD NATIONAL PARK

Technically, Redwood National and State Parks consist of the national park and three California state parks: Prairie Creek Redwoods, Del Norte Coast Redwoods, and Jedediah Smith Redwoods. The state parks were initially established in the 1920s, while the national park was designated on October 2, 1968. The area has been cooperatively managed by both National Parks and California State Parks since 1994.

SIZE
131,983 acres (206 sq. mi./534 km²)
Size rank among National Parks: 38 of 63

ELEVATION
Highest point: Coyote Peak (3,170 ft./966 m)
Lowest point: Pacific Ocean (sea level)

GEOLOGY
A few miles south of the park and a few miles offshore, three tectonic plates collide: The Pacific Plate shifts northward along the North American Plate, and from the northwest the Juan de Fuca Plate approaches the continent. In the frontal collision, this plate dives under the Pacific and North American plates, which are lifted and unfolded in the process. This ongoing process started about 65 million years ago, and formed the Coast Range, in which Redwood National Park is located.

FLORA AND FAUNA
Redwoods, believed to have been on earth for 240 million years, are the flagship of the temperate rain forest ecosystem. They have such dense canopies hardly any sunlight penetrates to the ground, and they suck most of the nutrients from the soil, so there is little understory in the forests. The lack of light makes the trees less attractive to mammals and birds. But the park also protects a landscape of vast plains, oak woodlands, wild rivers, and coastline, which are home to a variety of diverse species, including rare rhododendron species and the resident Pacific giant salamander—making Redwood National Park one of the most biodiverse ecosystems in temperate latitudes.

CLIMATE AND WEATHER

The coastal region is characterized by a maritime climate that brings moderate temperatures and little seasonal variation. The greatest amounts of precipitation are distributed over the mild winter months; the summers, from June to September are relatively cool and dry, but frequent fog in the forests ensures consistently high humidity. Spring and fall, with generally clear, cool days, are the most pleasant seasons on the coast.

CONSERVATION

Unlike most other national parks in the United States, Redwood National Park was not created to protect a geological formation, but to protect the last remnants of coastal redwood forest. Voices to save the redwood groves were raised as early as 1872 when Yellowstone was established. However, the idea was met with stalling resistance from business interests. That changed when the Save the Redwoods League was founded in 1918 by California civic dignitaries. The state of California contributed its own land, redeemed logging licenses, and established the State Parks between 1923 and 1929.

BEFORE YOU GO

While Redwood National Park isn't as frequented as Sequoia, it is one of the most popular destinations in California and often crowded. Remember that the park's greenery doesn't happen by chance: especially from October to April, there's a lot of rainfall, so be sure to bring rain gear and non-slippery shoes. There aren't any lodges in the park, and campsites should be reserved well in advance.

BEST TIMES TO VISIT

Temperatures in Redwood National Park remain relatively consistent throughout the year, but precipitation increases dramatically between October and March. The driest and sunniest months are June, July, and August.

HIDDEN GEM

The Flint Ridge campground is a "backcountry" camp, but is only a quarter mile hike from the parking lot, so it offers a high level of solitude without the intensity of a backpacking trip. The campground overlooks the Klamath River's exit into the ocean, and also provides access to the Flint Ridge Trail, which meanders through a quiet redwood forest.

INTERESTING FACTS ABOUT THE PARK

- Scenes from *E.T.* and *Star Wars Episode VI—Return of the Jedi Knights* were filmed in this area.
- In 1997, activist Julia Hill climbed a 1,500-year-old redwood and lived in a tiny tree house for 738 days to stop logging in the area.

Stephen C. Sillett

REDWOOD RESEARCHER

Ever wondered what it feels like to climb a redwood all the way to the top? Ask Stephen C. Sillett. When it comes to tall trees—and redwoods in particular—there are few people as knowledgeable as he is. Redwood canopies have long been a mystery. They are packed with epiphytes (plants that live on other plants), and some even resemble hanging gardens, with layers of soil that support even larger plants like the huckleberry bush. Sillett was the first scientist to explore this world high above the forest floor. The botanist, who says he wants to "give trees a voice," specializes in studying old-growth forests and the biodiversity found in their canopies. He pioneered novel methods for climbing, exploring, and studying the redwoods. His passion for science was first stirred by his grandmother, an avid bird enthusiast. In his undergraduate years as a biology student, he began climbing Douglas fir trees as part of his field research. During his Masters program, he studied the cloud forest canopy in Costa Rica. And when he moved to northwestern California to teach at Humboldt State, he became the first scientist to climb up the old-growth redwood forest canopy. To climb one of these giants, Sillett sets a climbing line with an arrow, then ascends using a modified arborist-style safety swing that involves ropes, leather harnesses, and pulleys. Once in the canopy, Sillett and his crew—he often climbs with his wife Marie Antoine, who is a fellow forest canopy researcher—lightly move over branches on climbing ropes, a style known as "skywalking." Like in rock climbing, Sillett moves between adjacent trees by deploying a Tyrolean traverse to reach outlying branches. The botanist used these scientific excursions to understand the limits of tree height.

Lassen Volcanic

The steaming, sulfurous fumaroles here serve as reminders of the power below the earth's crust.

In the spring of 1914, the 10,457-foot (3,187-meter) Lassen Peak began to awaken from its dormancy, ejecting steam and ash into the air and creating a small crater on the summit. The volcano continued in this fashion for the next year, slowly coming back to life with additional steam explosions carving out more and more of the crater until it measured 1,000 feet (304 m) across. Yet this was all just a warm-up: on May 22, 1915, there was an explosive eruption, blasting rock fragments and pumice high into the air above, creating an enormous column of volcanic ash that could be seen as far as hundreds of miles away in Eureka, California.

A pyroclastic flow—a fast-moving mixture of solidified lava pieces, volcanic ash, and hot gas so hot it burns anything in its path—worked its way down the mountain and changed an entire landscape in the process. An avalanche of melted snow and rock charged down the east side of the mountain, and a layer of pumice and volcanic ash spread out 25 miles (39 km) to the northeast. Almost 300 miles (480 km) away in Elko, Nevada, fine ash rained from the sky.

The eruption of Lassen Peak, the southernmost active volcano in the Cascade Range, was the impetus for creating the national park. Called Kohm Yah-mah-nee, or "snow mountain," by the Maidu people, the mountain and its surrounding area have been an important hub and sacred place for the Atsugwei, Yana, Yahi, and Maidu people, who for thousands of years gathered and hunted here during the warmer months.

Today, steaming thermaroles and bubbling pools are a reminder of the power that lies below the earth's crust. The Bumpass Hell Trail takes visitors into the heart of this volcanic landscape, with a boardwalk perched above the colorful soils and turquoise pools. Here visitors get an up-close look at the largest hydrothermal area in the park. The smell of sulfur from the mineral-rich waters is strong, and nothing here is safe to touch or swim in. In fact, the trail is named after a pioneer who stepped through the crust of a mud pot into boiling water, leading to the

CALIFORNIA

amputation of his leg. Big Boiler, the largest fumarole in the park and one of the hottest in the world, reaches temperatures above 300 °F (148 °C).

Gentler landscapes can be found here too, and during the summer, vibrant wildflowers like snow plants and silverleaf lupine blanket the mountain hillside. The park is dotted with 200 different lakes and ponds and several creeks, perfect for cold alpine dips. At night, far away from light pollution, the Milky Way shines bright. The park even hosts an annual Dark Sky Festival for avid stargazers.

Just like the volcanic explosion changed the landscape in the earlier 1900s, in 2021 the Dixie Fire worked its way across the park, in what was the largest wildfire in its history. Although the park was only moderately affected, a dozen park structures were either damaged or destroyed and several hiking trails were forced to close.

PARK AT A GLANCE

On May 6, 1907, Cinder Cone and Lassen Peak were both established as national monuments under President Theodore Roosevelt. A year after Mount Lassen's main eruption, the two monuments were combined, and Lassen Volcanic National Park was established on August 9, 1916, the fifteenth national park in the system.

SIZE
106,598 acres (166 sq. mi./429 km²)
Size rank among National Parks: 40 of 63

ELEVATION
Highest point: Lassen Peak (10,457 ft./3,187 m)
Lowest point: Hot Springs Creek (5,275 ft./1,607 m)

GEOLOGY
A landscape shaped and defined by volcanic activity, every rock in the park is volcanic. All four types of volcanoes in the world can be found here—shield, composite, cinder cone, and plug dome—and Lassen Peak is one of the largest plug dome volcanoes in the world.

FLORA AND FAUNA
The park encompasses three distinct ecological zones and a variety of habitats. A total of 57 mammal species like high elevation dwelling pikas and the rare Sierra Nevada red fox, 216 species of birds, and 6 amphibians live within the park's borders. The terrain is rich in smaller organisms too, like insects and spiders, and is home to 350 species of invertebrates, including the abundant orange and brown California tortoiseshell butterfly.

CONSERVATION
The park preserves a unique volcanic geology, which offers both recreational and scientific opportunities. Hydrothermal and volcanic features in the park might offer insight into what life on Mars once would have looked like, and NASA runs an astrobiology student intern program in partnership with the park.

BEFORE YOU GO
With all the geothermal activity, it is essential to stay on marked trails and boardwalks, as veering off course can lead to severe injury. There are seven campgrounds in the park.

BEST TIMES TO VISIT
Summer, when the snow has melted and all roads and facilities are open. Camping is popular, so reservations are recommended. Winter and spring offer activities like skiing and snowshoeing, but vehicle access is limited.

Yosemite

An icon of America's majestic beauty, Yosemite attracts visitors and mountaineers with its quiet grandeur, massive cliffs, and mighty waterfalls.

Yosemite icon and hiker's challenge, Half Dome rises above the park wilderness. Keen climbers embark in a 14–16-mile (23–26 km) round-trip to ascend the 8,836-feet (2,693-m) monolith and are rewarded with magnificent views across the park.

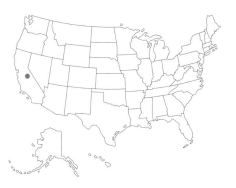

CALIFORNIA

Yosemite is so iconic, it's easy to think you've already been before you ever step foot in the park. Located in the heart of the Sierra Nevada, the park boasts picture-book (or, let's say, Mac OS wallpaper) landscapes with vistas so famous they turned the park into one of the most heavily visited in the country. Established in 1890, the park is brimming with landmarks, each more legendary than the last. And countless enthusiasts, ranging from early conservationist John Muir to legendary photographer Ansel Adams, have come to document their beauty over the years, capturing its flower-filled valleys, beautiful grasslands, thundering waterfalls, ancient sequoia groves, and glacially polished granite domes.

Reports of the valley's rare beauty sparked interest as early as 1855 when the first tourists arrived. But humans had lived in the area for nearly 4,000 years. With the arrival of trappers and prospectors (the so-called Forty-Niners), the native Miwok Tribe, which used to spend the hot summer months in the cool Yosemite Valley, was pushed out. Environmentalists raised concerns that the commercial exploitation of the land would degrade the environment and advocated for its protection. The geologist,

LEFT: The park's highest waterfall, Yosemite Falls, plunges more than 2,425 feet (739 m); ABOVE: Grizzly Giant, one of several giant sequoia trees in the park's Mariposa Grove. Some trees here, including Grizzly, are around 3,000 years old. OPPOSITE: Half Dome.

botanist, and travel writer John Muir, influenced by the works of Alexander von Humboldt, was the first to publicize the region and generate scientific interest through his writings.

The first parts of the national park were placed under protection as early as 1864. The Yosemite Grant, signed by President Abraham Lincoln, was the first time in history that land was set aside for the purpose of public use and preservation. It is viewed by many as the birth of the National Park System because it predates the establishment of Yellowstone National Park, which was officially the first national park. Following the understanding of nature conservation at the time, though, it was mainly the visual appeal of the iconic landscape that was preserved. Protecting biodiversity was only a side effect. Yosemite eventually became a national park in 1890 and was extended in 1906—after John Muir took Theodore Roosevelt out camping here.

While the park covers 1,200 square miles (3,100 km²), most visitors don't see more than a tiny fraction of that land—they stick to Yosemite Valley. Although the centerpiece only makes up one percent of the park's total area, most visitors flock to this spot, where you can observe how the glaciers pushed their way through the valley during the Ice Age. Towering over the densely forested valley is the mighty El Capitan (7,569 feet/ 2,307 meters), the largest granite monolith on earth, and Half Dome (8,836 feet/2,693 meters), the park's signature landmark. Their rounded mountain tops appear as mighty, chunky "domes," sculpted by glaciation. In the snow-free months, legions of climbers can be seen scaling their near-vertical walls to dizzying heights.

From Yosemite Valley, the Tioga Road leads through the park's highlands, along mountain lakes and flowering meadows, to the steppe landscape of the High Sierra. Further inside the park, an extensive network of trails crisscrosses coniferous forests rich in wildlife, mountain ridges, and creeks that turn to rushing rivers, depending on the season. The park's many vertical slopes, ledges, and hillside valleys are also home to many waterfalls, such as Yosemite Falls, one of the world's largest, while the south and west entrances to the park host groves of venerable giant sequoias (*Sequoiadendron giganteum*). The trees are remnants of a long-gone epoch, before Yosemite had become the poster child of American beauty.

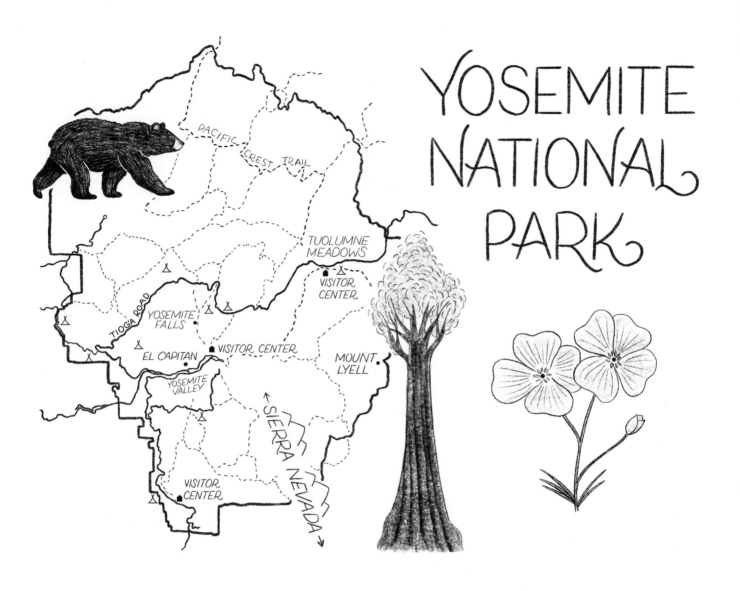

YOSEMITE NATIONAL PARK

When President Abraham Lincoln signed a bill in 1864 that created the Yosemite Grant, it was the first time parkland had been set aside specifically for preservation and public use by the U.S. federal government. Yosemite became a national park on October 1, 1890, and in 1984, it was designated a UNESCO World Heritage Site.

SIZE
759,620 acres (1,187 sq. mi./3,074 km²)
Size rank among National Parks: 16 of 63

ELEVATION
Highest point: Mount Lyell (13,114 ft./3,997 m)
Lowest point: Merced River (2,105 ft./642 m)

GEOLOGY
Yosemite is famed for its towering granite cliffs and domes, which were ground and gouged by the Ice Ages. Created about 10 million years ago when the Sierra Nevada was pushed upward by the Sierra fault, the land eventually tilted, forming the less steeply sloping western slopes and the steep eastern slopes. The uplift formed deep, narrow canyons from the streams and riverbeds. The movement of the ice masses

(some as thick as 4,000 feet or 1,200 meters during the early glacial period) hollowed out the valley, creating a U-shape.

FLORA AND FAUNA
The park represents one of the largest and least fragmented habitats in the Sierra Nevada, home to an abundance of plants and animals. Because of its elevation range, it contains five distinct ecosystems. Of the approximately 7,000 plant species native to California, about 50 percent are found in the Sierra Nevada, with more than 20 percent located within the park area. One of the most notable trees is the giant sequoia. Animal life is plentiful: About 90 different species of mammals are native to the park, and more than 250 species of birds have been reported here. Large mammals include mule deer, black-tailed deer, bighorn sheep, black bears, coyotes, and foxes.

CLIMATE AND WEATHER

The park has a dry-summer subtropical climate. Summer days are warm (up to 90 °F, or 32 °C, in the valley), but nights are cool, especially at higher elevations. Afternoon thunderstorms can be expected in late summer. Precipitation is highest between November and March. From November to May, most of Yosemite National Park is covered with snow.

CONSERVATION

The park protects the impressive granite cliffs, waterfalls and clear streams, groves of giant sequoias, and biodiversity. In 1864, President Abraham Lincoln signed a law granting legal dominion over Yosemite Valley, along with a redwood grove, to the state of California. The act set the precedent for the creation of Yellowstone as the nation's first national park in 1872. The law creating Yosemite as a national park was passed in 1890. Today, large numbers of visitors cause significant problems, especially in the limited Yosemite Valley, and there has been a cap on visitor numbers since 2014.

BEFORE YOU GO

The valley is the park's central hub, where masses of visitors literally throng. Here you'll find most of the lodges and campgrounds, several stores, numerous cafes, snack bars, and restaurants. Traffic in the valley is often jammed and parking lots can already be overcrowded in the morning, so it is worthwhile using the (not less crowded) shuttle buses that run from morning to evening. There are two visitor centers: one in Yosemite Valley (open year-round) and another near the Tioga Pass entrance (open seasonally).

BEST TIMES TO VISIT

The park is very crowded during the months of July and August. April and May in Yosemite are stunning, with waterfalls running full bore and the higher peaks still covered in snow. Winters in the Yosemite Valley are relatively mild, and this usually packed part of the park is empty of visitors.

HIDDEN GEM

A trip to Tuolumne Meadows will offer some reprieve from the valley crowds, while a backpacking journey deeper into the park will offer even more solitude.

INTERESTING FACTS ABOUT THE PARK

- The Miwok people who lived in the Yosemite Valley called the valley Ahwahnee, meaning gaping mouth-like place. They called themselves Ahwahnechee.
- For a few minutes at sunset during mid-to-late February, light reflection makes Horsetail Fall appear to be flowing with lava. The phenomenon is called "firefall".

Shelton Johnson

PARK RANGER

Shelton Johnson stepped out of the bus in Yellowstone National Park, and it felt like an awakening. In 1984, while on break from college, Johnson applied to be a dishwasher at Yellowstone's Old Faithful Inn. It was only a summer job, but it would bring him to the wilderness, a space he had longed for since he was a child. Johnson's first awakening happened in a national park far away—in the Bavarian Alps in Germany. As he stood surrounded by snow-covered peaks, gripping his parents' hands as clouds floated below his feet, young Johnson realized that the mountains were his home. Several decades later, Johnson is now one of the National Park Service's most popular rangers, and a face for Yosemite, where he has worked for more than 25 years. It's a career he never expected, given his background in classical music, poetry, and literature—not to mention the fact that he's not white. Many African Americans, he says, don't feel that national parks are relevant to them after a long history of slavery and industrialization. Just 6 percent of Yosemite's visitors are black. That's why Johnson relays the story of the "Buffalo Soldiers"—Black cavalrymen who protected the park at the turn of the century, long before the National Park Service was established and barred them from returning. Reintroducing African Americans to the wonders of America's national parks became a fulcrum of his work. Johnson invited Oprah Winfrey to camp in Yosemite (she came), and he spoke with Barack Obama about diversity in the parks. By keeping a narrative alive that has been widely forgotten, he promotes a new kinship with the earth. When asked why he didn't seek a promotion, the Detroit native shrugged and said, "I didn't join the Park Service for money. I get paid in gasps."

Pinnacles

A story of rebirth for the California Condor among the jutting remnants of an ancient volcano.

Covering just over 26,000 acres (105 km²), Pinnacles is the smallest National Park in California. Despite its humble acreage, the park is teeming with diversity in the cracks and crags of its rocky landscape. The park's namesake pinnacles were created 23 million years ago by a series of dramatic volcanic eruptions in present-day Lancaster, California. The powerful San Andreas fault triggered a great geologic migration, moving this immense volcanic landmass 195 miles northwest to a new home situated between Monterey and Fresno. Here the constant forces of wind, rain, and ice have eroded the volcanic stone over time, leaving behind giant walls, pillared precipices, and crimson monoliths colored with lava flow bands and pockets of green volcanic glass. This tremendous symphony of natural events set the stage for the majestic Pinnacles National Park we have today.

With over 30 miles of trails, Pinnacles offers plenty of options for hiking and climbing, whether you're looking to scale an exposed rock face or stroll through the park's cheery woodlands. The popular High Peaks hike is a steep cliffside traverse up carved steps of granite, leading to stunning vistas of the canyons below. For less seasoned hikers, the easier Bench Trail follows meandering creeks through the canyon bottom, with

views of the stately pinnacles floating above. To explore the park's dark, subterranean passageways, follow the Bear Gulch trails into the talus caves. Here visitors are dwarfed in "rooms" created during the last Ice Age when massive boulders fell from cliffs above. As the fallen boulders piled up, they created caves in the negative space between the rocks. The two most famous talus caves of the park, Bear Gulch Cave and Balconies Cave, are home to 14 species of bats.

The caves are just one feature of the park's unique terrain, which hosts an abundance of flora and fauna. Over 160 bird species nest in the high bluffs, and over 400 species of bees keep the lush wildflower pastures blooming in the springtime. Chaparral, chamise, and manzanita grace the sloping hillsides while blue oaks and gray pines dot the grassy woodland.

CALIFORNIA

PARK AT A GLANCE

In January 1908, President Theodore Roosevelt designated 2,080 acres (8.4 km²) of land as the Pinnacles National Monument. When President Barack Obama elevated Pinnacles' status to a national park on January 10, 2013, the newly minted park had grown to 26,606 acres (108 km²).

SIZE
26,606 acres (42 sq. mi./109 km²)
Size rank among National Parks: 57 of 63

ELEVATION
Highest point: North Chalone Peak (3,304 ft./1,007 m)
Lowest point: 824 ft./251 m

GEOLOGY
The park's pinnacles and spires are eroded remnants of half an ancient lava field. The San Andreas fault split the Neenach Volcano 23 million years ago, pushing one half to the central coast and the other to Southern California. The giant cracks and crevices created by these shifting tectonic plates have shaped the park's idyllic canyon streams and talus caves.

FLORA AND FAUNA
The park's diverse terrain and elevations are home to an array of plant communities, including woodland willows, fire-resistant chaparral, creekside sycamores, and high mosses. Among the greenery and streams also resides a host of insects, endangered native frogs, mountain lions, bats, condors, and endemic salamanders.

CONSERVATION
The park showcases the striking rock formations of ancient volcanic and tectonic activity from millions of years ago, preserving the unique habitats of many endemic and endangered species. A unique sanctuary for plants and animals alike, the protected wilderness is especially notable for its California Condor Recovery Program and extensive bat monitoring.

BEFORE YOU GO
Most of the 30 miles (48 km) of trails in the park are unshaded and steep, so plenty of drinking water and sun protection are a must for hikers. Bear Gulch Cave is usually closed from mid-May to mid-July to protect the bats during breeding season.

BEST TIMES TO VISIT
Spring and fall temperatures are the most pleasant, though winters are mild with moderate precipitation. Because of extreme temperatures, summer is the park's off-season.

The endangered California red-legged frog thrives in the verdant wetlands of the canyon floors. And up high, lichen and moss provide the necessary nutrients to the unique soil culture of the rock and scree, as well as nesting material to the menagerie of birds living in both the woodlands and cliffs.

Among these hosts of birds—horned owls, wrens, warblers, vultures, and woodpeckers—is the endangered California condor. Before Pinnacles became one of three condor release sites in 2003, condor populations had plummeted to a mere 22 wild specimens in the 1980s. Today, the program co-manages over 90 birds. For the Amah Mutsun, the Indigenous people of the land, the condors escort spirits of the deceased into the next world; their return is a promise of rebirth and redemption among the towering rocks they call home.

Kings Canyon

Ancient trees, alpine lakes, and granite peaks blend together in what John Muir called "a rival to Yosemite."

In 1924, a man named R. J. Senior stood at the base of the second-largest tree in the world, an ancient sequoia called the General Grant Tree. This *Sequoiadendron giganteum* was part of a sequoia grove that, 34 years earlier, had been the impetus for creating the General Grant National Park, the third national park to be signed into law. As R.J. Senior stood looking up at the enormous trunk, a little girl next to him exclaimed, "What a wonderful Christmas tree it would be!"

Inspired by this, Senior, who served as the President of the Chamber of Commerce in the nearby town of Sanger, California, worked with fellow Chamber of Commerce Secretary Charles E. Lee to put a plan in motion: to commemorate the tree for Christmas. Held at noon on December 25, 1925, the inaugural celebration spurred President Calvin Coolidge to designate the tree as the Nation's Christmas Tree.

An annual tradition was born, and the Sanger Chamber of Commerce hosts a seasonal "Trek to the Tree" every December. Named after Ulysses S. Grant, the victorious Civil War general and former president, the tree does more than serve a seasonal, celebratory purpose. In 1956, Dwight D. Eisenhower declared the tree a national shrine to service members killed in war, and the tree became the country's only living national shrine.

At 268 feet (89 m) tall it might be the most famous organism in Kings Canyon National Park today. On the way into General Grant Grove, there's proof of the logging threat that spurred the park's original creation: the Big Stump. Known as the Mark Twain tree, its base was 16 feet (4.8 m) in diameter when it was felled in 1891. Shipped to New York and London, the dead giant was used simply to prove to the rest of the world how enormous these trees were. All that's left today is a stump graying with age, and a wooden ladder attached so visitors can stand on top.

The majestic, ancient sequoias are only part of the park's richness. There are deep glacial canyons, like the park's namesake, Kings River Canyon. At over 1.5 miles (2.4 km) deep, it's one of the deepest canyons in the country. Clear alpine lakes reflect the granitic peaks of the Sierra Nevada in a wilderness area that's reminiscent of the iconic Yosemite National Park just to

CALIFORNIA

PARK AT A GLANCE

To protect the sequoias in General Grant Grove, General Grant National Park was established in 1890. Almost exactly 50 years later, on March 14, 1940, President Franklin D. Roosevelt created the new national park Kings Canyon, expanding the park in the process. It is jointly managed with the adjacent Sequoia National Park.

SIZE
461,901 acres (722 sq. mi./1,869 km²)
Size rank among National Parks: 21 of 63

ELEVATION
Highest point: North Palisade (14,242 ft./4,340 m)
Lowest point: North Fork Kaweah River (3,480 ft./1,060 m)

GEOLOGY
At about 10 million years old, the Sierra Nevada is a young mountain range in geological terms. The range consists of mostly granitic rocks like granite, diorite, and monzonite, which are fairly resistant to erosion. While dark to light gray from afar, they are flecked with tiny flecks of minerals like quartz, feldspar, and mica.

FLORA AND FAUNA
With a vast difference in elevation, there's a wide range of wildlife and plants. The lowlands, covered in oak woodlands and dense chaparral shrubs, provide shelter to gray foxes, bobcats, and black bears. Higher up, trees shift to pine, incense-cedar, red fir, and lodgepole pine, with animals like mountain lions, mule deer, and white-throated swifts. Alpine areas are home to higher-elevation animals like marmots, pika, and the endangered Sierra Nevada bighorn sheep.

CONSERVATION
Kings Canyon National Park protects ancient sequoias, including the 2,558 acres (10.5 km²) of Redwood Mountain Grove, the largest sequoia grove on earth. In 2021, lightning sparked the KNP Complex Fire, a wildfire that ripped through the area, destroying up to one-fifth of the giant trees.

BEFORE YOU GO
The General Grant Grove sits in a section of the park that's right at the edge of Sequoia National Park on Highway 180. The road is open year-round, but the rest of the road into the heart of Kings Canyon is closed in winter. There are several campgrounds open year-round in Grant Grove Village, and the John Muir Lodge is open seasonally.

BEST TIMES TO VISIT
September and October when temperatures are still warm, the seasonal road is still open, and the summer crowds are dwindling.

the north. In fact, King's Canyon offers some of the same majesty as its world-famous neighbor but with much smaller crowds.

In an 1891 article entitled "A Rival of the Yosemite," John Muir, a naturalist and environmental advocate instrumental in the protection of the Sierras, wrote, "In the vast Sierra wilderness far to the southward of the famous Yosemite Valley, there is a yet grander valley of the same kind. It is situated on the south fork of King's River, above the most extensive groves and forests of the giant sequoia, and beneath the shadows of the highest mountains in the range, where the canyons are deepest and the snow-laden peaks are crowded most closely together."

Muir would never know the crowds that Yosemite draws today, and if he did, he would perhaps be drawn to the lesser-visited King's Canyon, with its ancient trees, rugged Sierra wilderness, and ample space for solitude.

Death Valley

The place is brutal, yes. But don't let that put you off: in Death Valley, there's much more to experience than just hot air.

OPPOSITE: The iconic outlook, Zabriskie Point, at sunset. Its jagged Manly Beacon is the highest point, at 823 feet (251 m) and offers stunning views across the Badwater Basin salt flats (pictured on pages 258–259).

CALIFORNIA

Furnace Creek—could there be a more apt name for a place where the temperatures recently reached a scorching 129.9 °F (54.4 °C)? Not to mention the surrounding park's name: Death Valley. The largest national park outside Alaska is a long and narrow stretch of uninhabited terrain. It's filled with mountain-high sand dunes, lush forests, blinding salt flats, snow-capped peaks, mysterious "sliding" rocks, and technicolor canyons.

The valley's formation began about 3 million years ago when forces within the earth broke the surface into blocks, creating an alternating mountain and valley pattern. Lakes formed in the basin during the Ice Age. When those lakes dried up, they left behind vast, blueish-white salt flats that persist to this day.

OPPOSITE: Mosaic Canyon twists and turns between rock walls that have been polished smooth over millions of years by debris-laden water. LEFT: Rarely, in spring, and only in the right conditions, Death Valley breaks out in a superbloom—a vibrant display of wildflowers. BELOW: Salt crystals at Badwater Basin.

Badwater Basin, one such remnant of a prehistoric lake, lies 282 feet (86 m) below sea level. It's not only to the deepest point in the Western Hemisphere but also the hottest and the driest. Nowhere else can the relentless heat of the desert be felt as clearly as here, where even a breeze is anything but refreshing. Make sure to bend down and taste the salty surface, but you'll also want look up: you might spot the whitesea-level marker etched onto the cliffs high above.

People of the Timbisha Shoshone Tribe, who lived in this area for 9,000 years, call the region Timbisha, or "Valley of the Red Ochre." The rather eerie name "Death Valley" was coined only in 1849, when a group of gold prospectors set out from Salt Lake City to trek along the old Spanish Trail to California. Unfortunately, the prospectors got lost when they attempted a shortcut that strayed from the historical trade route. As a result, over 100 wagons were trapped in the valley for several weeks. To survive, they had to burn their wagons and eat their cattle. When they finally found a way out (with only one fatality), they left the 140-mile-long (224-kilometer long) valley with the words "Goodbye, Death Valley." Today, ghost towns and ranches offer a glimpse into the harsh reality of life back in the day.

Death Valley owes its popularty to its views and vistas more than most National Parks. The reason is apparent: any activity amid the barren and heat-drenched desert requires extreme physical exertion. Luckily, Death Valley has more miles of road than any other national park. Around 1,000 miles (more than 1,600 km) of paved and dirt roads connect the park's iridescent sand dunes (Mesquite Flat Sand Dunes), crusty salt flats, craggy peaks (Golden Canyon), and magnificent overlooks (Zabriskie Point). And be sure not to miss Artists Drive, a winding, narrow side road that brings visitors past rocks shimmering in rainbow colors, thanks to the oxidation of metals such as iron, mica, and manganese.

Despite the adverse environmental conditions, more than 1,000 different plant species thrive in the park, 23 of which are found nowhere else on earth. In spring, rare rainstorms fill the valley with a sea of golden, purple, pink, and white wildflowers (so-called "super blooms") and create lush sporadic oases that harbor fish and other wildlife. Moreover, Death Valley is a refuge for 400 animal species, including bighorn sheep, desert kit foxes, and jackrabbits, all of which have adapted to the harsh climate. Perhaps the most incredible example of this is the kangaroo rat, which has evolved to survive without ever drinking water over millennia to survive without ever drinking water.

DEATH VALLEY NATIONAL PARK

EUREKA DUNES

VISITOR CENTER

MESQUITE FLAT SAND DUNES

AMARGOSA DESERT

FURNACE CREEK

ZABRISKIE POINT

GOLDEN CANYON

ARTIST'S DRIVE

LAS VEGAS →

VISITOR CENTER

TELESCOPE PEAK

BADWATER BASIN

OWLSHEAD MOUNTAINS

Death Valley was first designated a national monument in 1933 and expanded several times in the following decades, including the incorporation of the small enclave Devils Hole, located further east in Nevada. On October 31, 1994, Death Valley was redesignated as a national park and in 2013 was also recognized as an International Dark Sky Park for its pristine views of starry skies.

SIZE
3,422,024 acres (5,347 sq. mi./13,848 km²)
Size rank among National Parks: 5 of 63

ELEVATION
Highest point: Telescope Peak (11,043 ft./3,366 m)
Lowest point: Badwater Basin (282 ft./86 m below sea level)

GEOLOGY
Death Valley has not always been a valley. In fact, the region was originally part of a warm, shallow sea that fell into a rain shadow due to the uplift of the Sierra Nevada and slowly receded. What remained was a huge salt crust. Later, volcanoes appeared, blanketing the region with numerous layers of ash and cinders (resulting in the vivid colors of the hills of Artists Palette and Death Valley's famous borate mineral deposits). Even today, the basin continues to subside, and the mountains rise ever higher.

FLORA AND FAUNA
Despite its name, the fauna in Death Valley is surprisingly diverse, with more than 400 species. It is possible to encounter solitary roaming coyotes, which feed on almost all small animals and plant parts. Other mammals include kit foxes, bobcats, cougars, and mule deer. The park is also a staging and resting place for many migratory birds: swallows, ibis, and mallards can be witnessed, especially in spring. Even fish live in the park, including the endangered, endemic Devils Hole pupfish. Of the over 1,000 plant species, many have adapted to survive. Some have roots as long as 50 ft. (15 m). During high amounts of rain, the desert floor transforms into a sea of blooms.

CLIMATE AND WEATHER

Although Death Valley is only a few hundred miles from the Pacific Ocean, it is one of the driest places on earth because the humid Pacific winds rain down on five ridges on their way from the ocean before they can pass over the park. While summers are extremely hot and dry, winters are somewhat milder with occasional storms.

CONSERVATION

President Herbert Hoover set aside almost two million acres (8,000 km²) and proclaimed a national monument in and around Death Valley in 1933. In the ensuing years, the Civilian Conservation Corps (CCC) developed infrastructure in Death Valley National Monument by building barracks, campgrounds, 500 miles (800 km) of roads, and installing water and telephone lines. Mining continued in the park on a large scale and was only limited in 1980. The last mine closed in 2005.

BEFORE YOU GO

Rule No. 1 in Death Valley: pack more water than you think you need (at least one gallon or four liters per day per person), fuel up before entering the park, and check your tires, otherwise this beautiful landscape can soon turn deadly—in this vast expanse, there might not always be someone to help out. If you plan on hiking, inform someone in advance about your plans. Watch out for dangerous animals including rattlesnakes, scorpions, and black widow spiders.

BEST TIMES TO VISIT

Death Valley is open all year round, but it is most pleasant to visit in winter, fall, or spring, as summer temperatures are extremely hot. Generally, the best times of day to visit the park are early morning and evening when the sun is low. October to April is the best time for hiking.

HIDDEN GEM

In the remote, northwest corner of the park are the Eureka Dunes, a field of sand dunes containing some of the tallest dunes in North America.

INTERESTING FACTS ABOUT THE PARK

- The mineral borax was discovered in the Death Valley area during the late 19th century.
- The Pacific Coast Borax Company built many of the park roads on which legendary teams of 20 mules pulled wagon loads of up to 40 tons.
- Charles Manson and his cult were tracked down and arrested at the park's Barker Ranch in 1969.
- Parts of Death Valley were used by director George Lucas as locations for two films in the original *Star Wars* trilogy.

Mary DeDecker

BOTANIST AND CONSERVATIONIST

Mary DeDecker (1909–2000) discovered her passion for plants quite late in life. She was 58 when she met Mark Kerr, a Californian naturalist who made an exhibit of native plants used by the Paiute. He taught DeDecker about several local plants and encouraged her to become a self-trained botanist. Born in Oklahoma to a farmer, DeDecker had spent much of her life in Los Angeles, where she studied fine art, before relocating to Independence, just west of Death Valley, with her husband and two daughters. The family went on numerous camping and hiking trips, exploring this unique region. In the decades that followed, Mary DeDecker devoted her life to studying the flora that thrives in Death Valley, becoming a preeminent plant expert in the northern Mojave Desert and Eastern Sierra Nevada areas. As advised by Kerr, she sent unknown specimens to the Rancho Santa Ana Botanic Garden in Claremont and to the California Academy of Sciences in San Francisco. On her field trips, she collected more than 6,000 specimens for identification. Among them were six novel species—three of which are named in her honor: *Lupinus dedeckerae, Trifolium dedeckerae,* and *Dedeckera eurekensis.* The latter was probably the most exceptional: after all, discovering an entirely new genus of flowering plant in the contiguous United States after 1950 was (and is) quite rare. Constantly vigilant and armed with extensive knowledge, she helped stand up to bureaucrats and politicians to pass the California Desert Protection Act in 1994, which led to the designation of Death Valley National Park. DeDecker's writings (and the extensive herbarium she left behind when she passed away at the age of 91) continue to serve botanists today. The park's Dedeckera Canyon was named in her honor.

Joshua Tree

This almost biblical expanse of barren desert,
affectionately known by locals as "J-Tree,"
is a promised land for climbers.

TOP: Around 250 species of birds inhabit the park, many of them migrants. They include woodpeckers, swifts, and hummingbirds (pictured).
OPPOSITE: Looking out across the unique Mojave Desert landscape with its otherworldly Joshua trees.

CALIFORNIA

Year after year, almost two million people come to California to visit Joshua Tree National Park. At first glance, this desert consisting of over 2,000 square miles (5,189 km²) of wilderness may not seem like the most life-friendly place on earth. But a closer look reveals a fascinating variety of plants and animals who have made their home in this land shaped by the elements. Located just east of Palm Springs, the park links two deserts and two distinct ecosystems whose characteristics are defined primarily by altitude. The lower, eastern part of the park is dominated by the Colorado Desert, with scrubland, cactus gardens, and the occasional fan palm. Situated above 3,000 feet (900 m), the Mojave Desert encompasses the western part of the park, where it is somewhat cooler and humid.

An essential part of the ecosystem in the Mojave Desert is the Joshua tree. With its whimsical and overgrown branches, the park's namesake tree dominates the sparse landscape. The tall-growing plant is not technically a tree at all, but a large, tree-like succulent that can grow to be 900 years old. The Joshua tree,

TOP: The Mojave Desert attracts hikers and trailwalkers by day and stargazers by night. Designated a Dark Sky Park, the park's cloudless nights reward campers with spectacular star-filled skies.
RIGHT: The Joshua tree is just one of 750 resident plant species.

or *Yucca brevifolia,* was first discovered in 1844 by explorer John C. Fremont, who considered it the "the most repulsive tree in the vegetable Kingdom." Its name was allegedly coined by Mormon pioneers who crossed the Mojave Desert in 1850; the plant's unique shape, with its thin, upward-pointing branches, reminded them of prophet Joshua's upstretched arms, leading the Israelites to the promised land. However, no historical sources can prove this legend.

What's unique to Joshua Tree National Park is just how intimately visitors can experience the barren desert landscape here. Whereas you mostly drive through regions such as Death Valley due to the heat, the widely scattered granite rocks, especially in the northern part of the park, offer protection from the blazing sun. These unusual rock formations, some of the most interesting geological formations in all of California, attract climbers from the world over. The park boasts more than 8,000 official climbing routes, whose difficulty ranges from easy bouldering to sheer vertical crevasses. There are, however, strict regulations as to whether a climb is allowed within the wilderness or not.

Of course, you don't have to be a climber to enjoy the park. Although the tourist infrastructure is relatively underdeveloped,

basically all known viewpoints—each one more stunning than the next—can be easily reached by car. The main roads through the park are paved and in excellent condition. There are also several dirt roads, but four-wheel drive and high clearance are often required. One of the more famous roads is the "Basin Road," which runs from the park's southern end to its center, leading to hiking and mountain biking trails. If you are lucky enough to be in Joshua Tree during the week, you should try to spend a few minutes alone with yourself and the vast, untouched nature.

Unfortunately, though, the park's otherworldly splendor is increasingly endangered. Climate change is a constant threat for the Joshua trees. With rising emissions and temperatures, 80 to 90 percent of their suitable habitat could be lost by 2099. The park's proximity to large urban areas means that smog often blows into the park. Due to the chemistry of how smog reacts with heat, visibility is reduced from 160 miles to 100 miles (257 km to 161 km) on average and to 55 miles (89 km) on days with high pollution levels. The nitrogen-rich compounds in the soil facilitate the growth of non-native plants such as red bromegrass, which allows fire to quickly spread across the desert, making the park increasingly prone to wildfires.

JOSHUA TREE NATIONAL PARK

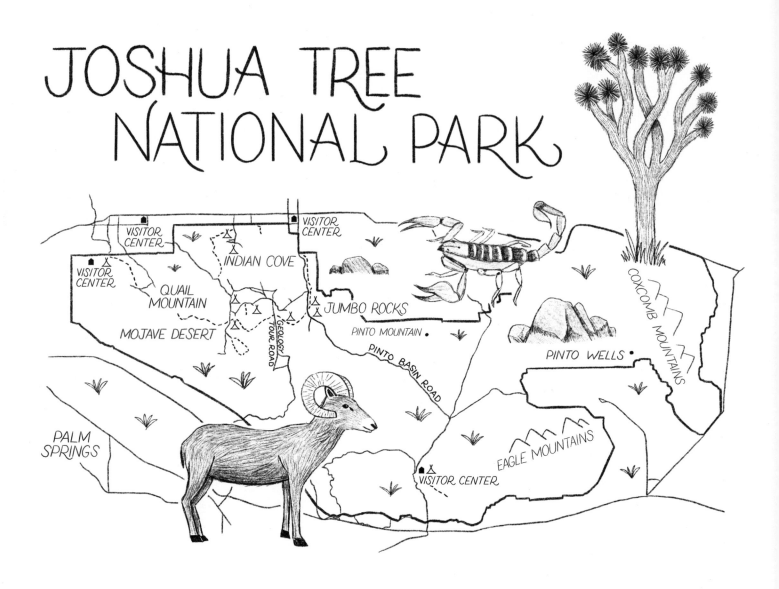

J oshua Tree in southern California was declared a national monument on August 10, 1936, and designated by UNESCO as a biosphere reserve in 1984. It was granted national park status on October 31, 1994, by the Desert Protection Act, which also increased the park's size by 234,000 acres. In 2019, the park was extended again. The Sand to Snow National Monument borders the park to the west.

SIZE
790,636 acres (1,235 sq. mi./3,200 km²)
Size rank among National Parks: 15 of 63

ELEVATION
Highest point: Quail Mountain (5,816 ft./1,773 m)
Lowest point: Pinto Wells (934 ft./285 m)

GEOLOGY
The rock formations in the park were formed about 100 million years ago when magma cooled and solidified beneath the earth's surface and was exposed by erosion after millions of years. Strong winds, unpredictable downpours, and climatic extremes have left their mark over millions of years, and the horizontal and vertical cracks loved by rock climbers were formed by numerous earthquakes. The most spectacular rock formations can be seen at Jumbo Rocks, Wonderland of Rocks, and Indian Cove.

FLORA AND FAUNA
The park is home to mountain lions, rattlesnakes, roadrunners, desert tortoises, scorpions, and tarantulas. Most are active during the evening and early morning. Coyotes can be seen patrolling near park roads, jackrabbits and shy kangaroo rats emerge from their burrows to forage for food in the evenings, and herds of desert bighorn sheep crisscross the landscape. Especially in spring and summer, a surprising variety of birds transit through the park via a migration route known as the Pacific Flyway. In addition to the wildlife, there are over 800 different plant species, including the memorable jumping cholla cactus, whose easily-dislodged spines seem to "jump" into the clothing and skin of passing hikers.

CLIMATE AND WEATHER

The climate is generally warm and exceedingly dry. Days are usually clear with less than 25 percent humidity. Temperatures are most pleasant in spring and fall, with averages between 50 and 85°F (10 to 29°C). Daytime highs in summer often reach 122°F (50°C). Winter brings cooler days with temperatures around 60°F (15°C) and freezing nights. It snows occasionally at higher altitudes.

CONSERVATION

Joshua Tree National Park owes its existence to Minerva Hamilton Hoyt, a Pasadena citizen who launched a campaign to protect the region in the 1920s (see right). After many years of bureaucratic struggle, the area was finally designated a national monument on August 10, 1936, thanks to President Franklin D. Roosevelt. In 1984, it became a Biosphere Reserve and finally a national park with the passage of the California Desert Protection Act in 1994.

BEFORE YOU GO

There are visitor centers at all three entrances, but no lodging, restaurants, or stores in the park. Trails will drag on more than you might think. In the desert, it gets very hot during the day, and temperatures can drop to freezing during the night. Bring more water than you think you need, at least one gallon (4 liters) per person, per day. Backcountry camping permits are free, and can be obtained by self-registration at one of the 13 backcountry boards located throughout the park.

BEST TIMES TO VISIT

Joshua Tree is best visited in October, November, March, and April. In spring, carpets of flowers cover the desert. Summer months can be extremely hot, while midwinter tends to be very cold and windy.

HIDDEN GEM

The Geology Tour Road offers a fun off-pavement adventure and provides access to several trails and rock-climbing areas. The road is a bit bumpy and sandy but can be navigated by most vehicles with medium-high clearance.

INTERESTING FACTS ABOUT THE PARK

- The Joshua tree looks like a tree, but it is in fact a member of the Agave family.
- It almost never rains in the park: on average, less than an inch of precipitation falls each year.
- Five oases of desert fan palms are scattered throughout the park, indicating those few areas where water occurs naturally and wildlife abounds.

Minerva Hamilton Hoyt

CONSERVATIONIST

In the early 1900s, cactus gardens were all the rage in L.A. Deserts were wild and unruly places, and people would go on joyrides in their newly purchased cars to dig up rare plants in the desert. One of the first people to take issue with this was Minerva Hamilton Hoyt. Born on a Mississippi plantation in 1866, she grew up in a privileged family and became a socialite who later married a wealthy surgeon in New York. Her passion for gardening brought her to the deserts of the American Southwest, which she turned to for solace following the deaths of her infant son and husband. She admired the austere beauty and extraordinary inventiveness of desert plants that managed to thrive in the harsh climate, and she was horrified by the widespread destruction she witnessed. Minerva Hoyt began a relentless fight to protect these places in the 1920s. As Conservation Chair of the California chapter of the Garden Club, she arranged exhibitions of desert plants shown in Boston, New York, and London. Later, Hoyt founded the International Deserts Conservation League to establish parks to preserve desert landscapes. She hired well-known biologists and desert ecologists to prepare reports on the virtues of the desert regions to get the support of top politicians. While President Hoover followed her proposal to establish Death Valley as a national monument, he wasn't inclined to do the same for her proposed Desert Plants National Park. Instead, she persuaded Hoover's successor, Franklin D. Roosevelt, whose New Deal administration established national parks and monuments as a jobs-creation initiative. Hoyt found an ally in Roosevelt's Secretary of the Interior, Harold Ickes, and on August 10, 1936, the president signed a proclamation establishing Joshua Tree National Monument.

Sequoia

These giant trees grew in peace for thousands of years until loggers chopped them down by the thousands. Now protected, they are the gems of Sequoia National Park.

LEFT: The park's Tokopah Falls Trail leads through the granite cliffs of Tokopah Canyon and culminates at the 1,200 feet (366 m) Tokopah Falls where, in spring and summer, snow melt sends water flowing down the rocks.

CALIFORNIA

Thought to be 2,300 to 2,700 years old, General Sherman is not the oldest tree in the world—that distinction belongs to the Great Basin Bristlecone Pine. It's not even as tall as many coastal sequoias such as the Hyperion, found in Redwood National Park. Nor does it have the greatest girth—that title is claimed by an old cypress near Oaxaca, Mexico. And yet, the Giant sequoia *(Sequoiadendron giganteum)* holds a record: in terms of total wood mass, it is the largest known living tree on earth. Each year, General Sherman adds enough wood to form a completely new 60-foot- (18-meter-) tall tree.

Unsurprisingly, this massive tree is the central attraction of Sequoia National Park. Located in the heart of the Sierra Nevada, the park protects the last significant stand of giant sequoia, a giant tree species which thrives only on the western slopes of the mountain range in Central California. The first specimens were discovered in the area during an expedition in 1833, but people dismissed the crew's stories as "tall tales." Then in 1852, a newspaper article mentioned the giant trees, sparking a craze. It wasn't long until the first tree was felled—at first to measure if it was really as big as people said. Soon, the

Along with its neighbour Kings Canyon National Park, Sequoia National Park protects 40 sequoia groves. The biggest trees among them weigh around 58 billion times more than the tiny seeds from which they grew. Flying squirrels, tree frogs, salamanders, and bats are among their wildlife inhabitants.

"I'm in the woods, and they are in me—I wish I were wilder, so bless Sequoia I will be."

—JOHN MUIR, CONSERVATIONIST

trunks were shipped to places as far as Europe, as "evidence," but people on the East Coast initially thought it was a hoax since the tree segments had to be cut up for railroad transport.

The first settlers here encountered members of the Shoshone Tribe, who had lived in the park area since about the 9th century. The exchange was friendly, as trappers and mountain men often made friends with the Shoshone and adopted their ways of life. But, as elsewhere, the gold rush changed everything. Prospectors, adventurers, and settlers who flooded into the region in the mid-1800s pushed the tribes out of their valleys. Most of the Native population met an agonizing end around 1862 through scarlet fever, measles, and smallpox. The remaining survivors moved eastward across the Sierra Nevada.

As loggers began to clear-cut the forest, they encountered some unexpected problems: some trees gathered so much momentum as they fell that they smashed to bits on the forest floor. Furthermore, the wood was of such low quality that it could only be used for firewood or fence posts. Despite all this, the industry thrived. One of the few opponents of the development

was the gold prospector and cattle rancher Hale Tharp. He arrived in what is now the national park in 1858 and lived in Tharp's Log, the hollow trunk of a fallen sequoia not far from General Sherman. In 1875, conservationist John Muir visited Tharp while the lumber industry around them had its heyday. Whole tracts of forest fell victim to saws and axes. The two initiated the creation of a national park to protect the remaining sequoias. By 1890, their idea had become a reality: Sequoia National Park was the first of its kind to save not a geological feature but a specific living organism.

Though the trees are no longer at the mercy of a lumberjack's axe, today's sequoias face another existential threat—forest fires. Although their thick, spongy, and water-rich bark protects them from common wildfires often caused by lightning, they have had a hard time withstanding the increasingly intense wildfires and persistent droughts that have plagued their habitat in recent years. The devastating wildfires that ravaged California forests in 2021 destroyed thousands of Sequoias. Others have been so severely damaged that they will likely not survive.

SEQUOIA NATIONAL PARK

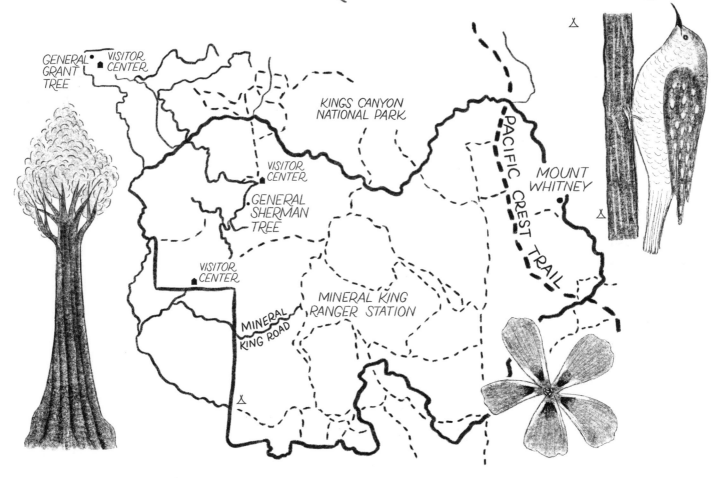

Sequoia National Park was established on September 25, 1890, as America's second national park by President Benjamin Harrison. Not far away, General Grant National Park was established one week later, which was then merged into Kings Canyon National Park, adjoining Sequoia to the north and northwest. Since there is no real border between the parks, both were placed under joint administration in 1943.

SIZE
404,063 acres (631 sq. mi./1,635 km²)
Size rank among National Parks: 22 of 63

ELEVATION
Highest point: Mount Whitney (14,505 ft./4,421 m)
Lowest point: Kaweah River (1,360 ft./415 m)

GEOLOGY
The Sierra Nevada mountain range forms the eastern boundary of both Sequoia and Kings Canyon National Parks and is the result of plate tectonic processes that went on for about 180 million years. When the Pacific Plate was pushed into the earth's interior beneath the North American Plate, deep volcanic activity formed the rocks that outcrop the two national parks today. Over time, the rock layers slowly lifted. Rivers carved deep, narrow valleys into the slowly uplifting rock strata, which glacial till widened into characteristic trough valleys over the past 2 million years.

FLORA AND FAUNA
Giant sequoias (*Sequoiadendron giganteum*) are obviously the showstoppers in this park. They often stand together in loose groups, so-called groves, and thrive exclusively on the western slopes of the Sierra Nevada. Animal life includes black bears, mule deer, gray foxes, squirrels, and other small mammals. There are also 17 species of bats. A few mountain lions and bighorn sheep live in secluded higher elevations, while several species of snakes, salamanders, and frogs thrive in the lower park regions.

CLIMATE AND WEATHER

The climate in Sequoia National Park ranges from pre-alpine to alpine. In other words: the weather here is a bit more bearable in summer than in neighboring Yosemite. Summers are warm, with cool nights, especially at higher elevations, while winters are severe, especially at higher elevations. Moderate precipitation falls evenly throughout the year.

CONSERVATION

Sequoia National Park was the first national park formed to protect a living organism: *Sequoiadendron giganteum*. The park's designation was largely thanks to cattle rancher and prospector Hale Tharp and early conservationist John Muir, who recognized the immense importance of protecting the giant sequoia trees from logging. By 1890, Sequoia National Park had become a reality and soon tripled in size. The park protects the last significant stand of giant sequoia in the world.

BEFORE YOU GO

There's only one road through the park, but it's best discovered on foot anyway, and there are many beautiful viewpoints and hiking trails. The John Muir Trail is probably the most famous, running north-south from Yosemite through Kings Canyon to Sequoia. If you camp between October and May, prepare for temperatures (sometimes significantly) below freezing.

BEST TIMES TO VISIT

Located at lower elevations, the Giant Forest and Grant Grove can be visited in the colder seasons to avoid crowds. (In spring, you will be rewarded with beautifully blooming dogwood trees.) However, high-elevation activities such as backpacking are best pursued from June to September.

HIDDEN GEM

Mineral King is a remote and rugged valley at 7,500 ft. (2,286 m) that can be accessed by the paved—but bumpy—Mineral King road. Along the road are two public campgrounds and a private lodge. From the trailhead, several hiking and backpacking routes can be accessed.

INTERESTING FACTS ABOUT THE PARK

- The Lindsey Creek tree, a coast redwood, had almost twice the volume of General Sherman. It was reportedly felled by a storm in 1905.
- Mount Whitney, the highest mountain in the contiguous United States, is located in Sequoia National Park.
- In the 1870s, the area was one of California's many gold rush centers. Mineral King, the gold-mining town in the southern part of the park, dates from that time.

Charles Young

FIRST AFRICAN AMERICAN SUPERINTENDENT

When Charles Young (1864–1922) was appointed superintendent of Sequoia National Park in May 1903, it was barely accessible. The park lacked Congressional funding, although it had been established over a decade earlier. The U.S. Army, which managed the park, was tasked with protecting the area from loggers, poachers, and ranchers who brought their grazing livestock. That changed with Charles Young. Born to enslaved parents at the end of the Civil War, he faced tremendous discrimination throughout his life. He was the first Black student to graduate from his high school in Ripley, Ohio, and was the third Black cadet to graduate from the U.S. Military Academy at West Point. At the time, Black soldiers often joined regiments called "Buffalo Soldiers," who were among the nation's first park rangers. In 1903, Young was asked to take his troops to Sequoia and the adjacent General Grant (now Kings Canyon) National Parks to become acting superintendent for the summer. During his brief tenure, Young achieved more than all of his predecessors. In one season, he supervised a company of Buffalo Soldiers and a team of local civilian road workers to construct the first road leading to Mount Whitney. They also completed an old wagon road to Giant Forest and extended the road to Moro Rock. He also successfully negotiated with private landowners to sell land, paving the way for the park's expansion. Soon after, Young went on to have a distinguished military career, where he served as the nation's first Black military attaché and became the first Black colonel. By making the park more accessible, Young effectively introduced tourism to the park. His determination to overcome adversity remains an inspiration to many.

Great Basin

This relatively young park is home to mysterious caves, the last remaining glacier in Nevada, and the oldest living organism on earth.

Just 300 miles (483 km) north of Las Vegas in White Pine County lies Great Basin National Park, a serene land where giant mountain peaks converge with star-filled skies, massive underground caverns play host to a kingdom of rock formations, and ancient trees keep watch over a solitary glacier. This diverse terrain welcomes visitors to witness the beauty of an unlikely wilderness sprouting in the Great Basin Desert.

The park's diverse and rugged landscape was shaped over the last 10,000 years by the currents of melting glaciers. Today, only the endangered Wheeler Glacier remains. To see this tenacious landmark, take the Bristlecone & Glacier Trail. Your hike begins in a grove of age-old bristlecone trees and finishes with breathtaking views of Wheeler Peak from the foot of the proud and defiant Wheeler Glacier.

NEVADA

Visiting the park's famous Lehman Caves transports visitors into a strange land filled with otherworldly limestone rock formations and a host of creatures found nowhere else on earth. The vast underground cave system contains a collection of ethereal and bizarre stalactites, stalagmites, speleothems, and flowstone. The various sections have names befitting their odd shapes: the Gothic Palace, the Lodge Room, the Inscription Room, and the Grand Palace. The caves were first discovered around 1000 to 1300 BCE by the Fremont people and records of their presence can be found in their artwork on display in the Upper Pictograph Cave. In 1885, a rancher named Absalom Lehman rediscovered the mysterious caves, helping them grow in popularity by turning them into a tourist attraction. Today guided tours are available year-round and offer stunning views of this geological masterpiece.

Hiking Great Basin's many trails is a great way for visitors to see the rich assortment of rare plants and animals in the park. The Bristlecone Pine Trail is a rocky and wooded 4.6-mile (7.4-kilometer) slope dotted with alpine wildflowers and millennia-old bristlecone trees. These are the oldest trees on the planet, with some specimens living for over 5,000 years. On backcountry

hikes along the Baker Loop Trail, the world's smallest rabbit, the pygmy, can be seen frolicking. And for easier hikes with low to no elevation gain, the Sky Island Forest Trail and the Alpine Lakes Loop Trail will take you along the park's beautiful sagebrush grasslands, home to many of the park's 238 known species of native birds.

And for eager stargazers, the park's low levels of light pollution provide some of the darkest skies in the United States, setting the stage for a window into the heavens. On cloudless nights, five planets can be seen with the naked eye and the Andromeda and Milky Way Galaxies are on full display in all of their splendor. The annual Great Basin Astronomy Festival held every September offers guided stargazing talks, astrophotography workshops, and the chance to gaze through powerful telescopes at the beautiful star-filled sky.

PARK AT A GLANCE

The mysterious and captivating beauty of the park's caves inspired President Warren G. Harding to create the Lehman Caves National monument in 1922. The surrounding area, including the Wheeler Glacier, was made a national park on October 27, 1986.

SIZE
77,180 acres (120.6 sq. mi./312.4 km²)
Size rank among National Parks: 43 of 63

ELEVATION
Highest point: Wheeler Peak (13,063 ft./3,981 m)
Lowest point: Mountain View Nature Trail (6,825 ft./2,080 m)

GEOLOGY
Over thousands of years, pronounced volcanic activity, severe earthquakes, and melting glaciers created the conditions for the Great Basin's unique mountain desert landscape. Within the next 20 years, extreme temperatures regularly reaching 100°F (38°C) in summer will melt the Wheeler Glacier, marking the end of the glaciation process that shaped the park's dramatic topography.

FLORA AND FAUNA
The park's varied elevations play host to a number of plants and animals. At higher elevations, spruce, pine, white fir, quaking aspen, and ancient bristlecone grow. In the valleys below, you'll find native sagebrush, saltbush, pinyon, and Utah juniper. These are just a few of the park's more than 800 species of plants. There are also 61 species of mammals, 18 species of reptiles, 238 bird species, and eight species of fish who call the park home.

CONSERVATION
The park's conservators are dedicated to protecting and preserving land that is home to the oldest trees in the world, the darkest skies in the United States, and a thriving cave ecosystem that is home to various plants, animals, and insects that live nowhere else in the world.

BEFORE YOU GO
For a quick trip through the park, the appropriately named Scenic Drive offers a beautiful 12-mile (19-kilometer) snapshot of the park, ascending 4,000 feet (6,400 km) through the diverse ecosystem.

BEST TIMES TO VISIT
Spring and summer are ideal for hikers. Winter attracts cross-country skiers from far and wide. For stargazers, the three-day Astronomy Festival happens every September.

Kobuk Valley

Explore a land of contrasts and extremes, where desolate sand dunes rise out of a lush river valley and where caribou make one of the longest land migrations on earth.

Entirely above the Arctic Circle in northwest Alaska, Kobuk Valley encompasses an immense landscape of mountains, boreal forest, sand dunes, and arctic tundra. There are no roads and no trails, and as John McPhee once wrote in *Coming into the Country*, the Kobuk Valley "was, in all likelihood, the most isolated wilderness I would ever see." While it may feel isolated, there is a long-standing human history here. People have lived, hunted, and fished on this land for at least 12,500 years. Those practices remain in place today and provide a way of life for the Inupiaq people.

Winding through the park is the Kobuk River. Its name an Inupiaq word for "big river," the 380-mile- (611-kilometer-) long river begins in the Brooks Range and empties into Kotzebue Sound. Today the river is one of the park's most popular spots for recreation and is especially beloved by boaters who come from far and wide to float down its slow and calm waters amid a backdrop of stunning wilderness. It takes about a week to float

ALASKA

through the park from the village of Ambler to Kiana. The area has long been an important corridor for wildlife and humans, largely because, unlike other parts of Alaska, Kobuk Valley was free of ice in the last Ice Age. Big game roamed the area—including the woolly mammoth—and this richness in wildlife has long provided a source of sustenance for local populations.

Paatitaaq, or Onion Portage, sits on the northern banks of the Kobuk River and is named for the wild onions that grow there. Told by local elders that they had been hunting caribou here for as long as they remembered, archeologist J. Louis Giddings led extensive archeological excavations from 1964 to 1967 to understand its history. The site revealed evidence that humans had been coming here for at least 10,000 years to hunt caribou as they crossed the river on their biannual migration.

PARK AT A GLANCE

Kobuk Valley became a national park on December 2, 1980, under the Alaska National Interest Lands Conservation Act, which included seven other national parks and increased the National Park System by 43 million acres.

SIZE
1,750,716 acres (2,735 sq. mi./7,083 km²)
Size rank among National Parks: 9 of 63

ELEVATION
Highest point: Mount Angayukaqsraq (4,760 ft./1,450 m)
Lowest point: Kobuk River (40 ft./12 m)

GEOLOGY
During the last Ice Age when continental glaciers covered most of North America, Kobuk Valley was left ice-free. The Kobuk River that flows through the area is one of the largest rivers in Alaska, and the park also has another important waterway, the Salmon River, designated as a National Wild and Scenic River.

FLORA AND FAUNA
Along with the caribou, the Arctic tern also migrate to the Kobuk Valley, all the way from Antarctica. The park is a protected habitat for other arctic animals like grizzly bears, wolves, porcupines, foxes, and moose. Many species of lichen thrive here and Kobuk locoweed is found only in the park. Ducks, cranes, loons, geese, and swans come in the warmer months, and the Arctic wolf and the ptarmigan are active throughout the harsh winter.

CONSERVATION
Kobuk Valley protects the central valley of the Kobuk River and the undeveloped arctic wilderness that surrounds it. The bluffs along the river hold permafrost ice wedges and ice age fossils, and the area is part of the migration corridor of the Western Arctic caribou herd, whose numbers have been decreasing in recent years.

BEFORE YOU GO
There are no fees or permits required for independent travelers, but the only way to access the park is by plane or boat in the summer, and by snowmobile or dogsled in the winter. The park's visitor center and headquarters are located 80 miles (128 km) southwest of the park in Kotzebue.

BEST TIMES TO VISIT
August and early September when the mosquitoes have died down and the river is still floatable. With its northerly latitude, it can snow at any point in the year.

Today Paatitaaq is considered to be one of the most important archeological sites in the Arctic.

Covering over 2,000 miles (3,200 km) in spring and in summer, the migration of the Western Arctic caribou herd is one of the longest land migrations on earth. They cross not only the river but also the Great Kobuk Sand Dunes, a rather unique feature for this part of the world. Rising up from the southern banks of the river, this vast stretch of sand was created during the last Ice Age, when glaciers high in the nearby mountains ground rock into sand, which was then blown by strong winds into the ice-free Kobuk Valley where it still sits today. The largest sand dunes in the Arctic are a popular place for backcountry camping—and relatively easy to reach, given that air taxis are able to land on them.

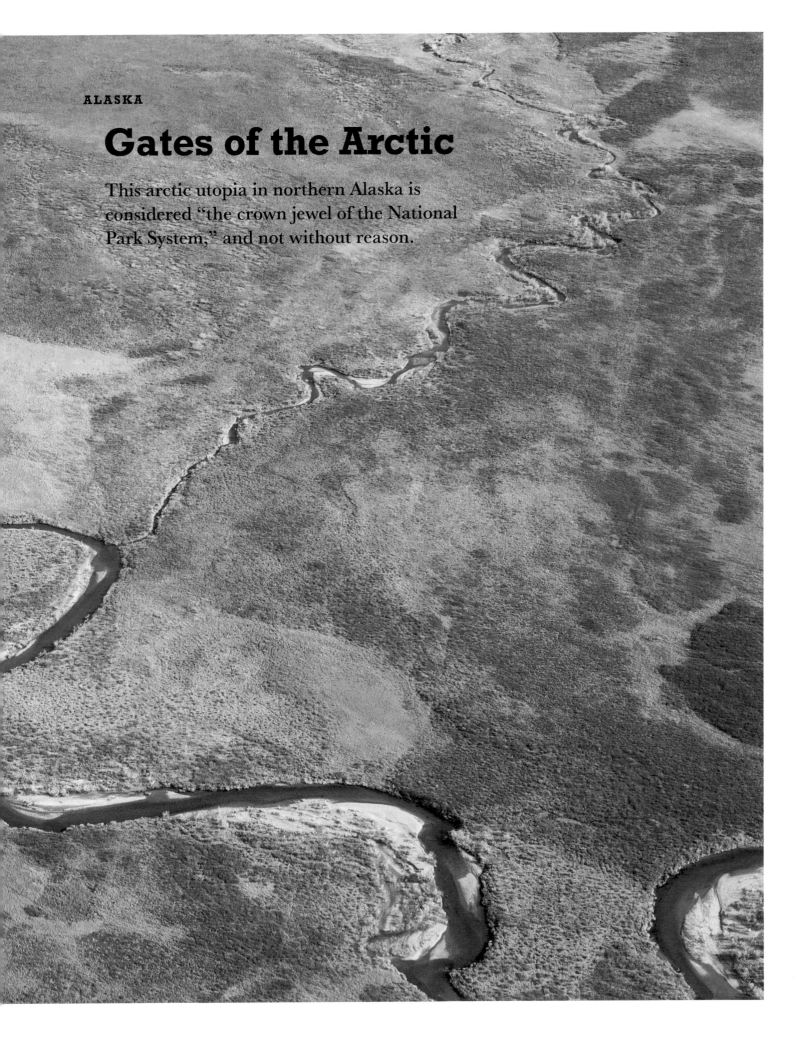

Gates of the Arctic

This arctic utopia in northern Alaska is considered "the crown jewel of the National Park System," and not without reason.

OPPOSITE: A major attraction at Gates of the Arctic are the six designated wild rivers that have carved their way through the arctic tundra terrain. Aerial views show how the waterways twist and turn as they navigate the paths (see also, pages 292–3 and 298–9).

ALASKA

Gates of the Arctic is not only the most remote national park on the continent, but also the least visited. It welcomes just about 10,000 people annually—that's 99.83 percent less than the Grand Canyon. If you go the extra mile, however, pure backcountry and one of the most jaw-dropping wilderness areas in the world await. Without roads, trails, or even visitor services, the vast and secluded terrain in the Far North is as challenging as it is rewarding for any wilderness-loving traveler. Visitors will discover a pristine yet harsh landscape, where the boreal taiga of central Alaska transitions to a treeless tundra that stretches all the way to the Arctic Ocean. It's one of the last places on earth where you can experience pure solitude.

Needless to say, a trip to this park needs thorough preparation. No matter if you want to spend your days fishing at alpine lakes, wandering through the boreal forest, or setting up camp next to a wild river—all visitors must be genuinely self-sufficient in this demanding environment. (If you're not ready for an expedition, consider booking a scenic flight or a remote overnight campout.) In most cases, transportation to the park will need

A major feature of the Endicott Mountains that lie at the park's heart are the Arrigetch Peaks, a run of impressively jagged granite pinnacles that rise 3,000–4,000 feet (900–1,200 m) above the tundra landscape. Half a million caribou migrate through the Brooks Range annually, moving north in summer and south in winter.

The park sees just about 10,000 people per year—that's less than the Grand Canyon on a single summer day.

to be arranged with an air taxi operator. Once you've arrived, you can then set out on foot or raft, following one of the park's many rivers (six of them designated wild rivers), which have been byways for wildlife and humans for centuries. Very few visitors come in winter, even though conditions theoretically allow for dog mushing or cross-country skiing.

The park's roots date back to 1929, when Bob Marshall, a prominent wilderness advocate and forester, arrived to "escape the strangling clutch of a mechanistic civilization." Between 1929 and 1939, he frequently traveled the North Fork Koyukuk River looking for "blank spaces on the map." He used forest research as a pretext for mountain climbing, mapping uncharted waterways, and mingling with the native Nunamiut people, who have lived here for thousands of years, sustaining themselves by fishing the waters and hunting caribou and sheep. Today, roughly 1,500 people live in 10 small villages within the park.

The designation as a national park, however, did not come until 1980, after a last-minute intervention by Jimmy Carter. In the years following the Second World War, local community members feared that irreversible changes were being made to the

land north of the Arctic Circle. This stirred a largely homegrown Alaskan conservation movement, which fought mining and petroleum behemoths who were pushing for a much smaller park, split down the middle by a pipeline corridor. Luckily, the park that was signed into law was in no way small—and free of pipelines. But the fight is not over: the "Ambler Road Project," headed by the mining company Ambler Metals, promotes building a road through the park, leading to a proposed copper mine.

Scientists and conservationists are concerned that the road would pollute previously untouched places and impact the Western Arctic caribou herd. Half a million of these animals migrate annually through the park. To observe them is a spectacle in itself. The Gates of the Arctic National Park and Preserve not only provides a refuge for Alaska's traditional Native and pioneer lifestyles, but it also preserves over eight million contiguous acres of exuberant wildlife: muskox, moose, wolves, and grizzly bears. In addition, it houses rare species like black bears, great horned owls, bald eagles, golden eagles, and snowshoe hares. Trout thrive in its streams, rivers, and lakes, as do native fish species such as Arctic grayling and char.

GATES OF THE ARCTIC NATIONAL PARK

ALASKA'S NORTH SLOPE

BROOKS RANGE

ANAKTUVUK PASS

VISITOR CENTER

ENDICOTT MOUNTAINS

MOUNT IGIKPAK

WALKER LAKE

VISITOR CENTER

KOBUK VALLEY

VISITOR CENTER

DALTON HIGHWAY

Gates of the Arctic was initially designated as a national monument in 1978. Upon passage of the Alaska National Interest Lands Conservation Act, it was redesignated as a national park and preserve on December 2, 1980. A large part of the park is protected wilderness, and with adjoining areas forms the largest contiguous wilderness in the United States.

SIZE
8,472,506 acres (13,238 sq. mi./34,287 km²)
Size rank among National Parks: 2 of 63

ELEVATION
Highest point: Mount Igikpak (8,276 ft./2,523 m)
Lowest point: Kobuk River (280 ft./85 m)

GEOLOGY
The park lies just north of the Arctic Circle in the Brooks Range, America's northernmost mountain range, covering glaciated valleys, barren, rugged mountains, and expanses of the arctic tundra. The Endicott Mountains, a part of the central Brooks Range, make up the park's heart. Like much of Alaska, they were formed when large sections of the earth's crust were transported here through plate tectonics.

FLORA AND FAUNA
The southern slopes of the mountains are blanketed with boreal forests of white spruce, aspen, and birch—similar to the Alaskan interior. The taiga in the north is a polar desert, barren and treeless with sparse black spruce forests. Wildlife is varied but widely dispersed; in the wilderness, animals accustomed to the cold climate have found refuge. Significant parts of the habitat of the Western Arctic Caribou Herd is located in the park, and in spring, migratory birds join the few resident bird species.

CLIMATE AND WEATHER
South of Brooks Range below timberline, summers are pleasant yet short and often cloudy, and winters are long and severe. North of it, summers are cooler and winters slightly warmer due to prevailing cold air inversions. The

weather is extremely unpredictable, and snowfall is possible at any time of the year.

CONSERVATION
The purpose of the park and preserve is to protect and maintain the cultural resources, as well as the wild and undeveloped character of Alaska's central Brooks Range and its habitats. (Within the park, subsistence hunting by local residents is permitted.) Proposals for a national park in the Brooks Range first emerged in the 1960s, but it took two more decades for the park to be established. Although the park is a shining example for environmental preservation worldwide, its ecological integrity is often at stake. Plans for an Arctic Transportation Corridor across the Brooks Range, as well as proposals for roads and pipelines are constantly being brought up by oil and mining companies.

BEFORE YOU GO
The Dalton Highway runs along the eastern edge of the park, but there is no direct road access. A visit has to be arranged via air taxi (intrepid hikers can also walk, but it takes a very long time). The park doesn't offer any accommodation; however, camping is permitted throughout the park except in Native Corporation lands, where visitors might need permission. When renting watercraft from a local vendor, making arrangements prior to arrival is advisable. There is no cell phone reception in the park.

BEST TIMES TO VISIT
The brief Alaskan summer from June to September is the best time to visit, when you can take advantage of warmer temperatures and basically 24-hours of sunlight. Even though the summer is more "mild," be prepared for cold temperatures, biting insects, and high rivers.

HIDDEN GEM
Gates of the Arctic is the most remote and least-visited park in the United States, so you are not going to encounter many crowds in this park. Choose a mode of adventuring that best suits your skills—such as paddling, hiking, climbing, or flying—and you're likely to see more wildlife than humans.

INTERESTING FACTS ABOUT THE PARK
- In 1968, President L. B. Johnson was asked to designate Gates of the Arctic as a national monument. He declined.
- The park's name was coined by wilderness activist Bob Marshall when he encountered a pair of mountains (Frigid Crags and Boreal Mountain) on two sides of a river.
- Some of the lichens in the park take as long as 150 years to reach maturity.

Rachel Riley

ELDER AND CULTURE ADVOCATE

For NPS staff at Gates of the Arctic, Rachel Sisoulik Riley (1941–2015) was a vital link between Western culture and the Nunamiut way of life. The elder was born along the Killik River, some 70 miles (112 km) west of Anaktuvuk Pass. Riley was only eight years old when her parents decided to join other families from Sulupaat, a camp near the mouth of April Creek in the Killik River valley, moving eastward from the river. As many people in their village had died from the flu, they wanted to join another group at Tulugaq Lake in the Anaktuvuk Valley. In summer of 1949, the group set out on an dog-packing trek. The strenuous endeavor took more than two weeks and led over uncharted terrain. "The Long Walk," as it came to be known, marked a final destination for many of the previously nomadic Nunamiut ("people of the land"), a pivotal moment in their history. But some things stayed the same, like caribou hunting: "Caribou meat has been our meat since I was born," Riley remembered. "I was raised with it. The skin was my clothes. The meat was my diet, and the broth was my drink. Without caribou meat, what would I eat?" A skilled sewer, she used to make caribou-skin masks by drying the leather over a wooden frame, a method that originated in the 1950s and is still used today. She took on the most prominent role in the country's only predominantly-Nunamiut village as she grew older: preserving Inupiaq language and culture. Riley taught at the Anaktuvuk Pass school and helped create educational books in Inupiaq. She took her students on camping trips to pass on her knowledge of traditional practices like hunting, skinning, butchering, and sewing. Throughout her life, the elder graciously shared her subsistence knowledge, serving on the Gates of the Arctic National Park Subsistence Resource Commission the last 16 years of her life.

Denali

Denali's twin peaks are the star of this pristine stretch of Alaskan wilderness. But they don't reveal themselves to just anyone.

LEFT: A challenge for mountain climbers, around half of those who try to climb Mount Denai do not make it to the top. This is largely due to low oxygen levels on the upper slopes, perilous crevasses, and below-zero temperatures.

ALASKA

In 1867, Russia sold Alaska to the United States for $2.7 million, much to the chagrin of American taxpayers who saw their tax dollars squandered on a worthless, ice-covered wasteland. Or so they thought. Today, Alaska's unspoiled beauty attracts millions of visitors, and for many, it's a visit to Denali National Park that makes it the trip of a lifetime. Here they discover a land where animals roam freely and where nature's forces are on powerful display. Others come to get up close to the giant that gave the park its name. Majestically towering over the scenery, Denali's snowcapped peaks jut into the clean, crystal-clear sky—if you're lucky. Most of the time, they get lost in the clouds.

At 20,310 feet (6,190 m) above sea level, Denali's South Summit is North America's contribution to the so-called Seven Summits, the highest mountains on all continents. Denali, which means "The Great One" in the ancient language of the Athabascan people, is only one of many striking mountains in the Alaska Range, home to enormous glaciers and countless miles of untouched wilderness. The park's northern region consists of hilly, expansive tundra, where ice-cold glacial streams flow in braided channels through broad gravel creek beds. Encompassing over 6 million acres

OPPOSITE: A transit bus wends its way across Denali National Park. Passengers can choose from one of four destinations on the route: Toklat River for hiking and wildlife; Eielson Visitor Center for excellent views of Denali and various ranger-led activities; Wonder Lake, with its incredible mirror-like surface; and Kantishna, a deserted gold-mining town.

> **"Don't hesitate or allow yourself to make excuses. Just get out and do it. You will be very, very glad that you did."**
>
> —CHRISTOPHER MCCANDLESS, ADVENTURER

(including the adjacent preserve), Denali National Park is the third largest in the United States and one of the largest and longest protected ecosystems in the world.

Even today, the park's fauna and flora have been largely spared humanity's impact on nature, whether through introduction or eradication, which has become all too commonplace throughout the world. The park is home to no fewer than 750 different species of plants, 39 species of mammals, and 165 species of birds, including the golden eagle, which is rare even in Alaska. Among the animals most commonly seen here are grizzly bears, caribou, moose, mountain goats, Dall sheep, wolves, foxes, otters, and marmots. The permafrost of the soil and the short summers have produced an unexpectedly rich variety of flora, in color and form. An impressive 425 different species of wildflowers alone have been identified in the park, making it a destination for flower enthusiasts.

A single road makes the entire park accessible to visitors. It's only open from mid-May to mid-September. To best manage the rush of visitors, the National Park Service has limited private vehicle traffic. The park operates guided buses, which shuttle visitors to sites such as the Drunken Forest, where spruce pines lean and slump toward the ground as if drunk, a result of the soil's eternal freezing and thawing. Other sights include the Polychrome Pass, which offers a superb view of the mountain range with its colorful lava hills and the vast tundra below.

The cleanliness and freshness of Denali National Park's air are of a quality you will rarely experience elsewhere, so make sure to breathe deep wherever you go. In the winter, you will find enough snow for skiing, snowshoeing, and dog sledding, and in warmer months, visitors can hike or bike through the park (beware of bears, though) or go tubing on the river. Avid (and highly trained) mountaineers can also climb Denali. Or you can witness just how pure the air and water are by visiting the world-famous Wonder Lake; here, the majestic beauty of Denali mountain is reflected in the lake's surface, which is so still you can take a picture, turn it upside down, and not know which way is up.

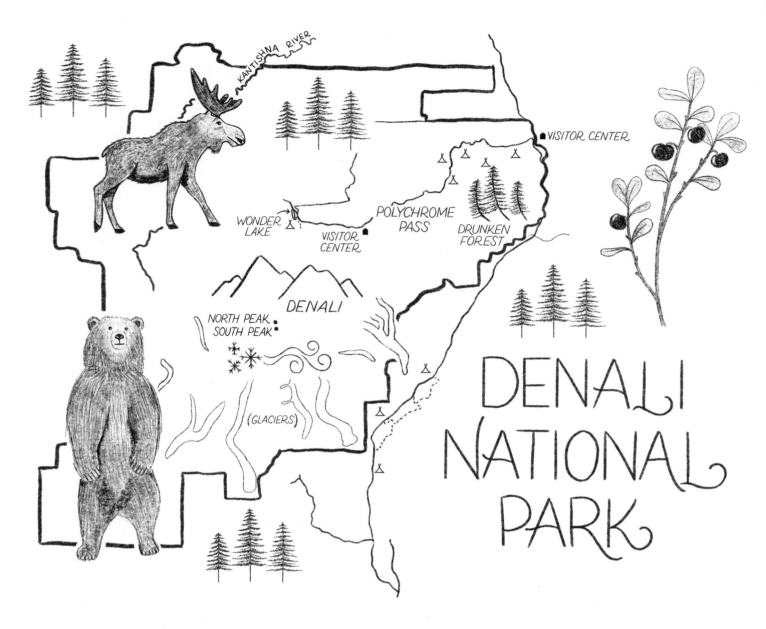

Originally established in 1917 as Mount McKinley National Park after the mountain's name at the time, on December 2, 1980, the Alaska National Interest Lands Conservation Act changed the park's status and renamed it Denali National Park and Preserve, based on the name given to its tallest mountain by the Koyukon people. The legislation enlarged the park from two million acres to its present size to preserve the habitat of the area's wildlife. It is also a UNESCO Biosphere Reserve.

SIZE
4,740,911 acres (7,408 sq. mi./19,186 km²)
Size rank among National Parks: 3 of 63

ELEVATION
Highest point: Denali (20,310 ft./6,190 m)
Lowest point: Yentna River (240 ft./73 m)

GEOLOGY
Denali National Park and Preserve is located in the central area of the Alaska Range, a mountain chain that began forming hundreds of millions of years ago when the Pacific Plate subducted under terranes and immense forces lifted up rocks that eventually became mountains. The formation process continues to this day—the Denali mountain is growing by about 0.02 of an inch (.5 mm) each year.

FLORA AND FAUNA
The Alaska Range has a strong influence on the park's ecosystems. With a tree line at 2,500 feet (760 m), most of the park is tundra. Even in the lowland, most trees and shrubs do not reach full size in the unfavorable climate. Wildlife still thrives: wild blueberries and soapberries make up a good part of the diet of bears, who are part of the "Denali Big Five"— moose, caribou, Dall sheep, wolves, and grizzlies. In spring and summer, many migratory bird species reside in the park. And there's even one amphibian: the wood frog.

CLIMATE AND WEATHER
The park's subarctic climate is influenced by two of Alaska's major climate zones—the maritime zone south of the Alaska Range and the continental zone in the interior, north of the range. Summers are short, humid, and usually cool. The days

are long and the skies are often cloudy. While winters are drier, they are long with short and bitterly cold days—temperatures below -58 °F (-50 °C) are not uncommon.

CONSERVATION

The park was established primarily to protect Dall sheep from overhunting, but preserves the entire wilderness today. Its creation is closely associated with the names of two wilderness men, Charles Sheldon and Harry Karstens. In the early 1900s, the conservationists studied the behavior of wildlife in today's park area. Aghast by ruthless gold miners and big-game hunters who were exploiting the land, Sheldon conceived the idea of preserving the Denali region as a national park as early as 1906. As the political climate at the time was unfavorable, Mount McKinley National Park only came to fruition in 1917. It took another four years for the government to approve a loan for the park, and Karstens became the first park superintendent.

BEFORE YOU GO

Denali National Park is easily accessible by car or railroad. The park is open year-round, yet most facilities are seasonal. Campgrounds, food, and shuttle-bus services are generally only open from late May to early September. (Because of its location just south of the Arctic Circle, it does not get dark at the end of June and beginning of July.) Most of the accommodations are outside the park. Within the park itself, there are a few wilderness lodges at the end of the gravel road in the Wonder Lake and Kantishna areas.

BEST TIMES TO VISIT

Late May to mid-September is the primary time to visit for mild temperatures and access to facilities such as the Denali Park Road.

HIDDEN GEM

The Denali Park Road is closed to private vehicles beyond the Savage River Check Station at mile 15, but is open to park shuttles, hikers, and cyclists. Consider a day or multi-day bike trip to view the scenery at a pleasant pace.

INTERESTING FACTS ABOUT THE PARK

- Denali's summit isn't the world's highest—but its rise from base to summit is the tallest of any above-sea mountain in the world.
- Denali was known as Mount McKinley, named after the former U.S. President. The name "Denali" stems from "deenaalee," the Koyukon people's original name for the mountain—it translates as "the great one." The name was restored in 2015 by President Barack Obama.

Donald "Don" Edward Sheldon

BUSH PILOT

Simply calling Donald "Don" Sheldon (1921–1975) an aviator doesn't even come close to capturing his legacy. In Denali, he was no less than a legend. At 17, he left the wilds of Wyoming to seek employment and adventure in Alaska. Pre-statehood, the raw and rugged region still felt largely uncharted. Sheldon eventually arrived in Anchorage, and after a short stint as a dairy truck driver, he and a friend decided to fathom how far north the $12 they had could take them. They ended up in Talkeetna, where Sheldon learned to fly. In the wake of Pearl Harbor, he was soon accepted into the military's Civilian Pilot Training program, and during the Second World War, he flew missions as a tail gunner in Europe. Sheldon returned with a military surplus plane and started a local airline in 1947. From Talkeetna, he ferried climbers, hunters, fishermen, and sometimes just a case of dynamite or a bottle of Jack Daniels to places previously inaccessible. Able to land in niches and on high glaciers all over the mountains, he became the go-to man for researchers. Armed with an extraordinary understanding of aerodynamics, topography, and meteorology—coupled with good business sense—there was nothing, it seemed, that Sheldon and his Piper Super Cub couldn't do. With retractable skis on the bottom of one of his planes, he pioneered the technique of glacier landings and helped the Boston Museum of Science map the area. But there were also dozens of troubled climbers, shipwrecked boaters, and lost hunters who owe their lives to him. When called, he would venture out in any weather, at any time. Sheldon died of cancer before being able to finish his dream of building a fully-fledged chalet to open up Denali's jaw-dropping grandeur to even more people. In 2018, his children and grandchildren made his vision a reality.

Lake Clark

Glacial lakes framed by active volcanoes are part of the watershed that supports the largest sockeye salmon fishery in the world.

There are no roads leading to Lake Clark National Park, so getting there requires a plane or watercraft. Many come to this remote wilderness in southwest Alaska to discover the true meaning of solitude. The park, which doubles as a nature preserve, protects over 4 million acres (16,187 km²) of pristine nature, an area about the size of Hawaii. Within its boundaries, you will find enormous mountains, two active volcanoes, tundra-covered hills where bears, caribou, and moose roam free, and last but not least, the headwaters of the largest sockeye salmon fishery in the world.

Qizhjeh Vena, also known as Lake Clark, was formed more than 10,000 years ago. Its turquoise glacial waters are a sign of the last Ice Age, which occurred around the same time as the first human settlers arrived in the area. The ancestral home of the Dena'ina people, Qizhjeh Vena means "lake where people gathered," and the village of Qizhjeh, built on its shores, thrived for almost 900 years. However, in the early 1900s, a flu and measles epidemic brought by European settlers decimated the population, and survivors decamped to another area to the south-west. By 1909, Qizhjeh was completely abandoned.

In more recent history, the park was home to famed naturalist and writer Richard Proenneke, who built a remote cabin in the area in the late 1960s and lived there for over 30 years. Constructed with mostly local materials and handheld tools, the cabin still sits on the shores of Upper Twin Lake and is open to visitors. Proenneke's story was the subject of the film *Alone in the Wilderness*, filmed in the park.

The land continues to provide for Alaskans today, and most of the park's rivers and streams are part of the Kvichak watershed, a crucial habitat for sockeye salmon. About half of the some 40 million sockeye salmon caught in Bristol Bay are spawned here. Given the fundamental role salmon plays in the Alaskan economy and culture, the need to protect these waters was one of the reasons the park was established.

Surrounded by mountains, Lake Clark is the hub of the park. The park's visitor center is located near its shores in the small lakeside town of Port Alsworth. Accessible only by plane, this is the jumping-off point for exploring the park, whether on an intrepid backpacking excursion or down one of the area's three National Wild and Scenic Rivers. There are only 6.9 miles (11.1 km) of maintained trails, but the entire park is open to adventurous and self-sufficient travelers who map their own routes. When the

ALASKA

PARK AT A GLANCE

Lake Clark was first designated as a national monument by President Carter on December 1, 1978, and upgraded to a national park two years later on December 2, 1980, under the Alaska National Interest Lands Conservation Act.

SIZE
2,619,713 acres (4,093 sq. mi./10,601 km²)
Size rank among National Parks: 7 of 63

ELEVATION
Highest point: Redoubt Volcano (10,197 ft./3,108 m)
Lowest point: Chinitna Bay (sea level)

GEOLOGY
Sculpted by glaciers, Lake Clark is nestled between the Aleutian Range to the southwest and the Alaska Range to the north. As the mountains approach the ocean, they descend into the waters of Cook Inlet. The coastal cliffs here contain 150-million-year-old fossils, buried in one of the best-preserved Jurassic sedimentary rock sections in the world.

FLORA AND FAUNA
Iconic moose, caribou, and wolves roam the tundra, bald and golden eagles soar in the air, and black and brown bears forage for spawning salmon. The waters of the park provide a pristine habitat for 25 species of freshwater and anadromous fish like salmon and rainbow trout.

CONSERVATION
Besides the vast swathes of untouched wilderness, the park also protects an essential watershed for Bristol Bay salmon fisheries and oversees the crucial task of ensuring water quality in the park. Glaciers have been the area's principal architects and provide visual proof of the significant impacts of climate change, which has caused the Arctic to warm much faster than other parts of the world. Since the 1950s, over 81,000 acres (328 km²) of glacial ice in the park has melted.

BEFORE YOU GO
Lake Clark National Park is not on the road system, and the most common access is by plane. Port Alsworth offers some lodging, but there are no grocery stores. There are no facilities or designated campgrounds in the park, and visitors who overnight in the backcountry need to take precautions for camping among bears.

BEST TIMES TO VISIT
June to October when the weather is warmer, and more transportation and guide services are operating.

conditions are right, the park's isolated location makes it a prime spot to see the *aurora borealis*. There's also world-class bear viewing here, particularly in Chinitna Bay and at the park's most visited spot, Crescent Lake.

The area is dominated by the Neacola and Chigmit Mountains, and rising from their ranks are two active volcanoes, Mount Redoubt and Mount Iliamna, part of the Pacific Ring of Fire. Rocks in the park show that volcanic activity has been present in the area for around 180 million years, but the two volcanoes are fairly young (at least in geological terms). Mount Redoubt is a "mere" 880,000 years old and has erupted four times in recorded history. In 1989, a KLM Boeing 747 on its way to Anchorage got caught in the ash cloud at 28,000 feet (8,500 m), leading to a complete failure of all four engines. Miraculously, the plane was able to safely land.

Wrangell-St. Elias

America's largest national park is also one of its wildest, with soaring peaks, immense glaciers, and vast stretches of untouched wilderness.

Boasting The United States' largest glacial system—featuring more than 100 glaciers in total—Wrangell St.Elias is around 35 percent covered in glaciers. They include the Nabesna Glacier, which at 53 miles (85 km) long is the world's longest interior valley glacier.

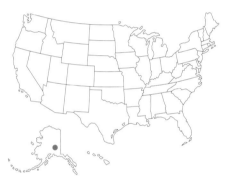

ALASKA

Most people seeking refuge in the austere beauty and solitude of "Wild Alaska" look no further than Denali. What a shame. While Denali might be home to the highest mountain in the United States, there's another park that is by no means inferior. Wrangell-St. Elias National Park and Preserve boasts the greatest collection of peaks above 16,000 feet (4,880 m) on the North American continent. And the superlatives don't stop there. The park is also the largest in the National Park System. Equal to the size of Yellowstone, Yosemite, and Switzerland combined, it encompasses a gigantic mountain world with shimmering turquoise glaciers and raging streams that seamlessly connect to Kluane National Park across the Canadian border.

Unlike most other parks in Alaska, Wrangell-St. Elias is relatively well connected to the road network, but only two gravel roads lead into the park, and most rental companies prohibit their use. Hearty adventurers looking for backcountry hiking, mountaineering, or rafting prefer to take a bush plane into the wilderness. Luckily, the restricted access has spared the park

A curious sight on the park's slopes, the copper-mining town of Kennecott has become a landmark in its own right. The National Park Service has repurposed a number of buildings—notably the General Store and Post Office and the General Manager's Office—using them to relate the town's history.

from mass tourism—for the time being. If you are willing to explore this vast area on your own, you will soon discover that there are still regions on earth that have remained practically untouched by human civilization. That is, except for two abandoned settlements in the park, reminders of the glory days of copper mining.

The park's most peculiar sight is Kennecott, a National Historic Landmark today. Within a few years of discovering copper deposits in 1899, this remote mining town sprang up as if from thin air. The dusty outpost quickly became a magnet for fortune seekers, adventurers, and people with nothing left to lose. Mining reached its heyday with the opening of railroad tracks in 1911. At the time, Kennecott was the richest copper mine on earth. The town thrived until 1938, when copper prices plummeted and operations were shut down. People were given 24 hours' notice to pack their belongings, and Kennecott became a ghost town overnight. The hasty departure is apparent in every corner. Only in the neighboring settlement McCarthy, where miners came to drink, gamble, or hook up, do a small number of residents still live year-round.

Its picturesque red houses, which bear witness to its former prosperity, stand against a dramatic mountain-and-glacier backdrop. Four major mountain ranges—Chugach, Wrangell, St. Elias, and the eastern reaches of the Alaska Range—converge in the park, giving Wrangell-St. Elias National Park the nickname "Kingdom of Mountains in North America." Within the park boundaries lies the namesake giant Mount Wrangell (14,163 ft./ 4,317 m), one of the largest active volcanoes in the world, whose plume of smoke, on a clear day, can be seen for miles around. Mount Saint Elias, the second-tallest mountain in the United States, is also said to have the world's longest ski run, with an astounding 18,008-foot (5,489-meter) descent.

As the St. Elias Range merges with the Wrangells in the heart of the park, it forms the highest ocean-front mountain range on earth. Nine of the 16 highest peaks in the United States rise into the skies here, including Mount Bona (16,550 ft./ 5,005 m), Mount Blackburn (16,390 ft./4,995 m), and Mount Sanford (16,237 ft./4,949 m). More than 100 huge glaciers stretch from the mountains toward the Gulf of Alaska, covering more than a third of the parklands. Spawning several large glaciers, the Bagley Icefield in the Chugach Mountains is the largest in the park and all of North America. It feeds the Bering Glacier, which is both the largest and the longest glacier in North America, covering roughly the size of Rhode Island.

WRANGELL—ST. ELIAS NATIONAL PARK

T he area that is now Wrangell-St. Elias National Park and Preserve was proclaimed a national monument in 1978. It was established as a national park on December 2, 1980, by the Alaska National Interest Lands Conservation Act–a law signed by President Jimmy Carter and the single largest expansion of protected lands in U.S. history. The park abuts Kluane National Park and Reserve in Canada. Together, the two parks form one of the largest remaining wilderness areas in the world and were designated a UNESCO World Heritage Site in 1979.

SIZE
13,175,799 acres (20,587 sq. mi./53,320,57 km²)
Size rank among National Parks: 1 of 63

ELEVATION
Highest point: Mount St. Elias (18,008 ft./5,489 m)
Lowest point: Pacific Ocean (sea level)

GEOLOGY
The park is revered for its geological diversity, attracting researchers from all over the world to study volcanism, glaciation, plate tectonics, and quaternary geology. According to geologists, the bedrock underlying the mountains formed much further south than its present position, perhaps off of California. When the terrane moved northward and collided with other crustal plates, the four mountain ranges (which constitute the park today) were formed. Plate tectonics remain a powerful force of change even today.

FLORA AND FAUNA
Wolves, grizzlies, moose, and herds of bison roam the dense backcountry of this vast wilderness—every now and then, you can even spot a puma. In addition, one of the largest populations of Dall sheep (about 13,000) live here. In the lowlands, dense deciduous and coniferous forests stretch to the horizon. Man-high ferns proliferate like weeds, their bright green colors competing with the darker mosses and lichens. The coastal waters are home to whales, sea otters, seals, and sea lions.

CLIMATE AND WEATHER
Despite the park's coastline, high mountains and icefields bar the ocean's moderating influence, resulting in long and

extremely cold winters, and short, warm, relatively dry summers. In any season, the weather can change rapidly.

CONSERVATION

Wrangell-St. Elias National Park and Preserve was established along with nine other national parks to maintain the natural scenic beauty of the diverse geologic, glacial, and riparian dominated landscapes and protect the attendant wildlife populations and their habitats. While the park's glaciers are threatened by climate change, its boreal forest is one of nature's biggest natural fighters—these forests store twice as much carbon as tropical forests.

BEFORE YOU GO

The park is relatively easy to reach by car, but inside there are just two gravel roads, and not all car rental companies allow driving on them. You should check road conditions at the visitor center, located 10 miles south of Glennallen on the Richardson Highway, before going. There are only a few maintained hiking trails in the park, but a wide array of operators offer guided backcountry tours for multiple days, which can include hiking, rafting, hunting, mountaineering, or ice climbing. Independent travelers can arrange to be dropped off with air charter operators.

BEST TIMES TO VISIT

Winter stays late and arrives early in Alaska, so the main season to visit the park falls between mid-May and mid-September. Peak season starts in early June when both temperatures and vegetation bloom and, unfortunately, mosquito numbers peak.

HIDDEN GEM

You are unlikely to encounter many crowds in this enormous park, and even less likely if you venture out on a backpacking trip. While most backcountry itineraries require chartering a bush plane, there are a few that can be accessed by vehicle. One noteworthy adventure is a trip to the Nugget Creek Cabin, a rustic cabin located 15 miles into the wilderness. Advance reservations are required.

INTERESTING FACTS ABOUT THE PARK

- The park contains North America's largest glacier— Bering Glacier.
- The two prospectors who fought their way through the seemingly impassable wilderness to discover some of the richest copper veins on the entire continent were actually looking for gold.
- The fishing community of Yakutat in the far southeastern portion of the park boasts some of the best surfing outside of Hawaii.

Katie John

FIGHTER FOR SUBSISTENCE RIGHTS

In 1964, five years after Alaska joined the United States, the Alaska State Board of Fisheries closed subsistence fishing in the village of Baltzulneta and nearly all other sites along the upper Copper River, in what is now Wrangell–St. Elias National Park. The ban, imposed in the name of "conservation," came as unwelcome news to the Ahtna people, who had relied on the salmon (dried, boiled, fried, or roasted) for much of their food for generations. Despite being protected by federal law and despite hundreds of thousands of salmon being fished for sport and commercial uses further downstream, customary fishing by Natives in Baltzulneta was met with harassment by state officials. But some people were willing to stand up for their right to practice subsistence hunting and fishing, just as previous generations had done before them. One such person was Katie John (1915–2013). In 1984, she requested permits to reopen subsistence fishing, which were denied. The decision set the stage for a decades-long legal dispute between federal, tribal, and state interests. In 2011, Tony Knowles, the governor of Alaska at the time, met her in Baltzulneta, where she told him all she wanted was to provide for her family as generations before her had. "On that day," Knowles later said, "I learned more than is written in all the boxes of legal briefs in this long-lasting court battle." Represented in court by the Native American Rights Fund, Katie John ultimately prevailed. In 2014, the Supreme Court refused to hear the case, cementing the lower court's ruling that subsistence hunting and fishing should be allowed on all federally managed waters in Alaska. Unfortunately, she did not live to celebrate her hard-won victory, as she had passed away the year before at the age of 97.

Katmai

Welcome to a land that's home to more brown bears than people and the largest runs of sockeye salmon on the planet.

Rising some 7,600 feet (2,530 m) Mount Grigg's is one of four stratovolcanoes in what is known as the Katmai Cluster, a dense group of volcanic vents within 9 miles (15 km) of Novarupta.

ALASKA

During the summer of 1912, residents in what would later become Katmai National Park and Preserve noticed something strange going on. As they prepared for the upcoming fishing season, the earth kept shaking almost every day. While earthquakes are not uncommon in Alaska, the frequency and magnitude of these quakes were unprecedented. Then, around 1 p.m. on June 6, as the skies darkened and the sun disappeared for 60 hours, it became clear why: a previously unknown volcano called Novarupta spewed tephra (ash particles) all over the Alaska Peninsula in what turned out to be the world's largest eruption of the 20th century.

Within days, the ash plume had devastated much of the plant and animal life in Southern Alaska. It turned the lush Ukak River valley into an ash-filled wasteland, burying it under 600-foot- (200-meter-) thick deposits of extremely hot pumice and ash. Groundwater trapped beneath the ash superheated and worked its way to the surface, discharging from thousands of cracks and fissures, so-called fumaroles. Explorer Robert Griggs

BELOW: It seems that volcanic activity is not the only force that has brought change to the landscape at Katmai. It is thought that the Savonoski Crater, a circular depression now filled by a lake, may have been formed by a meteor impact.
OPPOSITE: A river flows through a ravine.

"Our feeling of admiration for the valley soon gave way to one of stupefaction. We were overawed. For a while we could neither think nor act in a normal fashion."

—ROBERT FISKE GRIGGS, EXPLORER

and a team of explorers with the National Geographic Society could hardly believe their eyes when they witnessed the steaming landscape in 1916, eventually calling it the "Valley of Ten Thousand Smokes."

Convinced of the valley's uniqueness and its scientific significance, Griggs successfully lobbied to protect the area. The fumaroles, he thought, could easily rival the geysers of Yellowstone National Park. However, the valley floor has since cooled, and very few fumaroles are left today. This is hardly an issue for visitors, though, as there's a new spectacle to marvel at: bears. While the park is noted for its pristine lakes, wild rivers, and craggy mountains, it now owes its enormous popularity primarily to the park's large population of brown bears (*Ursus arctos horribilis*).

Each July and September, as the salmon make their annual run, as many as 2,000 resident bears congregate for a feast along the Brooks River. At Brooks Camp, the park's most visited area, viewing platforms allow you to observe the skillful hunters feeding on the salmon from just a few feet away. Usually, the bears don't

have to do much more than stand in the water and open their mouths to catch the jumping fish. The bears' survival depends on eating a year's worth of food in six months, as the salmon is crucial for the bears to gain enough fat to get them through hibernation. Each September, the NPS holds a "Fat Bear Week" contest, championing the chunkiest bear via an online poll (chubby cubs were also added to the competition in 2021).

The excellent salmon runs also attract sport fishers. In fact, before Katmai was known for bear watching, most visitors came to the park to fish, and many of the facilities were built for fishermen. Rainbow trout, Arctic char, and grayling can be found in many of the park's lakes and rivers, as well as five species of Pacific salmon. Not into fishing? Canoe, kayak, or rafting trips are options, as is backcountry hiking. Katmai covers an area of almost 5,800 square miles (18,800 km²) of wilderness, making it the fourth-largest unit in the National Park System. The vastness offers only a few marked hiking trails, but with thousands of square miles of wilderness at your feet, who needs those anyway?

KATMAI NATIONAL PARK

Katmai was designated a national monument in 1918. On December 2, 1980, the protected area was expanded and a national park was established through the Alaska National Interest Lands Conservation Act. A small portion to the north was declared a National Preserve, where hunting is permitted with the required licenses and permits.

SIZE
3,674,529 acres (5741 sq. mi./14,870 km²)
Size rank among National Parks: 4

ELEVATION
Highest point: Mount Denison (7,606 ft./2,318 m)
Lowest point: Shelikof Strait (sea level)

GEOLOGY
Katmai lies on the Ring of Fire, so the majority of its higher mountains are of volcanic origin. Its characteristic ponds and lakes were created when water filled the depressions left behind by large blocks of ice from melting glaciers, and they are fed by rivers draining in from the highlands. The park is pock-marked with deep valleys and rippled with glacial moraines. The eruption of Novarupta in 1912—one of the most powerful volcanic eruptions ever recorded—shaped the area, forcing Mount Katmai to subside and collapse and forming the Valley of Ten Thousand Smokes.

FLORA AND FAUNA
Sure, most people come for the brown bears, but Katmai's rivers and streams, rugged coastlines, and glacial valleys host plenty of other wildlife too. The hundreds of different types of vascular plants found in the park form the foundation of Katmai's ecosystems. From coast to tundra, 42 species of mammals have been documented, including caribou, gray wolves, and red foxes. Moose live throughout the coastal and lake regions, while along the coast you can find sea lions, sea otters, and sometimes even beluga whales and orcas. As well as sockeye salmon, there is an abundance of pike, pollock, cod, and rainbow trout in Katmai's streams and rivers.

CLIMATE AND WEATHER

Summers are cool and cloudy in Katmai, with frequent strong winds and rain. The weather can vary greatly in the course of a single day, shifting from heavy rain to cold winds, to warm sunshine. Winters are generally freezing cold and snowy, and the highlands are covered with snow until spring.

CONSERVATION

Scientific expeditions funded by the National Geographic Society contributed to the creation of the Katmai National Monument. It was originally designated to preserve the geological features resulting from the Novarupta eruption and especially the famed Valley of Ten Thousand Smokes. While still being famous for its volcanoes, today's park focuses on the importance of wildlife, including the protection of brown bears and the water habitats vital to spawning sockeye salmon.

BEFORE YOU GO

Katmai is one of the most remote national parks. It's not connected to any road system, so visiting the park requires some effort, extra cost, thorough planning, and timely reservations. The park administration is located in King Salmon, some 300 miles (480 km) southwest of Anchorage. A seaplane can take you from King Salmon to Brooks Camp, which has a lodge (because of high demand there's a lottery for overnight accommodations) and campground. The viewing platform has a maximum capacity of 40 people, so wait times can reach two hours during peak season.

BEST TIMES TO VISIT

For those who aren't hardened winter explorers, May through September is the best time to visit to take advantage of the brief Alaskan summer. July is best for bear viewing at the iconic Brooks Falls.

HIDDEN GEM

Katmai only contains six miles (10 km) of maintained hiking trails, but hundreds of miles of rivers and waterways. Consider exploring by boat to find extreme solitude and remote gems. Book a guide, or rent a boat if you're sufficiently experienced.

INTERESTING FACTS ABOUT THE PARK

- Fourteen active volcanoes and over 20 seismic monitoring stations are located within the protected area.
- When Novarupta erupted, it was reported that for two days the air was so thick with ash that a lantern held at arm's length could not be seen.
- In 1965 and 1966, NASA used the lunar-like Valley of Ten Thousand Smokes as a training ground for the Apollo astronauts.

Pelagia Melgenak

MATRIARCH

When ash from the famous Novarupta eruption drifted down, blanketing the region, Pelagia Melgenak (ca. 1877–1974) thought the world was coming to an end. It was the stories her ancestors shared over generations that helped her—and fellow villagers—to survive the volcano's explosive eruption in 1912. They knew they had to overturn boats to keep them from filling with ash. They knew they had to collect fresh water before it was contaminated. And they knew they had to protect their portable property from getting ruined. Without this emphasis on ancestral knowledge, the people of Savonoski village would likely not have survived the magnitude of the eruption nor would they have been able to resettle. Despite it being the largest volcanic eruption of the 20th century, nobody is known to have died in the explosion. Although the people of Savonoski lost their homeland, which became inhabitable due to the ash, most continued to live in the area, moving to a new settlement along the Naknek River that they called New Savonoski, where the ground remained so warm for a year that clothes were barely needed. There, Pelagia managed to spare her family from yet another disaster in 1918: a flu pandemic that killed a quarter of the villagers. She cut off contact between her family and other villagers while deploying traditional medicine made from local plants—skills she learned through family and cultural practices. Over the course of the decades that followed, she continued to teach and share her cultural knowledge, keeping alive the sacredness of shared traditions, the loving bonds of kinship, and the reverence for a spiritual connection with the land around her. She was not only a matriarch of her family, but also of her community and culture.

Kenai Fjords

The deep fjords here, sculpted by glacial ice, offer an intimate view of a shrinking landscape.

Here where land meets sea, the scenery is shaped by mountains, deep fjords, rocky islands, jagged headlands, and one of the park's most defining features: the Harding Icefield. Almost 40 different glaciers flow from this ice sheet, which covers 700 square miles (1,800 km²) of the local mountain range, as well as half of the park. Some of the glaciers formed here, like the Aialik Glacier, stretch all the way to the ocean's waters, while others, such as the Skilak Glacier, make their way into nearby lakes.

These rivers of ice are an essential part of the state's geography, and around one quarter (4.6 million acres/18,000 km²) of Alaska's glaciers exist within national parks. In Kenai Fjords, there's the rare opportunity for a "drive-up" glacier. The Exit Glacier can be seen from your car or is accessible by a short hike. It's one of Alaska's most visited glaciers, and its popularity makes it an icon of climate change. In 2015, President Barack Obama stood at the receding glacier to emphasize the importance of immediate climate action.

Beyond the Exit Glacier, visitors can also explore the Harding Icefield on an 8.2-mile (13-kilometer) round-trip hike. While strenuous, it takes hikers up to the edge of this massive icefield, the remnants of an even larger one that covered much of south-central Alaska. Look out over a sea of ice, the white

ALASKA

landscape accentuated by the occasional nunatak—solitary protrusions of rock that are in fact the jagged summits of mountains buried deep in the glacier.

If ice plays such an important role in the park, then so does water, and much of Kenai Fjords is only accessible by boat or floatplane. The coastal Sugpiaq/Alutiiq people have been traveling and subsisting off these waters for more than a millennium. Kayaking is still a popular way to explore this rugged wilderness, but it is not for beginners, and traveling with a guide is highly recommended.

Deep green hemlock and spruce forests hug the coastline, and evergreen trees perch atop high-cliffed islands that rise

PARK AT A GLANCE

President Jimmy Carter established Kenai Fjords as a national monument in 1978, and it became a national park when the Alaska National Interest Lands Conservation Act was signed on December 2, 1980.

SIZE
603,130 acres (942 sq. mi./2,441 km²)
Size rank among National Parks: 17 of 63

ELEVATION
Highest point: Unnamed peak (6,450 feet/1,966 m)
Lowest point: Pacific Ocean (sea level)

GEOLOGY
The park is shaped by plate tectonics, with the Pacific Plate subducting beneath the North American Plate. In 1964, the built-up pressure between these plates created the Great Alaska Earthquake. At a magnitude of 9.2, it caused the area that later became Kenai Fjords National Park to drop 3 to 8 feet (1 to 2.5 m) in elevation.

FLORA AND FAUNA
Iconic Alaskan animals like moose and black bears wander the park, as well as smaller animals, including five different species of shrews. Mountain goats and marmots thrive in the alpine environment, and the park helps protect marine mammals like seals, sea lions, whales, and other marine life.

CONSERVATION
In 1970, conservationists founded the Alaska Coalition, advocating and lobbying on behalf of Alaska's public lands. Under President Richard Nixon's administration in 1973, the coalition thought it had successfully lobbied to establish federally protected public lands in Alaska. However, these efforts stalled, overshadowed by the Watergate scandal. The land was eventually protected five years later. Kenai Fjords protects 545 miles (877 km) of Pacific Ocean coastline. The glacier ice is also an essential part of the local ecosystem.

BEFORE YOU GO
There's no entrance fee to the park, but much of it is only accessible from the water. In the summer months, daily boat tours operate out of Seward. The only part of the park accessible by road is the Exit Glacier area with a first-come, first-serve campground and trail access.

BEST TIMES TO VISIT
In summer, the conditions offer the most accessibility. In the winter, Exit Glacier Road is closed to cars but still accessible for winter recreation like snowshoeing and dogsledding.

abruptly from the water. Marine life is abundant here, from enormous humpback whales to king salmon and sea otters, an important keystone species. The waters are also filled with all kinds of sea birds such as black oystercatchers or horned puffins with their brightly tipped bills.

In 1989, the Exxon Valdez oil spill severely impacted the park. The "dragon's breath of swirling death," as one national park report noted, left dead animals in its wake and altered an entire ecosystem. The transient AT1 group of orcas that passes through the park's waters lost over half of its members, and the few that live today carry some of the highest levels of industrial contaminants found in any marine mammal.

Glacier Bay

A kingdom of awe-inspiring glaciers signals a rebirth for this dynamic and thriving wilderness.

T o witness the roar of falling icebergs and the thunderous clap of vaulting humpback whales first-hand, you'll need to pack your bags for an adventure in Alaska. A visit to Glacier Bay National Park and Reserve transports you to an immense 3.3-million-acre (13,355-square-kilometer) wilderness defined by ethereal glaciers and lush forests.

The otherworldly beauty of the glaciers attracts over 500,000 visitors a year. But arriving in the land of ice and snow is no easy feat. There are no roads for cars to enter the park, so 80 percent of Glacier Bay's visitors arrive via cruise ship while the remainder fly into Juneau and hop on a ferry to the park. The cruise ships offer stunning views of the glaciers, but it's worth noting that there is no port of call or drop point for anchoring near the ice. So, hiring a water taxi or booking a kayak tour is essential if you plan on seeing the stunning mountains of ice up close. For those seeking a lofty vantage point, specialized local flights are also available for aerial sightseeing and photography tours. These flights offer captivating views as they pass over clear blue glaciers, white tundras, snow-capped mountain peaks, rugged coastlines, deep fjords, and temperate rainforests.

To explore the mainland at Bartlett Cove, you'll also need to hire a smaller boat to ferry you to shore. Vessels like the Glacier Bay Day Boat offer great sightseeing opportunities for

ALASKA

taking in the beautiful flora and fauna while getting up close to the park's key tidewater glaciers. This 150-passenger catamaran docks at Bartlett Cove and sails up through Glacier Bay's West Arm en route to the stunning Margerie Glacier. The boat operates during summer months when humpback whales return to the area. This seasonal migration is a huge attraction for visitors hoping to catch a glimpse of the massive whales defying gravity as they launch themselves from the glistening turquoise waters.

For campers, the National Park Service Campground offers free backcountry camping permits to those willing to complete a mandatory orientation. This is to prepare you for the very real threat of bears, bitterly cold weather, and persistent rains.

PARK AT A GLANCE

Glacier Bay was made a national monument in 1925, and was redesignated as a national park on December 2, 1980. Part of a binational UNESCO World Heritage Site since 1979, it was designated as a Biosphere Reserve in 1986.

SIZE
3,223,384 acres (5,037 sq. mi./13,045 km²)
Size rank among National Parks: 6 of 63

ELEVATION
Highest point: Mt. Fairweather (15,325 ft./4,671 m)
Lowest point: Pacific Ocean (sea level)

GEOLOGY
Upper Glacier Bay is composed of steep glacial fjords, tidewater glaciers, and newly deglaciated meadows. Lower Glacier Bay is a wet tundra with remote eastern and western southern borders housing temperate hemlock rainforests with mild climate, low snowfall, and the most rainfall within the park's borders.

FLORA AND FAUNA
The park contains more than 300 species of plants, ranging from giant conifer trees to rare, small orchids. The park is also home to a plethora of land animals including brown and black bears, timber wolves, moose, deer, foxes, bald eagles, golden eagles, and various species of hawks and falcons. A variety of marine animals also call the park home including sea otters, seals, sea lions, dolphins, orcas, and humpback whales.

CONSERVATION
The park was founded to study plant succession—the process of plant life returning to land as a result of a major event like glacial retreat. It has since become a biosphere and is part of the world's largest protected marine waters. This living laboratory is home to numerous studies focused on separating natural environmental changes from those caused by humans.

BEFORE YOU GO
There are no main roads leading to the bay, so if you're planning a visit, it will likely be via a cruise ship or kayak. There is no cell phone service in the park except near the Visitor Center. Wi-Fi is available at the lodge.

BEST TIMES TO VISIT
April to June are the driest months, but due to year-round rains, warm clothing and rain gear are always recommended. Peak season is May to September and best for spotting whales.

For those looking for something slightly less rugged, the Glacier Bay Lodge is the only hotel and restaurant in Bartlett Cove. This legendary lodge is a massive and welcoming refuge for backpackers, kayakers, and travelers from all over the world looking for a warm respite from the great outdoors.

Despite the very cold weather, Glacier Bay has been the sacred homeland of the Huna Tlingit people for generations. In 2020, the National Park Service and the Huna Tlingit partnered to designate 150 acres (.6 km²) within the park as a protected cultural site. Take a tour of the Xunaa Shuká Hít, a large cedar lodge where visitors can discover the rich history of Huna Tlingit through their traditional food, art, crafts, and dance.

Channel Islands

Five picturesque islands off the coast of Ventura offer a glimpse of what native California looked like before Disneyland and freeways.

Between them, the five Channel Islands encompass a diverse range of habitats, from coastal dune and bluff through grasslands and woodlands to riparian areas and open sea, each with its own distinct flora and fauna.

CHANNEL ISLANDS

Dubbed "the Galápagos Islands of North America," this national park consists of five islands, forming the eponymous Channel Islands archipelago. Although the park seems tantalizingly close to the hustle and bustle of Santa Barbara and L.A., it's one of the least visited in the United States; the islands are not populated, and visitor numbers are regulated. You can reach the islands by private boat, but navigation can be treacherous with large surf, fog, and reefs. That's why most people take dedicated concessionaire boats. Once ashore, you can explore on foot or by kayak—arguably the best way to get up close and personal with the islands' sea caves and seaweed forests.

If the islands appear smaller than the roughly 390 square miles (1,010 km²) the park officially encompasses, it's because more

than half of the park actually lies underwater. There is a unique wealth of species off and on the islands. From plankton to dolphins, California pelicans, cormorants, sea lions, gulls, and blue whales, the park is home to over 2,000 species of plants and animals. A total of 145 species, among them lizards and lichens, are endemic to the islands.

If you make the hour-long journey by boat from Ventura, the first island to emerge from the turquoise sea will be tiny Anacapa Island. It is the most visited and consists of three small islets of volcanic origin. Pelicans and seabirds find ideal breeding conditions here. Keep your ears open and listen to the melancholy horn of the island lighthouse, built in 1932 to keep ships off this treacherous coast. From a viewpoint, you can see the two larger Anacapa islets and, beyond them, the bigger Santa Cruz Island.

Santa Cruz is the largest island in the national park (and in California), but only a quarter of it belongs to the park. Almost all the landscapes of the Golden State are reflected here. Santa Barbara Island, by contrast, is the park's smallest and probably loneliest island, with only a dozen or so boat trips a year. Its cliff-hewn coastline and vegetation offer stunning views year-round, and in springtime, a sea of bright yellow flowers blankets the island. Located far to the south, this tiny piece of land jutting out of the blue sea nevertheless has a remarkable 5 miles (9 km) of hiking trails through gently rolling grasslands.

Solitude can also be found in California's second-largest island, Santa Rosa, home to some of the rarest tree species on earth. A must-do hike is to Lobo Canyon, with its native flora, eroded sandstone formations, and fossils of dwarf mammoths trapped inside. The crossing from Ventura takes three hours each way, so day trips are not feasible, but the island has an airstrip with regular flights. It's easier to reach than San Miguel, the fifth of the islands. For seals and sea lions, San Miguel is a paradise—and definitely easier to reach than for humans; it has the harshest and most volatile weather conditions of all five islands, and you can only reach its shores after transferring to an inflatable boat.

An incredible place in which to explore the natural world, the five Channel Islands offer visitors a wide program of activities from camping and hiking to boating, diving, and snorkeling. Animals lovers can spend their time birdwatching, whale watching, and seal and sea lion viewing. For plant lovers, peak blooms occur in late winter through spring.

CHANNEL ISLANDS NATIONAL PARK

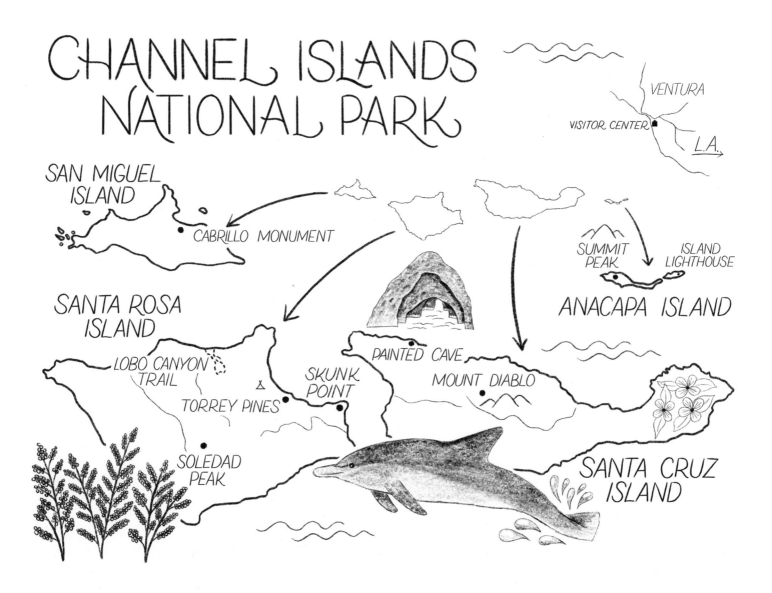

VENTURA

VISITOR CENTER

L.A.

SAN MIGUEL ISLAND

CABRILLO MONUMENT

SUMMIT PEAK

ISLAND LIGHTHOUSE

SANTA ROSA ISLAND

ANACAPA ISLAND

LOBO CANYON TRAIL

SKUNK POINT

PAINTED CAVE

MOUNT DIABLO

TORREY PINES

SOLEDAD PEAK

SANTA CRUZ ISLAND

The islands of Anacapa and Santa Barbara were declared a national monument in 1938, and all eight islands became a UNESCO Biosphere Reserve in 1976. On March 5, 1980, five of the islands–Anacapa, Santa Barbara, Santa Cruz, San Miguel, and Santa Rosa–became constituents of to the new Channel Islands National Park. A marine sanctuary protects six nautical miles of water around the park itself.

SIZE
249,561 acres (390 sq. mi./1,010 km²)
Size rank among National Parks: 27 of 63

ELEVATION
Highest point: Devils Peak (2,429 ft./740 m)
Lowest point: Pacific Ocean (sea level)

GEOLOGY
The Channel Islands rose from the ocean about five million years ago as the result of microplate tectonic forces. During the Ice Age, the northern islands were one giant island, known to geologists as Santarosae. Back then, the sea level was much lower, and the seabed today was land, but it's unlikely the islands were also connected to the mainland. With the melting of continental ice sheets, the islands separated.

FLORA AND FAUNA
The islands have always been separated from the mainland and developed a unique flora and fauna that is home to more than 2,000 species, ranging from rare sea birds to elephant seals to colorful wildflowers. Notable is the endangered island fox with gray and rust-colored fur, which in contrast to its mainland counterpart roams during the day. The best chance of seeing one of these creatures, which are a little larger than domestic cats, is on the island of Santa Cruz. Bald eagles, which were native to the islands, almost vanished in the 1960s with the use of insecticides, but, after decades-long restoration programs, have been breeding again in the park since 2006. In summer, large numbers of blue whales congregate in and around Channel Islands National Park—about 10 percent of the world's blue whales!

CLIMATE AND WEATHER

Forget the sunny Southern California weather, it's somewhat different (and much more unpredictable) on these islands. Although the Mediterranean climate is mild year-round and temperatures are quite stable, high winds, fog, and sea spray can occur at any time. Weather conditions differ greatly from day to day and island to island.

CONSERVATION

Channel Islands National Park protects the unique and fragile ecosystems on the eponymous islands. Over the years, non-native species were introduced to the islands, threatening the natural balance of the ecosystem. Hogs, rabbits, feral sheep, and cats led to the extinction of some native plants. The island fox was considered endangered in 2004, but a breeding program and other conservation measures have now led to a stable population.

BEFORE YOU GO

Visiting the park requires some advance planning. There are no hotels or other permanent accommodations on the islands, but all five islands offer camping. Some islands are completely treeless, so don't forget sun protection. The park administration maintains two visitor centers on the mainland in Ventura and Santa Barbara, where permits for visitation are issued.

BEST TIMES TO VISIT

The park can be enjoyed year-round with relatively mild temperatures, although the winter months are generally cooler and wetter. Summer and fall are great for those wishing to engage in watersports such as kayaking, surfing, or scuba diving. Spring is an excellent time for wildflower and wildlife viewing.

HIDDEN GEM

Contrary to what the name might suggest, Skunk Point on Santa Rosa Island is a remote stretch of beach with tidepools, shipwrecks, and unique rock formations. Some areas are closed seasonally to protect nesting birds.

INTERESTING FACTS ABOUT THE PARK

- The platform on which the islands are located first trended north-south like most mountain ranges in California, but eventually rotated.
- Evidence of human habitation on the islands goes back as far as 13,000 years when native Chumash peoples crossed from the mainland.
- The bones of the "Arlington Springs Man" were found on Santa Rosa Island. Over 13,000 years old, they are the oldest bones to have been excavated in North America.

Alan Salazar

CHUMASH AND TATAVIUM ELDER

Alan Salazar has spent much of his adult life sharing his Native American culture the traditional way: through oral storytelling. A founding member of the Kern County Native American Heritage Preservation Council and the Chumash Maritime Association, Salazar worked for over two decades as a probation officer and now serves as a Native American consultant and monitor helping to protect ancestral sites. A member of the California Indian Advisory Council for the Santa Barbara Museum of Natural History, he teaches and shares his culture throughout the area. As Salazar has said, "Native stories need to be told by Native peoples," and he has been a featured speaker in the park and the surrounding region, ensuring that the stories of his people are passed along. The Chumash people were deeply connected to the water, and the Native inhabitants of the Channel Islands would travel from island to island in tomols (a kind of traditional canoe), hunting, fishing, and trading. These deep wooden canoes, built for the open waters of the ocean, were constructed and paddled by the Brotherhood of the Tomol, a group that disbanded in 1834. Tomols aren't just a mode of transportation; they are seen as a central part of Chumash culture. As a member of the Chumash Maritime Association, Salazar helped to build a working traditional tomol in 1997, and the 26-foot- (8-meter-) long vessel was named 'Elye'wun, the Chumash word for "swordfish." In 2001 he was on the first tomol crew to make the crossing from the mainland to the islands in over a century. Since then, Salazar and fellow members of the Chumash Maritime Association have continued the crossing almost every year, reviving ceremonial and cultural practices of the past and preserving the tradition for future generations.

American Samoa

Halfway between Hawaii and New Zealand, this often-overlooked tropical reserve is a pristine haven, brimming with natural beauty.

Rugged landmasses covered in lush rain forest vegetation and ringing with tropical birdsong are the hallmark of American Samoa, one of the United States' most remote national parks.

AMERICAN SAMOA

In the middle of the South Pacific, thousands of miles away from the North American continent, lies what is likely the most unusual national park in the United States: American Samoa, a tropical paradise with coral reefs, rain forests, and dazzling white-sand beaches. The journey is long (14 hours from L.A. with a stopover in Honolulu) and by no means cheap, but once you've arrived, you'll feel like you've stepped onto the edge of the world. Some sections of the national park look as if no human has ever set foot here—no lodges, no kiosks, no snack bars, just unspoiled nature.

Despite covering very little landmass, the islands of Samoa actually belong to two different states. The larger, eastern part of the archipelago proudly calls itself the "Independent State of Samoa," or just Samoa, since gaining independence from New Zealand in 1997. The smaller, western part of the archipelago is a foreign territory of the United States and is consequently called

Visitors to American Samoa will find countless opportunities to witness secluded villages, to behold coral sand beaches, and to take in truly striking vistas of land and sea. The wildlife on and around the islands includes flying foxes and fruit bats and up to 800 species of native fish.

From jagged mountain peaks to colorful coral reefs, this tropical paradise in the middle of the Pacific is no short of sights to marvel at.

American Samoa. The territory's national park (locally known as "Paka O Amerika Samoa") was officially established in 1988.

The national park stretches over three islands, the largest and most developed of which is Tutuila. The island is covered with a network of well-maintained hiking trails. Some lead up to the 1,610-foot- (491-meter-) high Mount 'Alava, passing emerald rain forests and fantastic viewpoints, accompanied by the polyphonic chirping of countless tropical birds. But it's not just spectacular hikes you'll find here: American Samoa is also famous for its snorkeling and scuba diving. Over 4,000 acres of the park are underwater, where divers can catch a glimpse of the park's hundreds of native fish and coral species.

A particular paradise for divers is the island of Ofu, reachable by small plane or by boat. There are no dive centers here, so you'll need to bring your own equipment, but the coral reef, with its colorful inhabitants, is all the more pristine and breathtaking for it. The third island, Ta'ū, is covered in dense rain forest. Its foothills flow out onto the rugged coastline in impressive cliffs that are

among the highest in the world. The adventurous can climb Lata Mountain (3,169 ft./966 m), which boasts the highest elevation in American Samoa National Park. The island is bisected by a single permanent watercourse, the Laufuti Stream, which plummets almost 1,000 feet (305 m) at the Laufuti Waterfall.

Inside the park boundaries, there are no lodges or camping opportunities. That is because the land is actually owned by the Samoan people, who lease it to the U.S. National Park Service. (Some trails pass through private property, and it's generally considered respectful to ask for permission to hike these trails.) The first people to have reached the Samoan islands made the journey by sea from Southeast Asia some 3,000 years ago; the Samoan culture is considered the oldest in Polynesia. Today, ancient Polynesian traditions and typical American lifestyle peacefully coexist here. A unique way to discover local customs and learn cultural practices and courtesies is a homestay with a Samoan family on any of the three islands, which can be arranged through the park's Homestay Program.

AMERICAN SAMOA
NATIONAL PARK

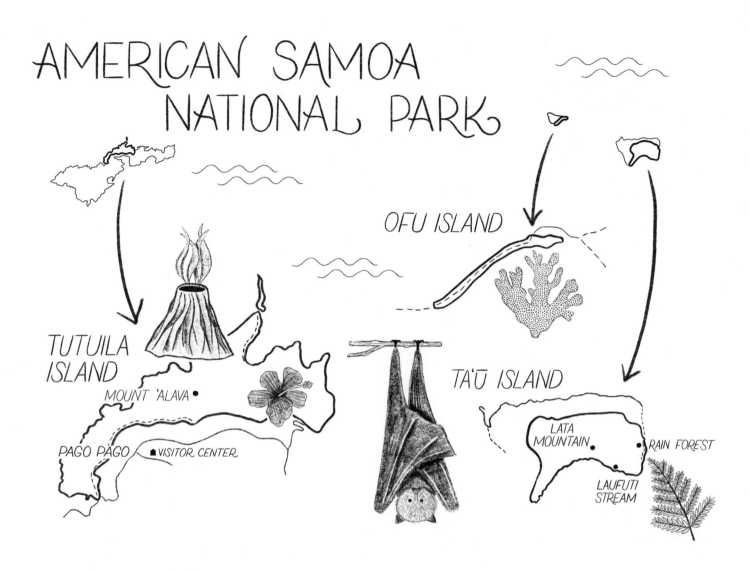

OFU ISLAND

TUTUILA ISLAND

MOUNT 'ALAVA •

PAGO PAGO · ▲ VISITOR CENTER

TA'Ū ISLAND

LATA MOUNTAIN •

• RAIN FOREST

LAUFUTI STREAM

Located some 2,600 miles southwest of Hawaii in the South Pacific Ocean, the National Park of American Samoa is the only United States national park in the Southern Hemisphere. Established on October 31, 1988, the protected area stretches over three islands: Tutuila, Ta'ū, and Ofu. Congress approved an expansion of the park in 2002.

SIZE
8,256 acres (13 sq. mi./33 km²)
Size rank among National Parks: 61 of 63

ELEVATION
Highest point: Lata Mountain (3,169 ft./966 m)
Lowest point: Pacific Ocean (sea level)

GEOLOGY
American Samoa is quite young by geological standards. The series of broad shield volcanoes have formed within the last few million years, when the Pacific Plate moved over a stationary hotspot deep in the earth. Although the volcanoes showed no activity for centuries, the tectonic hotspot is still active, and they may erupt again. Intense weathering and erosion has shaped the extremely steep topography

and created the world's tallest sea cliffs, which soar up to 3,000 feet (914 m) above the ocean in the park.

FLORA AND FAUNA
The park is primarily home to winged animals such as the flying fox, a fruit bat with the wingspan of a barn owl. The park's sole specie of snake is the Pacific boa. The reefs are home to more than 900 species of fish and 200 species of coral; humpback whales pass by on their journey from Antarctica. The rain forest protects hundreds of plant species and is home to 35 species of birds.

CLIMATE AND WEATHER
Samoa's climate is dictated by its location in the South Pacific close to the equator. The climate is warm and wet year-round. There is a long, wet summer season (October through May)

and a slightly cooler and drier season (June through September). The mountainous interior is often shrouded in low clouds. Rain showers are frequent and may last from a few minutes to a full day.

CONSERVATION

The national park was established in 1988 to protect the unique ecosystem of American Samoa on land and at sea. Because the park was not able to purchase traditional communal land, it was only in 1993 that the NPS signed a 50-year lease agreement with eight participating villages. The park's ecosystems are at great risk from climate change. If not reversed, the coral reefs off the coast could die within the next 100 years. They are severely threatened by rising temperatures and increased levels of carbon dioxide in the seawater. But the park not only safeguards nature, it also helps protect the customs, beliefs, and traditions of the area's Native communities. The Samoan culture, Fa'a-Samoa, is roughly 3,000 years old. Many travelers experience the local culture via homestays or tours with local guides.

BEFORE YOU GO

Although the park lies in United States territory, you need a passport to visit—even as a U.S. citizen. It is advisable to contact the park before visiting. Trails are often rugged and steep and medical care is fairly limited; seriously injured people have to be flown to New Zealand, Australia, or Hawaii. The visitor center is located in the town of Pago Pago on Tutuila Island and features an American Samoa exhibit.

BEST TIMES TO VISIT

The climate of American Samoa is warm and wet year-round. The wetter, warmer season runs from October to May, and tropical storms are more prevalent during this period. June to September is drier and a bit cooler.

HIDDEN GEM

Take the short journey by plane to Ofu Island to explore pristine shorelines and lagoons. The Ofu Lagoon's remote location means you're unlikely to encounter crowds.

INTERESTING FACTS ABOUT THE PARK

- The National Park of American Samoa is the United States' only park south of the Equator.
- Samoa means "sacred earth."
- Saua, a village on the coast of Ta'ū, is thought to be the birthplace of the Polynesian people.
- During a tsunami in 2009, the visitor center in Pago Pago Harbor was destroyed and more than half of the exhibits on culture and nature were lost.

Bert Fuiava

HIGH TALKING CHIEF AND RANGER

As a local Samoan, Bert Fuiava holds the Matai High Talking Chief (HTC) title. Born and raised in the Manu a Islands, the easternmost islands of the U.S. territory of American Samoa, Fuiava is an active member of his village council and the Samoan community. He grew up with a self-sufficient lifestyle, living off the land, air, and ocean, amid Samoan culture and traditions that instilled a love and respect for Mother Nature and natural surroundings. Fuiava currently works at the National Park of American Samoa (NPAS) as the Manu a district ranger, responsible for managing park operations in the Manu a Islands. Fuiava started his journey with the Park Service in 2009. During his regular trips to the island of Ofu, he noticed most of the natural resources valuable to the ecosystems were understudied. New findings show that Ofu Lagoon is home to many coral species that are resilient to high water temperature and can withstand coral bleaching events. Fuiava has been supporting park's staff and partners in conducting studies within the lagoon, and operates a research laboratory in the district for use by visiting researchers and NPS staff performing inventory, monitoring, and other scientific work. As an active member of the community, Fuiava pours his energy into encouraging village and political leaders to support efforts to protect their natural resources, using his cultural and oratory skills to highlight these issues with community members and outreach programs in schools. He is dedicated to supporting ongoing efforts to protect natural resources and opportunities to give back to the park and the underserved Samoan community.

Haleakalā

A tropical paradise born from primordial lava flows is home to some of the rarest plants and animals on earth.

Located on the Hawaiian island of Maui, this relatively young national park is dedicated to protecting the unique and fragile ecosystem birthed from the raw power of Haleakalā, the magnificent and sacred volcano from which the park takes its name. The park's lush bamboo forests, tropical jungles, and stark volcanic landscapes are home to more endangered plant and animal species than any other national park. To save Maui's endemic flora and fauna from extinction, the park has been designated a UNESCO International Biosphere Reserve. As a result, visiting the park is carefully regulated to maintain this delicate island habitat.

The park's namesake volcano, Haleakalā, is an immense cultural and spiritual landmark for Hawaiians. According to Hawaiian legend, the volcano is where the demigod Māui trapped the sun, in order to make the days longer. Fittingly, sunrises from the summit are awe-inspiring and draw crowds for sightseeing, religious ceremonies, and spiritual cleansing. One example of the volcano's legendary power is a rare phenomenon called the Brocken Spectre: only possible at high elevations, this jaw-dropping illusion occurs when a person's shadow falls on the cloud cover below, creating an enormous, shadowy figure that

HAWAI'I

floats in the sky, encircled by a mystical rainbow halo. There are many ways to see Haleakalā's magic, including scenic drives, helicopter tours, and hikes along the Halemau'u and Keonehe'ehe'e trails. Many visitors opt for the Haleakalā Highway, a winding 37-mile (60-kilometer) climb that begins below sea level at the base of a subtropical rainforest and ascends through the clouds to the 10,023-foot (16,130-meter) crater pinnacle. There are steeper roads in the world, but no other highway on earth reaches such a high elevation in such a short distance. Six of the 14 world climates occur in the park's varied elevations, resulting in immense biodiversity, much of which is unique to the volcano. For example, the delicate yet resilient silversword is found nowhere on earth except in the black sands of the summit's moon-like crater. The plant's silver,

feathery leaves are the centerpiece of a fragile ecosystem of rare plants and endangered bird species.

While Haleakalā volcano is the park's star attraction, there are 30 miles (48 km) of additional hiking trails, camping, and guided tours through a myriad of waterfalls, gorges, ocean vistas, and tropical forests. Take the Pīpīwai Trail (3.8 mi./6.1 km) in the coastal Kīpahulu district for panoramic ocean views and a visit to the stunning 400-foot- (122-meter-) tall Waimoku Falls.

Haleakalā is known as "the house of the sun" but it is also one of the most popular destinations on earth for stargazing. Hawaii's first astronomical observatory was built on the summit of Haleakalā. Many also describe the volcano's barren landscape as "moonlike." So much so that in the 1960s, NASA sent its astronauts to train on Haleakalā.

PARK AT A GLANCE

*C*ongress established the Hawaii National Park in 1916, which included Haleakalā. It was made a separate park on July 1, 1961, and became a UNESCO International Biosphere Reserve in 1980.

SIZE
30,183 acres (47 sq. mi./122 km²)
Size rank among National Parks: 31 of 63

ELEVATION
Highest point: Puʻu ʻUlaʻula Summit (10,023 ft./3,055 m)
Lowest point: Pacific Ocean (sea level)

GEOLOGY
When the Pacific Plate drifted over a hotspot in the ocean floor more than a million years ago, the super-heated rock created rivers of lava that solidified into Haleakalā. It took millennia of erosion to sculpt the distinctive "Warrior's shield" shape it has today.

FLORA AND FAUNA
A total of 103 endangered species exist on Haleakalā, the most of any national park. There are 81 flowering plants such as the silversword plant, six non-flowering plants, and three native insects. The only native mammals on Haleakalā are a bat and a seal, and the only native reptiles are sea turtles. Of the island's 10 native birds, the Nēnē, or Hawaiian goose, is the official state bird of Hawaii.

CONSERVATION
Haleakalā stands 28,000 feet (8,534 m) above the ocean floor, making it the third-tallest mountain on earth. The national park protects not only the volcano, but also the diverse ecosystems it supports. Stewards of the park aim to preserve the natural resources that thrive here, while also sharing Native Hawaiian knowledge, traditions, and culture for future generations to experience and appreciate.

BEFORE YOU GO
There are no restaurants or gas stations in Haleakalā, so pack and plan accordingly. Due to the fragile nature of Hawaiian ecosystems, the law forbids hikers from stepping off the marked trails. Pets of any kind are prohibited on all trails. Due to high demand and conservation efforts, reservations and permits are needed for many hikes and experiences.

BEST TIMES TO VISIT
The park has steady temperatures year-round, but December to April are ideal times to visit, when the average high ranges between 80° and 83°F (27°–29°C).

Hawai'i Volcanoes

Two of the world's most active volcanoes
offer a glimpse into the earth's beginnings.

The landscape of the Ka'u Desert is a desolate one of cooled lava rocks, pumice, and volcanic ash. BELOW: With its flame-red flowers, the 'ōhia tree is as much a symbol of the park as the molten rock oozing from its fissures.

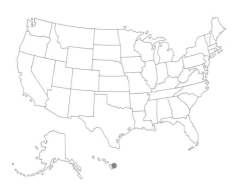

HAWAI'I

Established in 1916, Hawai'i Volcanoes National Park is one of Hawaii's most popular attractions and a sacred place for Native Hawaiians. The park on Big Island is marked by two active—or shall we say: very active—volcanoes: Kīlauea, which has had a continuous lava flow since January 1983, and Mauna Loa, which last erupted in 1984. Rising 13,677 feet (4,169 m) from sea level to its summit, Mauna Loa is one of the largest volcanoes in the world and marks the highest elevation in the state of Hawaii. On its southwestern slope, it borders Kīlauea, which is younger and significantly smaller. Each day, however, Kīlauea makes the Big Island a tiny bit bigger: every 24 hours, it spews out enough lava to resurface a 20-mile (32-kilometer), two-lane road.

Visiting an active volcano isn't everyone's cup of tea, but this being America, you can do it from the comfort of your own car. It's possible to skirt Kīlauea's caldera without stepping out of your vehicle, giving it the moniker "the world's only drive-in volcano." It would be a shame, though, to not venture out onto its slopes, where lush primeval rainforest is intercepted by young lava tongues. On the hot and dry southwestern slopes, the rain forest gives way to bare, desert-like lava fields. Underneath the earth, lava tubes have formed, such as the 40-mile (65-kilometer) Kazumura Cave, thought to be the longest in the world.

Mauna Loa resembles more of a volcanic wonderland. Rugged trails lead through the volcanic landscape of solidified lava in wildly twisted shapes, cinder cones, and open fissures. Volcanoes are visible evidence that the earth's surface is an endless work in progress, and scientists use the national park to explore the evolution of life on our planet. While they can only guess about the future of volcanic activity, many locals believe that the strong fluctuations stem from the mood of the powerful fire deity Pele. The elemental force behind the creation of these harsh landscapes, she is embodied by the lava and the untamed forces associated with volcanic eruptions.

Its geological past has made the Hawaiian archipelago the most geographically isolated group of islands on earth. The park is a treasure trove of endemic species like carnivorous caterpillars, happy face spiders, and colorful honeycreeper birds (which are, unfortunately, at risk of extinction due to forest clearing and avian malaria). Many of the fascinating native plants and animals in the park are critically endangered as a result of invasive species such as feral cats and mongooses. Protection of the local flora and fauna is one of the most essential tasks of the park administration. The island represents the last refuge for several native plant species that so far have successfully avoided extinction.

HAWAI'I (BIG ISLAND)

MAUNA LOA

VISITOR CENTER

KAZUMURA CAVE

KILAUEA

ALA KAHAKAI NATIONAL HISTORIC TRAIL

KAHUKU UNIT

HAWAI'I VOLCANOES NATIONAL PARK

Established as Hawaii National Park on August 1, 1916, today the park has more than doubled in size–although in 1961 Haleakalā National Park on the island of Maui was designated a separate entity. In 1980, the park became an International Biosphere Reserve and in 1987 a UNESCO World Heritage Site. Its name was changed to Hawai'i Volcanoes National Park in 2000.

SIZE
323,431 acres (505 sq. mi./1,308 km²)
Size rank among National Parks: 24 of 63

ELEVATION
Highest point: Mauna Loa (13,679 ft./4,169 m)
Lowest point: Pacific Ocean (sea level)

GEOLOGY
If you drained the Pacific, the Hawaiian Islands wouldn't be tiny dots but a range of massive mountains—perhaps the greatest mountain range on earth. They started to build up from the seafloor through thousands of volcanic eruptions about three million years ago when a fissure opened across the floor of the Pacific Ocean. As they started to lift out of the sea, the building forces of volcanism met the destructive

forces of waves, wind, and erosion. Today, the Big Island is the southernmost, youngest, and largest of the Hawaiian archipelago—and the only one with active volcanoes.

FLORA AND FAUNA
The variety of landscapes in the park safeguards a variety of plant species that have evolved over the past 70 million years in near-complete isolation. They have adapted to life without plant-eating mammals, often lacking defensive weapons such as thorns, poisons, and scents—there are mintless mints and nettleless nettles. That makes them especially prone to the introduction of alien, invasive species. The same goes for the tropical birds that abound in the park: at least two dozen species have become extinct since the arrival of Europeans in the late eighteenth century. In the park, they are protected from feral cats and mongeese.

CLIMATE AND WEATHER

The weather in Hawai'i Volcanoes National Park is quite unpredictable. Temperatures can vary from hot and humid (or hot and dry) to chilly, windy, and rainy. A difference of 10 to 15 degrees is not uncommon when climbing up a volcano. At higher elevations, snowfall can occur.

CONSERVATION

The purpose of Hawai'i Volcanoes is to protect, study, and provide access to Kīlauea and Mauna Loa volcanoes, while perpetuating endemic ecosystems and traditional Hawaiian culture. Initially, the park encompassed only a tiny portion of its present area. Most of it was in private hands; eruptions and lava flows drew adventurers and scientists to the region in the 1840s, leading to a sell-off of the volcano. Lorrin A. Thurston, who operated a series of hotels at the rim, was an early advocate for creating a park, and convinced John Muir and former President Theodore Roosevelt to endorse the idea. In 1907, Hawaii paid for 50 members of Congress to visit Haleakalā and Kīlauea—they were served a dinner cooked over lava steam vents. The park was eventually created in 1916, thanks to legislation introduced by Jonah Kūhiō Kalaniana'ole (see right).

BEFORE YOU GO

The best time to observe Halema'uma'u's glow is before sunrise, or after 9 p.m. A fitting spot to do so is the Volcano House, located at the edge of Kīlauea. Open since 1846, it's the only lodge within the park and offers multiple campsites.

BEST TIMES TO VISIT

Hawaii experiences a wet season from November to March and a drier season from April to October. A visit in April, May, September, or October will offer the best balance of dry weather and fewer crowds.

HIDDEN GEM

Visit the Kahuku Unit for a surprisingly lush, pastoral landscape on the flanks of the volcano. This area is one of the lesser-visited corners of the park and offers a variety of hiking trails.

INTERESTING FACTS ABOUT THE PARK

- Ancient Hawaiians settled in this area sometime between 1200 and 1450 CE.
- An unusually explosive eruption of Kīlauea in 1790 killed a party of warriors, women, and children. The footprints left by their last march were preserved in the hardened ash.
- Eruptions among Hawaii's volcanoes are actually quite rare. The reason for this is the relatively low overpressure in the magma chambers.

Jonah Kūhiō Kalaniana'ole

POLITICIAN AND LAST PRINCE OF HAWAI'I

In Hawaii, most people knew Prince Jonah Kūhiō Kalaniana'ole (1871–1922) simply as "Kūhiō"—or "Prince Cupid," his childhood nickname. For 10 consecutive terms, he was Hawaii's Congressional Delegate to the United States House of Representatives—and the only member of Congress born into royalty. When the Hawaiian kingdom was overthrown by American and European businessmen in 1893, Kūhiō was arrested for treason after participating in a failed counterrevolution. He was jailed for a year, and when his sentence ended, he left the island and vowed never to return. But under urgent persuasion, he returned to his homeland in 1901. Since the United States had annexed Hawaii in 1898, Kūhiō decided to run for election as the Hawaiian delegate to Congress. Kūhiō won the race but because Hawaii was only a territory at the time, he served as a nonvoting delegate, with no official say in congressional matters. Nevertheless, Hawaii's "Prince of the People" pushed through legislation like the Hawaiian Homes Commission Act, which gave Native Hawaiians a homestead to live and work on and encouraged them to become self-sufficient farmers, ranchers, and merchants. The prince was revered and respected for his efforts to preserve and strengthen the Hawaiian people and land: in 1916, he introduced the Hawai'i National Park Bill, which sought to establish a Hawai'i National Park covering land on Kīlauea, Mauna Loa, and Haleakalā. The director of the Hawaiian Volcano Observatory testified in support of the bill, and President Woodrow Wilson signed it into law. Although funding proved to be difficult at first (one Oregon congressman infamously said: "It should not cost anything to run a volcano"), it eventually became the country's 11th national park. Today, Prince Kūhiō's birthday, March 26th, is a Hawaiian state holiday.

Congaree, South Carolina
Text: Florian Siebeck
Images: Madison and David Bowman/
American Field Trip (28–31)

Crater Lake, Oregon
Text: Florian Siebeck
Images: shutterstock/Matthew Connolly (220/221),
NPS (222 left), shutterstock/M4Productions (222 right),
shutterstock/Sveta Imnadze (223), shutterstock/D Currin (224),
Andrew Wojtanik/liveandlethike.com (225)

Death Valley, California
Text: Florian Siebeck
Images: Christopher Zebo (258/259, 261),
Mohammed Raja Hamid (260), Madison and
David Bowman/American Field Trip (262, 263 bottom),
NPS/Dianne Milliard (263 top)

Denali, Alaska
Text: Florian Siebeck
Images: NPS/Kent Miller (302/303),
Madison and David Bowman/American Field Trip (304–307)

Dry Tortugas, Florida
Text: Anna Brones
Images: shutterstock/Mia2you (46),
shutterstock/Henryk Sadura (47)

Everglades, Florida
Text: Florian Siebeck
Images: shutterstock/allouphoto (34/35),
Valerie Noell (36–38, 39 bottom),
Madison and David Bowman/American Field Trip (39 top, 40/41)

Gates of the Arctic, Alaska
Text: Florian Siebeck
Images: Madison and David Bowman/American Field Trip
(292–295, 297 top), Mohammed Raja Hamid (296),
NPS/Zak Richter (297 bottom), NPS/Sean Tevenbaugh (298/299)

Gateway Arch, Missouri
Text: Anna Brones
Images: Paul Brady/Alamy Stock Photo (48)

Glacier, Montana
Text: Florian Siebeck (park text and facts),
Anna Brones (portrait)
Images: Madison and David Bowman/
American Field Trip (186–188), NPS (189, 191 bottom),
Erika Wiggins/Alamy Stock Photo (190),
Chris Robbins/Alamy Stock Photo (191 top),
NPS/Tim Rains (192/193)

Glacier Bay, Alaska
Text: Kevin Oberbauer, Yuko Shiroma
Images: NPS/Jakara Hubbard (334),
DamantisZ/Alamy Stock Photo (334), NPS (336)

Grand Canyon, Arizona
Text: Florian Siebeck
Images: Mohammed Raja Hamid (170–172),
Madison and David Bowman/American Field Trip (173–175),
Andrew Wojtanik/liveandlethike.com (176/177)

Grand Teton, Wyoming
Text: Florian Siebeck (park text and facts),
Anna Brones (portrait)
Images: Jessica Lim (120/121), Madison and David Bowman/
American Field Trip (122, 123, 125),
Andrew Wojtanik/liveandlethike.com (124)

Great Basin, Nevada
Text: Kevin Oberbauer
Images: Andrew Wojtanik/liveandlethike.com (286),
shutterstock/IrinaK (287)

Great Sand Dunes, Colorado
Text: Anna Brones
Images: NPS/Patrick Myers (116, 117),
shutterstock/Rosalie Kreulen (118)

Great Smoky Mountains, Tennessee / North Carolina
Text: Florian Siebeck
Images: Bart Smith (50/51, 53, 54 bottom),
Zoonar GmbH/ Alamy Stock Photo (52),
Madison and David Bowman/ American Field Trip (54 top, 55)

Guadalupe Mountains, Texas
Text: Anna Brones
Images: NPS/D. Buehler (88), Christopher Zebo (89, 90)

Petrified Forest, Arizona
Text: Anna Brones
Images: Danita Delimont/Alamy Stock Photo (168), Maciej Bledowski/Alamy Stock Photo (169)

Pinnacles, California
Text: Kevin Oberbauer, Pauline Ordonez
Images: Andrew Wojtanik/liveandlethike.com (250), NPS/Kurt Moses (251), Cavan Images/Alamy Stock Photo (252)

Redwood, California
Text: Florian Siebeck
Images: Madison and David Bowman/American Field Trip (228–232, 233 bottom), Mohammed Raja Hamid (233 top)

Rocky Mountain, Colorado
Text: Florian Siebeck
Images: Madison and David Bowman/ American Field Trip (98–103)

Saguaro, Arizona
Text: Anna Brones
Images: Andrew Wojtanik/liveandlethike.com (166), Bart Smith (167)

Sequoia, California
Text: Florian Siebeck
Images: Madison and David Bowman/ American Field Trip (276–283)

Shenandoah, Virginia
Text: Anna Brones
Images: Jon Bilous/Alamy Stock Photo (24), Andrew Wojtanik/liveandlethike.com (25, 27), NPS/Neal Lewis (26)

Theodore Roosevelt, North Dakota
Text: Anna Brones
Images: NPS/Mark Meyers (180), NPS/Janice Shanks (181)

Virgin Islands, Virgin Islands
Text: Anna Brones
Images: Courtesy of the National Parks Conservation Association (48 top), George Oze/Alamy Stock Photo (48 bottom)

Voyageurs, Minnesota
Text: Anna Brones
Images: Don Brenema/Alamy Stock Photo (72), shutterstock/Frank Kennedy MN (73)

White Sands, New Mexico
Text: Anna Brones
Images: NPS (94, 96), Efrain Padro/Alamy Stock Photo (95)

Wind Cave, South Dakota
Text: Anna Brones
Images: Dan Leeth/Alamy Stock Photo (184), shutterstock/Cheri Alguire (185)

Wrangell-St. Elias, Alaska
Text: Florian Siebeck
Images: Madison and David Bowman/ American Field Trip (314–319)

Yellowstone, Wyoming / Montana / Idaho
Text: Florian Siebeck
Images: Madison and David Bowman/ American Field Trip (128–133), Bart Smith (134/135)

Yosemite, California
Text: Florian Siebeck
Images: Madison and David Bowman/ American Field Trip (240–242, 246/247), Valerie Noell (243, 245), Andrew Wojtanik/liveandlethike.com (244 left), Valerie Noell feat. Arielle Bodenhausen (244 right),

Zion, Utah
Text: Florian Siebeck
Images: Madison and David Bowman/ American Field Trip (156–158, 162/163), Mohammed Raja Hamid (159, 160 bottom, 161), Valerie Noell (160 top)

United States vector map illustration:
shutterstock/Fourleaflover

The Parklands

Trails and Secrets from the
National Parks of the United States

This book was conceived and edited by gestalten
and Parks Project.

Design and layout by gestalten
In cooperation with Parks Project

Edited by Robert Klanten, Andrea Servert,
and Florian Siebeck
Contributing editors: Parks Project

Introduction letter from Keith Eshelman

Park texts by Florian Siebeck, Anna Brones,
Kevin Oberbauer, Pauline Odonez, and Yuko Shiroma

Feature texts by Jessica Dunham and Kevin St. John

Captions by Anna Southgate

Parks Research Specialist and editorial support
by Joe Gibson from Parks Project

Editorial Management by Lars Pietzschmann

Photo Editor: Valentina Marinai

Design, layout, and cover by Charlotte Bourdeix
Layout assistance by Melanie Ullrich

Illustrations by Devin McSherry (maps)
and David Sparshott (portraits)

Map design (pp. 2–3) by Bureau Rabensteiner

Typefaces: *Baskerville URW* by John Baskerville,
Trade Gothic Next by Akira Kobayashi and
Tom Grace, *Rockwell* by Monotype.Design Studio

Cover image by NPS/Kent Miller

Printed by Printer Trento S. r. l., Trento
Made in Europe

Published by gestalten, Berlin 2022
ISBN 978-3-96704-029-6

Die Gestalten Verlag GmbH & Co. KG, Berlin 2022

For more information, and to order books,
please visit www.gestalten.com

Bibliographic information published by the
Deutsche Nationalbibliothek.

The Deutsche Nationalbibliothek lists this publication
in the Deutsche Nationalbibliografie; detailed bibliographic
data is available online at www.dnb.de

This book was printed on paper certified according
to the standards of the FSC®.